James Arthur Ray received international fame for his contribution to the bestseller *The Secret* and now presents his practical, results-driven programme for becoming absolutely unstoppable in achieving what you want. He holds live events worldwide teaching methods proven to create true wealth in all areas of life: financially, relationally, mentally, physically and spiritually. This powerful programme, first introduced on the *Oprah Winfrey Show*, is now brought to you in *Harmonic Wealth*.

'*Harmonic Wealth* is a classic. James Arthur Ray did not just write a book, he went out into the world and made it happen, charting every move he made. This book is a map that clearly outlines how you too can literally create a life of harmonic wealth.'
—Bob Proctor, author of the international bestseller *You Were Born Rich*

'James Ray writes with the conviction and ease of a man who has lived the truths he wants to share. I find his observations on the relation between spiritual and worldly well-being particularly invigorating and relevant to my own experience and current teaching. I believe readers at any point on their life's journey will find this book full of practical and empowering ideas they can use right now to help make their lives more fulfilling and harmonious.'
—Zen Master Dennis Genpo Merzel, author of
Big Mind-Big Heart, Finding Your Way

'In this book, James Ray offers the world the life-changing tools that he himself continues to use to create opportunity out of every experience and actively achieve success.'
—Ivan Misner, *New York Times* bestselling author, and founder of BNI

'*Harmonic Wealth* is full of fascinating ideas and concepts. A compelling book that will teach you how to create abundance and wealth in your own life, *Harmonic Wealth* will show you how James Ray's philosophy of going 3 for 3 will help you create the life you've always wanted.'
—Scott Martineau, CEO, ConsciousOne.com,
and bestselling author of *The Power of YOU!*

'*Harmonic Wealth* unleashes James Ray's fearless, daring spirit—his thorough and unwavering conviction that you can create wealth and harmony in all areas of life! Read this book and James will show you step by step how to make this a reality in your life.'
—Pete Bissonette, president of Learning Strategies Corporation

'James Ray is a consummate teacher. He speaks from great life experience, honed by decades of in-the-trenches teaching experience—a combination not easy to find. We all want to lead more fulfilling and significant lives, but exactly how to do that is the elusive brass ring. In insightfully thinking through the many nuances involved in this quest, James has saved us all a great deal of time and many potential mistakes. Do read this fascinating book, and do take action on what James reveals in it. You'll be very glad you did.'
—Bill Harris, director, Centerpointe Research Institute, creator of Holosync meditation technology, and author of *Thresholds of the Mind* and *Managing Evolutionary Growth: How to Create Deep Change Without Falling Apart*

'A powerful book that will show you how to forge your own success in the world. *Harmonic Wealth* offers a new way to think about and create wealth in every aspect of your life.'
—Marci Shimoff, author of *Happy for No Reason*, coauthor of the number one *New York Times* best-seller *Chicken Soup for the Woman's Soul*, and featured teacher in *The Secret*

'*Harmonic Wealth* is an inspirational, thought-provoking, action-stimulating book that will help you build vibrant wealth from the inside out.'
—Dr John F. Demartini, best-selling author of *How to Make One Hell of a Profit and Still Get to Heaven*

Harmonic Wealth

Also by James Arthur Ray

PRACTICAL SPIRITUALITY:
How to Use Spiritual Power to Create Tangible Results

THE SCIENCE OF SUCCESS:
How to Attract Prosperity and
Create Harmonic Wealth Through Proven Principles

Harmonic Wealth

The Secret of Attracting
the Life You Want

James Arthur Ray

with
Linda Sivertsen

sphere

SPHERE

First published in Great Britain in 2008 by Sphere

A CIP catalogue record for this book
is available from the British Library.

ISBN 978-1-84744-176-8

Typeset in Bembo by M Rules
Printed and bound in Great Britain by
Clays Ltd, St Ives plc

Sphere
An imprint of
Little, Brown Book Group
100 Victoria Embankment
London EC4Y 0DY

An Hachette Livre UK Company
www.hachettelivre.co.uk

www.littlebrown.co.uk

Acknowledgments

Nothing of a large importance has ever been created without the collective efforts of like-minded and inspired people. As this book moves from pure inspiration to actualisation I'd like to express my heartfelt gratitude.

First and foremost the Creative Source. That energy that sustains and inspires me to step more and more fully into an awareness of who I am, who you are, and the things of which we're all capable.

Next, to all the teachings and teachers that have contributed to my life path, many of them are mentioned in this book, many of them are not.

To my loving parents, Dr A. Gordon Ray, a biblical scholar and man of vast wisdom, and Joyce Elaine Ray, a true saint and woman of vast understanding and love—my first and greatest teachers and mentors. This book is dedicated to you. Every single life it touches great and small is a result of your impact and teaching.

Dad, thanks so much for teaching me the value of reading and studying at such an early age. For being such a strong example of living your mission and purpose, for exemplifying what it means to follow a path of heart and the will of the Creator. For supporting my quest for truth even when and if it differed from your truth. And thanks so much for the countless late-night calls (way past your bedtime) to find the specific location of numerous biblical references I needed for this book. You are a powerful example of the masculine principle of wisdom in this universe.

Mother, you told me since I was just a little boy that I was special, and that I had something unique to bring to this world. While I didn't believe in myself for so long, and therefore didn't believe you for many years, you continued to believe and to support me nonetheless. No matter how many times I disappointed you and fell, you refused to let go of what you believed. I now know that we're all special, and we all have a unique gift to bring. If all mothers knew this as passionately, and lived it as completely as you, maybe more of us would step more fully into our true potential. You are a living example of the feminine principle of unconditional love and support in this universe.

To all the members of my amazing team at James Ray International. Without your skill, commitment, and support there's no way I could have completed this work. Most specifically, to Megan and Josh Fredrickson, my Director of Operations and Manager of Business Growth, respectively. You two are a power couple beyond description. My sincere gratitude goes out to you daily for believing in what appeared to many to be a crazy vision to impact the world in a powerful way—long before there was any major physical evidence. You two will leave a legacy in this world long beyond your earthly years.

To my brilliant writing partner and collaborator, Linda Sivertsen. Linda, your ability to take my collective thoughts, my tendency to be provocative, fun, and irreverent, and place them into a format that reads and 'sounds' like my voice is unsurpassed. Your commitment to this project obviously goes way beyond our business contract. Thank you so much for your energy and enthusiasm. I am eternally grateful.

To Bob Miller, Brenda Copeland, and the entire team at Hyperion. Thank you so much for your support and belief in my work. It's an honor to work with you.

Finally to you, the reader. As mystical as it may seem, I truly believe there are no accidents in this universe. Everything is perfectly orchestrated for your betterment, growth, and evolution whether you're consciously aware of it or not. For this reason, the fact that you're holding this book is because you're 'supposed' to read this book at this particular juncture of your journey. This means you and I at some level are kindred spirits, and we're both here to complete a special and similar purpose in the world. You are the one the world's been waiting for. I thank you for re-membering (reuniting) with this. Let's transform the world together.

Contents

Harmonic
Wealth

Welcome

Everything's About to Change

You're about to read a list of counterintuitive statements that will rock your world and alter everything you've ever thought about life and wealth. While reading this list, ask yourself how your life would change if every word were true. Would you move forward with more courage? Give yourself more freedom? Treat yourself with more respect and self-love? Walk through the world with less guilt? Experience more joy?

In short, what would you dare to dream for yourself and those you care about most? How would your actions, habits, and feelings – your *entire* life – transform if these statements were, without question, absolutely true?

1. Balance is bogus and you don't want it!

2. Positive thinking doesn't work, but optimists achieve more.

3. You always get what you're looking for – always – even the negative things you give your time and attention to.

4. All significant breakthroughs in life *must* be preceded by a breakdown.

5. All goals are spiritual goals – including abundant material wealth and mind-blowing sex.

6. Your current bank account isn't who you are; it's who you *were*.

7. When you pursue greatness, don't expect others to support you. You'll represent the courage, strength, and vision they don't yet have.

8. The greatest competition you will ever have is the competition between your disciplined and undisciplined mind. You must constantly
study, understand, and immerse yourself in that which brings you value
and power, and avoid at all costs anything that weakens you.

9. Your willpower will *never* be stronger than your unconscious mind,
no matter what.

10. Be the *real* you. Whatever is suppressed will be expressed, in later
days, in uglier ways.

11. If you don't love yourself, you'll never attract a soul mate who
truly loves you – not ever. When you think of yourself as unlovable in
any way, you're actually *in love* with that unlovable version of yourself,
and your relationships can only reflect that.

12. C students often own the businesses that B and A students work
for.

Do some of these statements seem counter to what you've been taught
or believe? Did they make you uncomfortable or maybe even a little
anxious? Good. My purpose is to challenge you . . . to get you to move
beyond your self-imposed boundaries, otherwise known as your comfort zone. That's the only way you'll grow. Unless you're ready to think,
feel, and act in different ways than you've done prior to now, you'll continue to live the life that you're living with the results you're getting. You
may be thinking, *Now, wait a minute, James, my life's pretty good in several areas!* It probably is. But I'll bet there's at least one area of your life (if not
two or three) where you know you deserve more than you're currently
getting. If this weren't true you wouldn't have picked up this book.
Congratulations. You do deserve more and I can help you to have more.
But you have to be willing to keep your mind open and to challenge
your current thoughts, beliefs, and assumptions.

So, back to our list of twelve counterintuitive statements. Guess what?
Each and every one of them is indeed true, as I'll prove in this book.
Intrigued? That's my intention.

We live in the most exciting time in world history. Right now. A time when spiritual traditions and scientific findings have stopped opposing one another and have become sister studies. The quantum physicists, the chaos theorists, and the biologists of today are the mystics of the twenty-first century, proving the timeless truths that mystics and spiritual elders have been teaching us since antiquity. They're doing it through hard scientific evidence.

But for all of the excitement, we're also at a turning point. Modern science proves that everything in our world is comprised of energy – everything. What appears to be solid – from your house, your car, to your body – at the quantum level is 99.99999 per cent energy or light. All energy vibrates and we call that a frequency. The fact is that you'll never create high-energy results from a low-energy vessel. Like attracts like. So it's imperative that we continue ramping up our vibrations, which can only happen by redefining what spirituality really means and by overhauling our views on wealth across the globe. We need to do this quickly, not out of fear, but out of enough already!

If you're anything like me, you're completely over the age-old belief that life is a struggle. And aren't you suspicious of the idea that virtuous, spiritual, or religious people – the very men and women we look to for inspiration, high ideals, and leadership – are supposed to suffer as paupers to somehow justify our trust, not to mention the guarantee of their cushy afterlife? Have you swallowed the pill that life is hard and then you die? I'm sorry, but I call that bullshit. I had that tablet caught in my throat for years, but I coughed it up and will help you do likewise.

If anything I've said rings true for you, stick with me. We've got a lot to cover. I'm going to show you a whole new way to think about and create wealth in every single aspect of your life. By the time you're done with this book, you'll know exactly how to create a fulfilling life of true wealth – what I call Harmonic Wealth®. I've been living and teaching this life for more than twenty years, and it's time you lived it right along with me.

And I'm not kidding when I say I want you to live this. Of course, I want you to read this book – to enjoy it, to feel it, to believe it, and question it, too – but I want more than that for you. I want you to participate in this book, to make it your own, a conversation with me and a dialogue with yourself. So, with that in mind, I've extended the book beyond its covers, so what you have here is actually so much more than what you're holding in your hands. Curious?

As you go through these pages you will notice icons throughout. These icons are a signal to you that further support material (worksheets, exercises, questions, and cues) is available online at www.harmonicwealthbook.com. In addition to the integrated workbook, this website also contains a special video component prepared exclusively for readers of this book. I urge you to make use of these resources to heighten the experience of this book. More than that, to heighten the experience of your life.

Harmonic Wealth is an experience of life that few have understood but that once grasped becomes second nature. I'm talking fulfilment in every area of your life, not just in one or two. This is what you and everyone on this planet really desires – and I'm here to tell you once and for all that you totally deserve it. You always have and you always will – but deep down inside you already know that, don't you?

Time is of the essence. Let's get started.

1

One Quest, Five Pillars

The mind is its own place, and in itself
can make a heaven of hell, a hell of heaven.

– JOHN MILTON

Harmony – The Elegant Whole

Maybe you know people who make millions of pounds a year but don't have
fulfilling relationships or good health. Or people who spend their lives committed
to religion or spirituality, literally touching the divine, but have holes in their shoes.
We all know people who have razor-sharp intellects but are out of shape and out
of touch. There's a much more integrated, fulfilling way to live: I call it Harmonic
Wealth.

Harmonic Wealth isn't just about material abundance – although that's a
fun and extremely necessary component. It's about abundance in all
areas of your life. Think of harmony as a musical performance, in which
different instruments move to weave a magical tapestry. Now, apply this
to your life. Wouldn't you like to have all the different parts of your life
moving towards an elegant whole that's more than the sum of its parts?
That's Harmonic Wealth.

Most people equate wealth with money. While money is a part of
wealth, it's so much more than that. True wealth is a state of harmony and
well-being. I know people who are multi-multimillionaires who would

gladly hand over half their net worth to have more health, loving relationships, or a personal connection with something beyond themselves.
A truly wealthy individual experiences harmony in all facets of his or her
life – a sense of fulfilment and well-being that transcends the momentary
happiness of lopsided achievements in one or two areas while neglecting
the others.

So, you're about to learn how to have an abundance of well-being in
the five key areas of life, what I call the Five Pillars of Wealth: Financial,
Relational, Mental, Physical, and Spiritual. Without these five pillars, you
might be rich, but you'll never be wealthy. Interestingly enough, I've
found that the more you reach this state of *true* wealth, the more money
rushes to you – and all that money can provide. The universe is at your
command and lines up in joyous support of your awakening.

Creating Harmonic Wealth brings an overall sense of well-being, fulfilment, even unity. Understand that your pillars are interdependent:
when you attend to each of them, all increase in strength. When you take
care of your health by working out regularly and eating well, you create
multiple benefits. Sexual relationships become enhanced by your greater
confidence and stamina. Business booms from your increased energy.
You're more alert and receptive in spiritual pursuits. You're more alive.
Similarly, spiritual growth translates to deepening intimacy in friendships
and romantic relationships, fuelling your desire to keep up with your
physical exercise.

Research in the evolution of consciousness now proves that cross
training is the key to exponential growth. This is a fundamental concept
we'll be dealing with in this journey. Through revealing personal stories
and case studies, ancient and cutting-edge wisdom, and simple but powerful exercises, we'll look at how to make the most of this integrative way
of life. What's more, we'll reveal how, with Harmonic Wealth, you can
create true wealth by going 3 for 3 in the five main areas of life. Going
3 for 3 is what happens when your thoughts, your feelings, and your
actions are all firing simultaneously and in alignment. I'll give you proven
action steps that are practical and easy to implement – the same steps that

have catapulted my life and work into the world. I'll keep them down, dirty, and simple, because if you're anything like me, you want your results yesterday.

Why Balance Is Bogus

I'm a great believer in harmony, but balance is bogus.

Many teachers talk about balance, and guess what? Not one of them is balanced. I know; I used to be one of them. The only people who are perfectly balanced are six feet under and it's not your time yet. Balance in this world cannot be achieved, so get over it.

Think of a scale. In perfect balance, nothing's happening. There's no dynamism, no life or vibrancy. Now, think of a jazz band in action – the life and vibrancy are palpable, aren't they? The performers in this band have less to do with playing the melody as written and more to do with improvising. They give life to nuance and the music takes shape in the moment. That's harmony. The different parts aren't balanced – sometimes the saxophone leads. Sometimes it's the bass, or the drum or guitar. Whatever instrument is out in front at the moment, they're all contributing, all creating that amazing thing called music. Each musician plays his part of a magical, magnificent whole.

I want to encourage you to think of your life like this. When you're in harmony, some days your parenting skills will lead. Other times it'll be your job or your school. On certain occasions your marriage will take centre stage. Sometimes you're going to be running on two hours sleep, having worn the same clothes three days in a row. It may not be pretty, but that may be just what it takes to finish the business plan that lands you the big money and the nourishing rest and relaxation that follows. If you had been in perfect balance, you never would have worked those crazy hours to begin with, and look at what you'd have missed. So, with my way, you're going to have to get used to the idea that you're never going to be in perfect balance, nor would you want to. Perfect balance is death, death of mind and spirit.

Hopefully I've just lightened your load if you're good at travelling on guilt trips on account of your lack of balance. It's time to get over it. Knowing that nothing dynamic's happening when you're in balance, why would you want to be? Harmony is where it's at; harmony is dynamic and full of life, even if you choose to venture temporarily into choppy seas. While it's true that you can't control the waves, who said you can't learn to surf?

If you're still tempted to strain for balance, you've been forewarned that it's always going to be an impossible dream. My prayer is that you'll see throughout the chapters how liberating it is to cease chasing this illusion.

You Always Succeed at What You Value

'James, I want to be more successful!' a man I'd never met told me over the phone. 'Can you help me?'

'Sure,' I said. 'Where are you already successful?'

'I'm not! That's why I need your help!'

'Okay, cool,' I answered. 'Now, tell me, where are you already successful?'

'James! You're not listening to me!' he wailed. 'The reason I'm calling you is because I need to be successful and I'm not.'

'Interesting,' I said. 'How's your health right now?'

'Well, I've never been more fit in my entire life,' he answered.

'How's your relationship right now?' I asked.

'My wife and I just celebrated our twentieth anniversary. She's wonderful. Our eldest daughter just got into Oxford.'

'So, fit, healthy, and in a loving connected relationship with happy kids?' I asked.

'Yes, and I can see where you're going with this, James. But my friend down the street is making ten times more money than I am and I can't figure out why. He just bought my brand-new dream car, a BMW, and it's driving me nuts!'

'That's really terrific for him,' I said. 'But how's his health?'

'Um, he had a heart attack last year and nearly died.'

'Interesting,' I said. 'How is his relationship?'

'He just went through a nasty divorce. He and his ex are fighting over custody.'

'Interesting. So, who's more successful?' I asked him.

I'm not here to tell you which path in life is right or wrong for you. That's not my role. You currently have the life you chose, based upon your values, and the actions you've taken towards those values – like my caller friend and his neighbour. Read that again. Even if you don't like this life (and I'll explain later why I believe you actually love it), for now it's enough to say that you've succeeded at creating what you value. The guy up the street clearly had a higher value for his business than my client. He valued materialism more than his family or his health. Conversely, the caller had a higher value for his health and his family than he did for his business. We always put energy where our attention is. There's a law in our universe that's backed up by physics, which states, 'Energy flows where attention goes.' Our challenge is to shift our attention to what we truly value . . . and keep it there.

If we take this focus and attention business one step further, we see that when we're constantly focusing on *I don't have it*, the universe says, 'Your wish is my command,' and we continue not having it. But that, too, is a story for later. For now, just know that I'm going to help you turn this type of thinking around to where 'right thinking' followed by 'right action' becomes your natural state – quickly.

We Are Energy, We Are Divine

I struggle a bit with the label *self-help*, even if that's the section where you found this book, because I come from the premise that you're *already* perfect, magnificent, and divine. To my way of thinking, self-help says that you're broke and need to be fixed. I prefer personal transformation. Personal transformation says that no matter how fantastic things are for you, you can always grow, expand, and more fully express yourself. There's always room to receive more of the richness and wealth the universe has to offer. If you're currently struggling in any area, it doesn't mean you're not perfect. It just means you're ready for a change. That's why you picked up this book.

To make that shift, you'll probably have to redefine your ideas about God, wealth, and spirituality. I was raised in a very fundamental Christian household with a Protestant minister as a father. He's one of my best friends and mentors and he always taught me to study and keep an open mind. I'm here to tell you that you're not going to hear the tired 'you've got to suffer to get into heaven' jargon from me. There isn't one ounce of belief in me that says you have to have a hard life to justify spiritual rewards. Nonsense! Ever since I was a kid I questioned – everything. Deep down inside I just knew that you could advance spiritually without giving up the joys of the earth. I looked around and saw that the people who were saying you couldn't be wildly successful and highly spiritual at the same time didn't appear to have authentic results in either area.

This is a new millennium and it's time to redefine what it means to be wealthy *and* spiritual. I believe, for example, that it's every bit as spiritual for Ronaldo to score a hat-trick as it is for me to sit in my living room meditating. Bill Gates has touched as many, if not more, lives with his inspirational vision as any modern-day teacher. Each person contributes and gives to the world from their own unique calling and gifts. Quantum physics as well as spiritual traditions tell us that all things come from the same source.

I'm not knocking meditation by any means; I meditate every day and have an outrageous story to share with you about doing so. That said, it's incredible hypocrisy to sit on a cushion all day, so connected and high, only to drive around in traffic an hour later and go ballistic. Heaven starts within, my friend, and true harmony can be had whether you smell the roses or the diesel fumes. I'm going to help you redefine spirituality in your own life while we uncover your purpose and get you on track to have an incredibly wealthy life on all levels.

To understand how I see spirit, start by understanding what you read in the welcome – that everything is energy. Everything – you, me, every-thing around us. We live in a vibrational universe. We all vibrate to our own frequencies, forming a massive energy field from which science tells us all form is created. Since everything in your universe (from a plant to a palace to a planet) is comprised of this same energetic source, this field is pregnant with unlimited potential and possibility. This field of unlimited opportunity goes by many names. Some scientists call it the quantum hologram, some call it plenum or the Zero Point Field. Some of these scientists are even calling it the mind of God. If you ask them to describe energy, they'll say something like, 'Well, it's omnipresent. It can never be created or destroyed. All that ever was or will be is already here. It's always moving into form, through form, and back out of form.'

Ask a theologian what created the universe, and you'll hear about God or the Creator, the Source, Universal Mind, Higher Self, the Holy Guardian Angel – the list goes on. Ask that theologian to define God, and he or she will say, 'God is omnipresent, can never be created or destroyed, was always here, and is always moving into form, through form, and back out of form.'

Notice anything? They're saying the same things! For the first time in recorded history, we now have a marriage between science and spiritual-ity. We need to drop these artificial distinctions between the spiritual and the material. It's up to us to see how these truths apply to our everyday lives and how we can integrate them for Harmonic Wealth in all areas.

But you and I aren't going to live in mystical abstractions. We've got real work to do. Spiritual mastery in today's world is about integration. It's about being able to have a great body and run a business, as well as meditate, give back, and everything in between. My goal has always been to soar into the realms of the mystic, while keeping my feet in the sand. You know, a practical mystic. There's no point in teaching you how to tap into the Zero Point Field if you can't bring it back to the third dimen-sion and create results in your life. My intention for you in this work is to give you insights, tools, and techniques to create the outrageous and amazing results you deserve in every area of life.

Trust me, the universe is going to support us in this. The laws of our vibrational universe are vast and varied, but they are immutable. The Law of Attraction is the understanding that everything in our universe is comprised of energy and like energies are attracted to each other and dissimilar energies repel, and I'll go into that in depth later. While people seem to want to force fit the entire universe into the Law of Attraction these days, our universe is governed by other equally powerful, distinct, and definitive laws. When you align with them, you win, and when you don't, you lose. It's just that simple.

Your Fellow Traveller

In case you haven't noticed yet, I'm eclectic (although I prefer the term integrated). That comes, I believe, from having thrived in the extreme mystical realms to executive roles in the business world – with a full spectrum of integrated living in between.

While I've always had a strong appetite for spiritual and mystical truth, I've never felt it necessary to shun the business world or the amazing joys this life has to offer. To me, integrated spiritual mastery is about embracing both worlds with equal enthusiasm and commitment.

The reason I'm so excited about bringing this information to you is because it's truly the 'best of my best' from everything I've learned and accomplished – a blueprint, if you like, for the success I've enjoyed on so many levels and helped foster in the lives of my clients.

My research in the field really began when I was still in high school. A voracious reader and seeker, I was never fully satisfied by the answers about the meaning of life I got from traditional religion. My strict upbringing gave me a certain perspective, yet my dad always encouraged me to think for myself. That said, it was still a little bizarre for the eighteen-year-old son of a Protestant minister to start lugging home books on Buddhism and meditation.

The voracity of my seeking increased with time, and I began travelling to sacred sites around the world, working with shamans and teachers. I've been honoured to have been initiated into three shamanic orders from the Incan culture as a Mesayoq – 'carrier of power' – as well as the supernatural Huna tradition of ancient Hawaii.

As awe-inspiring and insightful as these teachings have been, however, I still found that many of my questions remained unanswered. Whether I was in the rain forest of the Amazon, the sacred mountains of Peru, the islands of the South Pacific, or the deserts of Egypt, I found myself thinking during many a ceremony, 'These people are so pure, but almost childlike in their understanding and mentality.' Not to mention, I didn't love the idea that unless I wanted to give up money, food, and sex, I would never fully be able to tap the power of Eastern meditative practices.

In addition to my spiritual questions, I've lived and thrived in the more traditional business world too. I was one of AT&T's top sales managers for five years and spent four years as a personal and business growth expert with the AT&T School of Business. I spent four years working with best-selling author Stephen Covey, and thirteen years as an entrepreneur and business growth expert. But despite my successful corporate career, I knew I wouldn't be complete until I'd integrated the two different worlds in which I walked. I designed my work schedule to fit around my journeys, not the other way around. For twenty-five years, I've faithfully blocked off substantial weeks of time for yearly voyages and excursions.

The question that haunted me for years was, 'How do you apply these ancient methods to the modern Western world?' Deep down, a nagging feeling told me that our call is not to return to the old ways, but to bring their truths into today's world. I've spent years studying quantum physics, trying to translate the arcana of science into practical use. This book is the culmination of my efforts to do that: *Harmonic Wealth* distills success principles from across the globe, both old and new.

I, like you, remain a flawed student. I have struggled with my demons and have fought my dragons. Insecurity, fear of abandonment, lack of self-worth, and money identification have been my bedfellows, but I've pushed onward. Being a true student is about committing to diving deep and practising the disciplines of mastery versus just dabbling here and there as a 'tourist' until the going gets rough.

I teach with a passion for helping you avoid the hard knocks I've created, endured, and triumphed over. I'm someone who believes that admitting my flaws and challenges is a source of strength. I love to point them out because not only can you learn from them and avoid them, but then I don't have to live with such high standards in people's eyes. (Besides, if I don't get to them first, you might!)

How to Use This Book

As you'll see, this book is divided into five parts – one part for each of the Five Pillars – Financial, Relational, Mental, Physical, and Spiritual. Each section is comprised of chapters that offer facts, theories, anecdotes, and exercises. Don't just read the exercises; I *insist* that you *do* the exercises. But then again, once you do the first one, I won't have to lord it over you. You'll see almost immediately that they're fun and very different. I'm not into re-creating what you've done in other books and seminars. I'd stake my reputation on the fact that there are at least a few exercises that you'll be jumping out of your seat to start.

Harmony Starts Here

As you might have figured by this point, I believe in starting big. So take a deep breath, roll up your sleeves, and prepare to get busy. I promise that nothing worth accomplishing will come without focus and big action . . . but the prize is well worth the price.

You're reading this because you want – and know you deserve – more. More financial freedom, love, intellectual and emotional mastery, health, physical fitness, spiritual connection, joy, toys – you name it. It's all good and it's all spiritual – from a pine tree to a Porsche.

There are many ways to cross a river, but as I tell my students, 'The only way I know is my way.' Are there other ways to achieve Harmonic Wealth in life? Possibly, but I don't know them; I only know mine and I guarantee it works. So since you're holding my book, we're going to play by my rules. Meet me in five minutes with your notepad or journal, awake and ready to focus, and have fun mapping out your harmonically wealthy life.

'James. The old notepad thing?' If you're thinking, *Been there, done that, and I'm not in the mood,* get over it. Do it again. This is different. While you may have written down lists before – maybe even until your hand ached and carpal tunnel syndrome threatened – we're going to figure out right now exactly where you stand with the five key areas of Harmonic Wealth: Financial, Relational, Mental, Physical, and Spiritual, and what you choose to have in each. It's important to take stock of what you want – *or think you want* – now, because I want you to have a starting point. You should never start a journey without knowing where you're headed. And I also want you to have the powerful experience of seeing how things change once you've looked at your life and goals from the new, out-of-the-box perspectives to come. I think you'll be surprised by what is born of this process. So, at the risk of repeating myself, just do it. You'll be glad you did.

Intimidated? Let that go too. This disciplined approach is for your life and your life only. Resist any teachings that tell you you can just sit back and watch your life transform. Discipline always precedes dominion and anyone who's truly wealthy knows this. So, even if I do sound like a drill sergeant, don't worry about that. I love to tease, poke, and prod. But it's all in fun and meant in the spirit of changing lives; I always have your best interests in mind. I am honoured and humbled that you're taking this journey with me. That said, to the degree that you play full-on is the degree to which your life transforms. It's that simple – or not. It's your choice.

As I said, there's always a price to pay for the prize. The more you give, the more you get. The master embraces pain and pleasure in pursuit of his or her vision, dreams, and purpose. Don't wish for an easier life – that's illusion. Wish for greater capability and capacity to ease elegantly through life.

Do I hear you asking, 'But James, what if I'm not sure what my deepest desires are?'

I LOVE that question because, in truth, most people don't have a clue about what they really, really want. You're on common ground. I've been teaching this information in seminars, workshops, and keynotes around the world for over two decades, and I can promise you that most people have plenty more knowledge about what they *don't* want than about what will make them happy:

> Me: 'What do you want, oh kind-hearted seminar participant?'
> Seminar Participant: 'Well, I don't want to be fat anymore. I don't want to be broke another minute. I hate being unmarried at forty-five!'

See where I'm going with this? Do you ever do this? Answer someone's big-thinking question with a squeeze-the-fun-out-of-it, ignorant, fear-based, or downright depressing answer that's all about what you hate, what you don't want, what your life is full of? That's normal, I can assure you, but is that what you want – to be normal? I don't know about you, but the masses (with their high rates of divorce, obesity, and debt) have some serious challenges and 'normal' ain't cutting it. How can you commit 100 per cent to your spouse, your health, and your economics when *you don't even know what you really want?* You'll never be fully engaged in where you are or where you're going by settling for normal. Here's a fact: no one who was normal ever made history. Drop that fantasy like a hot potato!

I'm asking you to be willing to walk differently through the world, and I'll help you. The world isn't bad; people aren't bad. But there's a serious pack mentality on this globe – a certain level of consciousness, if you like, that must be surpassed to attain the Harmonic Wealth you seek. Breaking free starts with knowing who you are and why you're here. Most people I ask are hard-pressed to give me concrete details about what would make them jump out of bed in the morning. Given the finite amount of time you've got in this incarnation on this planet, doesn't that seem like a serious waste of time?

If your palms are sweating and your head's pounding, let me calm your nerves by saying that where you've been is not where you're going. I can help you figure out what you really, really want right now, and activate the Law of Attraction, as well as some other laws of the universe, to work wonders in your life, so stay with me.

You: A Visionary

I'm assuming your notepad has been in front of you for some time now, right? It's time to take a couple of minutes and write down the things you choose to create in your life. If you can get them down, I'll tell you how to achieve them. I want you to think harmonically, comprehensively, financially, relationally, mentally, physically, spiritually. What are the things you choose to create? Here's the thing: I'm not asking you to write down what you *think* you can get but rather what you would *dare to dream* if you knew anything was possible. Get it down – now. If you want to keep it short and sweet that's fine, you'll have the opportunity to go more in depth later. But for now, please commit to answering the following questions. ⓘ

ASSESS YOUR FINANCIAL WEALTH
- What's your ideal annual income?
- What's your dream net worth?
- How much do you want in your financial freedom account? (This differs from having a large net worth by including debt, like mortgages, since they're tied to payments.)

ASSESS YOUR RELATIONAL WEALTH
- Do you spend quality time by yourself? Do you enjoy your own company?
- Do you treat yourself the way you want other people to treat you? Please describe.
- What things do you do that contribute to your feeling joyous and fulfilled?
- Do you give yourself enough personal time?
- Do you have a dream mate?

• Would you know your dream mate if you met him/her? How specifically would you know?

• Who do you have to become to attract your dream mate?

• If you have a mate already, do you make time for that relationship, just the two of you?

ASSESS YOUR MENTAL WEALTH

• How many books do you choose to read per month, per year? (I bet this number changes after you've read the Mental Pillar.)

• How many seminars are you going to attend each year to invest in your number-one asset, your marvellous mind? Maybe there's a course you've always wanted to take that you've set aside for a long time.

• Are you the master of your own emotions or do they master you?

ASSESS YOUR PHYSICAL WEALTH

• What's your dream weight, dress size, suit size, body shape?

• How many days a week are you going to work out to stay in that shape? You know what that shape is. You know how you feel when you're healthy. How flexible do you want to be? I guarantee an inflexible body is a reflection of an inflexible mind.

• Do you have all the toys you want – that home you've always dreamed of, that car you've always wanted to drive?

• Where do you want to travel and explore? Do you want to drink fine wine in Paris? Visit the Great Pyramid in Egypt?

ASSESS YOUR SPIRITUAL WEALTH

• Have you discovered that one-on-one connection with your creative source? How do you define that? Be specific.

• What inspires you? *Inspiration* comes from the Latin word *inspiratu*, meaning 'divinely breathed into'. Are you inspired by great music, reading the classics, taking a walk in nature or a jog on the beach? Long baths with candles and incense? An evening at the Four Seasons in Maui? What would you want the divine to 'breathe into' your life right now?

I promise, when your vision on the inside becomes more compelling and powerful than what you observe on the outside, the universe is at your command. So, be specific, make it real, and fill in your vision with as many sensory details as possible. If you had it, what would it feel like, smell like, sound like, look like, taste like? You want to be able to recognise your intention when you create it at last.

Think big – really, really big. Don't censor yourself. I've shared this powerful strategy with thousands of people on all levels of the happiness scale, and the results are often extraordinary and life-changing when people truly let go of what they think is possible and write down their soul's desires.

Can you accomplish what you've just written down? It's going to take a tremendous amount of power for you to create this reality – more than you currently have. You might say, 'But James, you don't know me, how can you say that?' I know it's going to take more power than you currently have *because you don't have these things yet.* If you had enough personal power to attract your goals into your life and create them for yourself, you'd already have them. But make sure and give yourself credit for writing down your vision – I congratulate you. If you've done the work so far, you're already building up your power and energy with every page turned and exercise completed.

However, perhaps you're one of those people who will look at this list and think, *I just can't answer these questions.* Relax. I have a tactic created especially for you. As I said, I want your deepest focus to be on what you *do* want, but if you're truly stuck, the quickest way I've found to erase any confusion or doubt about your heart's true desires is to start with what you *don't* want.

On the *Oprah Winfrey Show,* I got the opportunity to work with a woman from the audience who said that she didn't know what her deepest desires were or her purpose. She was frustrated. Oprah and I agreed that the woman's dilemma was both 'big' and common. Perhaps like you, she didn't know the right questions to ask. Sometimes the most simple, most direct route to success is hidden from view.

Grab your notepad and write down everything you don't want, everything you really don't like about the life you now have: 'I don't want to be broke. I don't want to be overweight. I don't want to be alone' – whatever. Get it all down. Then use the Law of Polarity to your advantage. Just start down that list and ask yourself, 'What's the exact polar opposite of each statement?' Write it down as if you already have it. 'I don't want to be broke' becomes 'I have financial freedom.' 'I don't want to be overweight' becomes 'I am the perfect size and shape.' 'I don't want to be alone' becomes 'I'm in the perfect, loving relationship.' If you do this exercise, you'll get really clear on what you desire in your life.

Your 'Before' Life

Remember how you charted your growth against a doorframe of your childhood home so you could actually see how much you grew from year to year? Now it's time to gauge your current level of harmony on the five Harmonic Wealth columns. It just takes a few seconds. Rate yourself from 0 to 10 for each of the five pillars of Harmonic Wealth, with 0 being little or no satisfaction and 10 being the highest level of satisfaction possible. Drawing a straight line across the notches helps you rate your satisfaction levels and gain an immediate understanding of your level of Harmonic Wealth as it currently stands.

Now ask yourself the following questions:

1. Which areas need the most work in order to harmonise my life?

2. Why is this important to my overall success?

3. What do my pillars tell me about myself, my priorities, and my values?

4. What must I do differently to improve the strength of my columns?

5. If I had to choose one barrier to achieving harmonic wealth in all areas, what would it be?

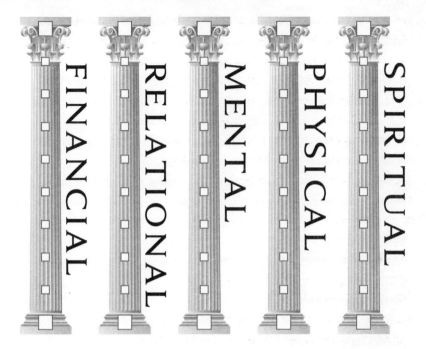

Are you concerned that your pillars vary wildly in height? Again, no worries. Honestly, if they're all perfectly 'balanced' at 9 or 10, you could be fudging the numbers (or standing with a foot in the grave). But seriously, depending on where your values currently lie, everyone will want and need different-sized pillars – and those will change as your life changes.

If you weaken any of these five pillars, however, the integrity of the entire structure starts to fall apart, either all at once or by bits and pieces. You can't strengthen the structure simply by reinforcing the strong pillars alone. Instead, you must attend to the weak ones, the areas of neglect. The key distinction is to realise that your pillars will never be equally strong all the time.

Realise that all five areas must have some attention all the time, but not all five areas demand all your attention all the time. Did you get that? If you're spending ten hours a day at work on a special project (remember our no-shower, three-day working binge example?), you're not going to be able to spend the same amount of hours at the gym or in quality time with your kids. That would be impossible. We'll cover how to handle these very real dilemmas in your everyday life, including how to make agreements with yourself and others, and planning for finite periods of focus and defocus but never total neglect.

Inevitably, by focusing on harmony throughout the chapters of the book, you'll either see a marked 'harmonic' improvement in each of the pillars, or have a more conscious, empowering awareness about which pillars need strengthening at different times when making your choices.

Let's Go

Harmonic Wealth will challenge everything you've been taught. Facing these truths will radically change your life. I know that because I've been teaching this information to thousands of students a year for over two decades, and I've seen these truths in action, truths now validated by physics and just starting to get major airtime in movies like *What the Bleep Do We Know!?* and *The Secret.* There will come a time in the not-so-distant future when their 'secret' knowledge will be accepted as the norm. But until that time, you're about to get on the inside track. People will look at your life and think, *My God, it's magic.* They'll be right: you created that magic.

2

My Journey

The road of life twists and turns and no two directions are ever the same.
Yet our lessons come from the journey, not the destination.

– DON WILLIAMS JR

Running on Empty

The dot-com crash of 2000 brought me to my knees. I went to bed one evening with a belly full of sushi, feeling comfortable and secure, and woke up the following morning to find that I was royally screwed. I had recently broken up with my girlfriend of five years – more than my girlfriend, she had been my brilliant accountant and business manager – and I didn't know who I was without her. We'd been a good team, but working together 24/7, our relationship suffered drastically. Every romantic dinner turned into a discussion of how to grow my company's assets and acquisitions, and that was cool for a time, but because we weren't experiencing harmony in other areas, we grew far apart. Oh yeah, we had the toys, the house, the cars, the 'life' for sure, but it had all grown stale. Now, aside from dealing with the intense emotional pain that accompanies a breakup, I was also dealing with the realisation that I would have to assume responsibilities that didn't come naturally to me. For the years we'd been together my girlfriend had handled my financial affairs masterfully, which left me free to concentrate on my teaching and my ever-growing appetite for acquiring more toys. Being unconcerned with money management, I focused on doing what I loved and doing it well. But faced with shouldering the added obligations of the fiscal side of the business, my

work stopped being fun. The adventure had become a burden, the desire, an obli-
gation.

I was at a place of spiritual emptiness. I had run out of inspiration. While I knew that I was here on this earth to run this business, I didn't like it anymore. I was at the top of the ladder, but it was leaning against the wrong wall. All I knew was that a tremendous longing in my spirit was pulling me away from everything I had built, urging me to divorce my-self from the world and soar to a new level. You can imagine that with this mind-set, paying attention to the mundane details of managing my finances felt impossible. Things began to unravel quickly.

In a flash, I was nearly bankrupt, broke, and alone. My serenity van-ished along with my stock portfolio. The divide almost conquered me.

Unable to pay off some major expenses, I had to sell most of my things. Tears filled my eyes as I handed my house keys to the agent. I said goodbye to my custom-built home library – the realisation of a lifelong dream – and a canvas I'd coveted since meeting one of my favorite artists. A fan of great art, I now felt as if my life had been rendered by Picasso in his cubist period – fractured, disjointed, everything in the wrong place. Yesterday I'd been a successful businessman known for helping tens of thousands achieve their material dreams in nationwide seminars. Today I wouldn't be able to afford a ticket to one of my own events.

I should have known better, but apparently I'd become addicted to consumerism. Although I wasn't famous, my beautiful multimillion-dollar home was higher up on Soledad Mountain than Deepak Chopra's, and I was foolish enough to think that might mean something. My intellect understood the futility of that ego-measuring stick, but that didn't stop the swell of pride rising in my chest each time I'd pass his street on the way up to mine. Who was I without my toys? Who was the James Ray who could barely afford the electricity that powered the twinkling lights of even one of the more modest homes below?

This wasn't the first time I would face financial ruin. I had, in fact, flirted with bankruptcy once before. But I had climbed back quickly from the previous near miss, and that had left me confident, smarter, and stronger. Now, near broke once again, I shook my head and laughed out loud. Was this a joke? If so, who was the joker?

We Teach What We Most Need to Learn

Every great spiritual teacher has said that life doesn't have to be a struggle. Jesus said, 'I come that you might have life and that you might have it more abundantly.' The Four Noble Truths in Buddhism reveal the existence of suffering. However, the word loosely translated as suffering is *dukkha*, which actually means a lopsided or bent wheel axle. The teachings basically say that there is *dukkha*. *Dukkha* arises, *dukkha* ceases, and there's a way *beyond dukkha*.

The teachings say that suffering, or being out of harmony, is a real thing, and yet there's a path beyond that disharmony. It brings to mind another great Buddhist teaching, that you aren't punished for your thoughts but rather by them. I was still bound by suffering, still in the all-too-familiar position of crawling on my hands and knees to drink from a dirty puddle. Ego aside, the bigger truth was that I was facing the greatest spiritual crisis of my life, one I would have to resolve if I was ever going to experience any kind of lasting joy or ever help anyone achieve authentic wealth. Was I up to it? At that moment, I wasn't so sure. I just really wanted out.

Ever since I was a kid, I'd always believed that you could be rich and spiritual. Weren't all the material goods I'd accumulated proof positive of that theory? After all, I did have an awesome amount of stuff and an awesome amount of freedom. It had to be because I meditated every day, didn't it? I had travelled to enlightening spiritual retreats. I had powerful, incredible friends, including spiritual leaders in other cultures. I could discourse on the concepts of God and spirituality with the best of them.

Of course, I had also spent a lot of my life not having toys, but I wasn't as spiritually evolved back then – or so I told myself. Now that I'd gone through this incredible spiritual evolution *and* lost all my material goods, what would life be like now? What could I learn from all this? What was I truly left with now?

It was time to test my theories on different turf, to try a hard-core experiment far away from home. I had nothing left to lose.

We all long for beauty, culture, finery. We're pulled towards these things, not out of greed or shallowness, but because they ignite within us who we are in our heart and soul. This elegance and beauty can be found in abundance throughout nature, where eye-popping fields of wildflowers, the carpetlike greenery of a seemingly endless forest from the air, or a school of fish a million strong remind us of the sheer scope and breadth of creation. It can also be found in man-made creations. I can't look at the streamlined simplicity of a space shuttle, the beauty of the Golden Gate Bridge, or the regal majesty of the Eiffel Tower and the Great Pyramid without pausing to soak it all in, marvelling at the creative genius of the human spirit.

Is there a spiritual difference between the glories of nature and the creations of man? It's true that nothing man-made has ever given me the same sense of expansion, of true wealth as, say, a view of a mountain or the Grand Canyon. But is there a difference between what man creates for his own pleasure and what man creates for the world, for others, for a higher good? Is a cathedral more spiritual than a castle? Are the gaudy McMansions of California less spiritual than centuries-old palaces built to stand the test of time? Is there something different about wealth that doesn't evaporate overnight?

These questions, large as they were, brought me back to my own situation, to the realisation that whatever I was doing clearly wasn't working – not completely anyway. I felt I had partial answers but part of the equation was still missing. My mind was weary but my eyes were open. As I turned to walk away from the life I knew, stumbling on humble legs towards the airport, I ached to see my world – *the world* – with fresh sight.

Call of the Spirit

My journeys, both inner and outer, haven't always made sense in the moment. They may seem impetuous – foolhardy, even. But I don't believe they are. The call of spirit is often totally illogical. You've heard of 'following the beat of a different drum'? Well, I follow the beat of my own marching band, and although it's loud and large, I'm usually the only one who can hear the marching orders.

You see, I believe there's nothing as important in this life as expanding one's consciousness. I also believe that the more we grow spiritually and mentally, the more we can create riches of all types on the physical plane. So, when I feel the need to get off the treadmill of my life and expand my mind, energy, vision, and creative powers, I'm known to hop on a plane, even when I'm cash poor. I'm not saying that's something you should do; everyone's path is different and I don't yet have the tug of family responsibilities in my personal equation. But I will say that I've never regretted roaming the planet. Not once.

So, even though I was on the verge of financial ruin, even though everyone was telling me that I should stay put and focus on the demands of my business and finances, defying logic, I decided to follow my heart. I got on that plane.

Coming into Focus

There was no mistaking that this was a defining moment, as if my entire life had led me to the places I visited during my trip. I'd gone to Europe thinking I was just too attached to my things, and I was. Since I'd been on a spiritual quest all my life, that realisation seemed like a natural epiphany, and it was true. Not that I had let my belongings and my status define me – not entirely. But I had to admit that they contributed a great deal to my sense of self. Still, while I knew that these things weren't who I was, I had resisted the idea of giving them up. Yet, something else was coming into focus. What if the problem didn't lie in the toys, but in the intent behind them?

I got a sense in that moment that I could have any house I wanted, even a palace, but if my wealth existed so that I could feel better about living higher up the hill than someone else, there was only one way to go from there, and it wasn't up.

There's a fine line between being grateful for what you have in life and

wanting more, and *needing* more because deep down you feel undeserv-
ing or that you're living as an imposter – out of your league. While I had
been living large, I had bought into my own publicity and thought my
multimillion-dollar life was a big deal. Yet, my whole mansion could
have fit into the foyer of this palace. What was my yearning for more,
bigger, better all about?

In the World, Not of the World

In many parts of the world a man is considered lucky if he owns a shirt,
a pair of shoes, and has access to clean water. It's important to know
that, to acknowledge it. However, when we widen our perspective to
consider those who have so little, wanting more can make even the
best-intentioned among us feel ungrateful and greedy. Perhaps that's
why so many of us don't ask for more. How can we justify our desires
when there's someone down the street pushing everything he owns in
a shopping cart? How dare we ask for more!

My next realisation hit me like a burst of wind after a thunderstorm.

I'd been feeling guilty for my arrogance and my success, and thus
thinking and acting too small, but in fact I should have been thinking and
acting bigger. Not because I needed another big house or library or art
collection (those things would take care of themselves when I righted my
thinking), but because of the man I'd have to *become* to sustain a bigger
life. My problem wasn't with things. My problem was with the identity
I had built for myself – that I was my house, my car, my bank account.
But I realised that I was so much more than that. It was time to be in the
world, but not of the world.

The loss of my material possessions was just a reflection of my past
thoughts and actions, a gauge of where I'd been, not where I was going.
I knew that I had to heal what was going on inside me so that I could
bring a fuller, more self-realised me into the world. Not a greedy me, but
an expanded, integrated me who could teach by example and help shed
light on this material/spiritual dilemma we all wrestle with. Spiritual
teachers throughout time have warned us that things won't make us

happy, and my life had proved just that. After all, we're all just temporary custodians of our things. No point in getting too attached to them. Was there a way to own things without being owned by them? To have wealth without hoarding resources? To celebrate all that God has given us without losing sight of the giver? The answers to these questions were the gifts of my debacle, the blessings I was now grateful for. I had been on a spiritual quest since I was a kid, and I was becoming more and more aware that it wasn't necessary to suffer to love God. Moreover, loving God didn't mean you couldn't appreciate a beautiful lifestyle. A wave of gratitude washed over me as suddenly it was becoming clear.

Longing for the Sacred

What I needed, what we all need, is a spiritual renaissance – a return to the elegant and sacred in our everyday lives. But this renaissance can't be centred entirely on the external; it has to focus on a higher awareness. We are about to usher in a whole new era. It can't be born from subjugation or fear of the past, and it can't be brought about by overindulgence. This new era can only come from celebration, recognition, and awareness of the expansive good that is true wealth in all its forms. It can only come from a new beginning. It can only come from Harmonic Wealth.

Choosing to see the loss of my belongings as an opening for the emergence of a bigger awareness helped me to trust that the symphony of my life was divinely orchestrated, that this crash was bringing me to an awakening.

In truth, I realised that I hadn't been all that attached to things until recently anyway. (Had I been, I might have paid more attention to what was happening with my finances.) I longed for the sacred, for the inspiration of spirit. I had built my career around bigger, better, best, but to be part of something meaningful and contribute at a greater level, it had to be about more than getting the toys. I wanted to have a lasting and profound impact on my own life and on those whose lives I touched.

It was on this trip that the concept of the five pillars of Harmonic Wealth – something I had been working on for years – came into sharper focus for me. I saw that they were incomplete in and of themselves; and yet completely necessary as a whole.

I needed time and fieldwork to test my theory of Harmonic Wealth, but first I needed to recover from the past few years. I was in so much psychological pain from the financial and emotional roller coasters I'd been riding that I couldn't move forward. I understood that pain is a signal to grow, not suffer, and I believed that I could emerge from this personal tragedy more successful than ever. Nevertheless, from where I stood, that was incredibly ominous and unsettling. I had so many financial obligations and yet it was under that pressure that I had to realign my teaching and thinking. I was frightened. Knowing me, I'd be asking myself to expand even further next time. I wasn't ready to tackle that soon.

While I was mostly sure I was hardwired for the challenge of overcoming my financial obstacles so I could bring that working blueprint back to myself and to my students, more than anything, I just wanted to run away. To go further inward. To heal deeper. Since it was my attitude towards my material possessions that had brought me to this place, I knew there was nothing else to do but give them up. I decided I didn't want to own a thing. Not even a bike. I wanted to feel what it was like to live like a snail with life on its back. I started by seeking out a wise kahuna in Hawaii and a Peruvian shaman 16,400 feet up in the Andes because I felt this strong pull to ancient wisdom. I had looked at many religious and cultural traditions in my years of study, and it seemed to me that the teachings from the prophets since our current world history had been recorded hadn't changed much. I wanted to go back to the beginning, back to the source, back to shamanism before wisdom had been watered down. I wanted the truth.

True Wealth

Now I was the student. Cradled in the embrace of ancient ways on raw land with big sky, I slowly nurtured myself back. I was shown a world of wisdom more simple and profound than my mind could often handle, and my first big lesson was that everything appearing in my world was of my own creation. Everything. That was big. Of course I'd heard this from self-help gurus for years, but when it came from the Peruvian shaman with eyes as old as time and a voice as pure as the wind, the truth of his delivery hit me at my core. I had no choice but to go deep and look at my life and ask, 'How have I created all this pain for myself? How have I gotten so hideously off track?'

I had seen myself as the king of the hill and had been taken down by the peasant-like thoughts of my own ignorance. I'd thought that because I'd eagerly studied spiritual texts and embarked on so many spiritual quests I was evolved, but now that I had to look at myself with honest eyes I understood that I wasn't nearly as evolved as I had thought. In fact, I began to think that I had been more *involved* than *evolved*. That's when it hit me: the quests don't make us spiritual; understanding and right application make us spiritual. I wasn't living as a spiritual person. I had only *thought* I was. Moreover, it wasn't my theory of being rich and spiritual at the same time that was faulty; it was my actions, and the intent behind them, that had been all wrong. True wealth is not what you have, it's what you're left with when all you have is gone. Maybe the lesson is that when you begin to think you're the bomb, the universe loves you enough to drop the bomb.

Thump.

PILLAR I

Financial

I've always been very mystical but also very, very practical. I love hard scientific evidence, and I love to make it applicable so you can grab it with your hands and put it to use. One of my teachers in Peru, don José Luis, once told me, 'Santiago, power is an empty vessel unless it grows corn.' That's really the point of this book. You may be able to tap into every theory in quantum physics, spirituality, psychology, philosophy, or anything else that can teach you about accessing your power, but if you can't use that power to create results in your life, it's pointless, useless, a total waste of time.

My intention for you in this work is to give you insights, tools, and techniques to create the outrageous and amazing results you deserve in every area. This isn't just going to be a 'write down your goals' book, but one that deals with the fundamental level of vibration and consciousness for profound, lifelong shifts.

Money is nothing more than a metaphor for the physical, material, and tangible. Your ability to attract money in your life is a reflection of your ability to manifest your God power into physical form. My ultimate intention is that you'll have enough money and material things in your life that you'll no longer waste one precious moment worrying about them. But it's more than just having these things, it's about knowing that no matter what happens, you have all the power and ability inside you to create them – and everything else – time and time and time again. You deserve this . . . It's your birthright. This I know.

Why such focus on money? Because money changes everything by magnifying your current state of affairs, tending to make problems (or joys) that exist in other parts of life even bigger. Money in and of itself doesn't provide fulfilment, but Harmonic Wealth does. If you find yourself constantly worrying about this pillar, you'll find it very difficult (if not impossible) to focus on the other four pillars of wealth. So let's get this one handled and get on with it. Are you ready?

3

Grandeur Is Our Birthright

Look at everything as though you were seeing it either for the first time
or the last time. Then your time on earth will be filled with glory.

– BETTY SMITH

Limiting Beliefs

We learn most of our limiting beliefs about money as children. I have a vivid
memory of at least one thing that got me tripped up. I'm eight years old, sitting
in the front pew in my father's church, the Red Fork Church of God, in Tulsa,
Oklahoma, when I hear the words that would play in the background of my mind
like annoying elevator music for years to come: 'It is easier for a camel to go through
the eye of a needle, than for a rich man to enter into the kingdom of God.'

That cannot be, I thought. I felt anger rise within my chest, making my
shirt feel two sizes too small, which was probably the actual case. Mum
and Dad didn't have money to buy nice clothes. In fact, we were too
poor to own a home, and lived instead in the office space attached to the
church. The hardest part of my childhood was reconciling how Dad
poured his heart into his work, how he helped so many people, and yet
couldn't even afford to pay for haircuts for me and my brother. Mum
would sit on the front porch to give us crew cuts while local kids would
stand nearby and laugh.

One evening my father helped an especially long string of people who just kept walking through our door and I thought, *What the hell? What kind of God takes so much and gives so little in return? How could a loving God keep me from the Cub Scouts on account of not being able to afford a uniform? How could a loving God make a baseball glove too expensive for our family to afford?*

I felt like a total flop.

What if I want to be rich someday, God? Did this camel business mean that God wouldn't let me through the pearly gates? Even at that age, I knew I wanted to see the world. But Mum and Dad made it clear that riding in planes took serious money – money we didn't have.

'Can we go to Disneyland?' I asked, eager and impatient as only a young boy can be. 'Greg just missed a week of school because his family went there, and he said it's the best!'

'Not right now, son,' Dad said matter-of-factly, so typical of a guy who'd learned discipline and limits in the navy.

'What about the Empire State Building?' I pressed on. 'We saw pictures of it in class and Mrs Davis says it's as tall as one quarter of a mile and millions of people go to the top of it every year!'

'We can't afford that either, honey,' Mum said, patting my head. She looked melancholy. Strangely enough, it was my beloved mother who was always the strongest advocate of this scarcity position. I understand today that this fear and lack mentality was a product of her extremely strict upbringing. The sins of the fathers and the mothers are gifted upon the sons and daughters. The endless cycle continues to self-perpetuate.

'Are all those millions of people who go there richer than us?' I asked.

'Well, I don't know about that,' Mum said. 'But you know that preachers don't make a lot of money. Your father is doing God's work.'

Thus began my confusion about God and money, and why the two were considered mutually exclusive when I knew in my bones they weren't.

So, where did it all get so mixed up? Where did it become sinful in our society, especially for pious folks, to want or love money? After learning about the plight of those living on the street, I would later come to think more in alignment with George Bernard Shaw's quote, 'Lack of money is the root of all evil.' As a child, when I compared the ease and freedom some wealthy parishioners enjoyed in Dad's church (and how they'd return from jaunts to the islands sporting tans and loud Hawaiian print shirts) with the enormous sadness and limitation on view in lines at the soup kitchen, it sure seemed to me that something other than right vs wrong or good vs evil was at work here. Bottom line? Here's what I know: it's a sin to be poor.

I loved God with all my might. I also loved and respected my dad. I was so proud of him. If anyone deserved to have money, he did. Unlike those whose entire lives are about the race for the prize, Dad's heart was always centred on the purity of his love for divinity. You could see it a mile away.

Maybe in solidarity for the father I revered, or maybe just to keep myself from going insane, I made a decision right there that I was going to solve this puzzle – to redefine, if you like, the relationship between spirituality and money. It was possible, even likely, that I wouldn't figure it out in time for Mum, Dad, my younger brother, and me to slap on our Mickey Mouse ears and go racing down the Matterhorn or get dizzy as drunken sailors (especially since that 'eye of a needle' comment was really messing with my head!), but some kid somewhere would benefit. I'd do it for him.

Keep in mind, this was more a general inner resolve than an actual plan. I mean, how do you go about designing the job description of 'one who helps expand mass consciousness'? I didn't have the first clue where I was headed back then, but I knew it was high time to make having lots of money a good thing, even a spiritual goal, and to show the masses that God was in full, no-holds-barred support mode.

Missing the Mark

We all have our complicated financial histories, and it doesn't help much that there's a poverty consciousness that hovers over us like a thick marine layer, whispering, 'Life's hard and then you die, so grab what you can, if you can, before someone else does. He who dies with the most toys wins.'

My drive to teach was building serious momentum when I hit my twenties, but the more I looked around, the more daunted I was by this self-imposed task. Money lies are everywhere, like blankets of fog rolling in and fingering their way through every conceivable crack, from attic windows and cellar doors to hearts and minds young and old. No one is immune. 'You can't be spiritual and love money.' Lie. 'Money doesn't grow on trees.' Lie. (Where do you think paper comes from?) 'Nice guys finish last.' Lie. 'Success has very little to do with fulfilment and is mostly about hard work.' Lie. 'The meek will inherit the Earth.' Lies. Lies. Lies.

Together humanity stands guard, willingly enforcing the 'facts' that hold these half-truths in place. Look, for example, at the difference in remuneration between an actor and a teacher. We can all agree that placing more value on our entertainment than on our evolution, transformation, and growth is bizarre at best. But then again, one measure of what we truly value the most is how much time we spend doing it. By that measure, it's crystal clear what we value most in our society – entertainment. As you'll see shortly when we cover the difference between pleasing activities and pleasing results, we also *always* throw money at what we truly value.

When I learned that the root word for *sin* is Greek in origin, referring to a term from archery meaning, 'to miss the mark', a lightbulb went on for me. I had the proof I needed to feel certain that most people, including my own family, were inadvertently fuelling the lies by missing the mark when it came to money. If my well-meaning, honest, and giving parents were doing it, who had a chance of breaking free from our foggy societal conditioning? No wonder we have no problem compensating sports figures in shorts with millions of pounds a year to chase balls around fields, while paying the people who enrich the minds of our children (not to mention our spiritual teachers) so little that many take second jobs just to survive. The lie, like the joke,

is on us. We've propped up faulty logic and called it gospel. Good
Lord!

Heaven Is Expansion

As I got older and started studying history, world religions, metaphysics,
and the world of financial systems, I was fascinated by the origin of our
beliefs, and how they were so masterfully crafted and manipulated, or at
the very least grossly misunderstood.

As for the '. . . it is easier for a camel to go through the eye of a
needle, than for a rich man to enter into the kingdom of God' line from
the Bible that had given me such stress, I about fell over when I learned
that the word heaven comes from the Greek *ouranos*, meaning 'expansion'. Then I remembered that when Jesus spoke of the kingdom of
God, he used parables about rising bread and the proliferation of mustard
seed and the like. Everyone knows that bread rises, *expands*, when it
bakes; likewise, tiny mustard seeds blow in the wind, *expanding* their
reach. Could it be, then, that heaven is the expansion and growth of consciousness, the evolution of who we are? After all, Jesus never talked
about heaven as an actual place. He actually referred to it only as 'being
within' and 'at hand'. So we're talking about the kingdom of expansion
within, not about somewhere on clouds. Jesus never promised clouds or
that we'd be issued wings and a harp and walk on streets of gold. That was
all made up by the people trying to control us through fear and future
promises.

Think about 'In my Father's house are many mansions.' Again, in
going back to the Greek for house, you get *oikos*, or 'family residence'.
Look up mansion and you get *mone,* meaning 'abode' or 'dwelling place'.
A translation could be: 'In my Father's world are many dwelling places or
many rooms,' maybe even many paths and approaches. To me that means
there's room for everyone. Get your heart, mind, and soul in the right
space and join me within, where heaven resides for everyone. All roads
lead to Rome.

What of that poor camel? Turns out the 'eye of a needle' was actually a gate our camel needed to pass through to enter the old city of Jerusalem. Merchants would enter this gate when bringing their wares into the city, bringing only what a camel could carry. By all accounts the gate was so small that camels had to get on their knees in order to squeeze through. Changes things, doesn't it?

So, look again more closely at Matthew 19:24. It doesn't say that it's impossible for the rich man to get to heaven, just that it's easier not to. Think about that next time you've saddled your camel down with bags full of ceramics, linens, and jewellery, and keep that image in mind because it's a metaphor for how very easy, how seductive it is to fall in love with your stuff and your money. When you do that, you often halt your expansion and your growth because you get seduced into all the external things that money brings – toys, power, fame, the works.

Start to focus on material objects over the daily journey and you'll believe that your joy resides outside of you in *things*. You'll lose the simple pleasures of being alive. Believe me . . . I have first-hand experience. We've all seen the difference between a toddler happily playing with a wooden spoon and a teenager bored out of his mind in a room full of video games and material luxuries. Same idea.

The Love of Money Is the Root of All . . .

Toys, power, fame, the works can be fantastic, and if that's what you want, you should experience it all. But the Darth Vader move, as I call it – the transition from a man of light to a monster of darkness – can happen at any level. Regardless of how high you grow and evolve, you can still fall. Even more so, when the seductions are everywhere. You need to guard against this as if your very life depends on it. It doesn't matter how much you grow and expand either; the allure of increasing wealth and fame is always a seductive reality, slithering around your ankles, ready to strike in the blink of an eye. It's even seductive for me, and I know what to watch out for, my antivenom always at the ready because it gets really comfortable receiving adulation and gifts, the accoutrements of success. Halting our expansion (our heaven within and without) is an easy detour when you get caught up in the physical trappings of life and take a sharp left, veering away from the path to your soul. The 'love of money' thus becomes 'the root of evil' when people start loving money and using people. I prefer to love people and use money.

Just to keep it *really* interesting, the word for hell comes from the Greek word *hades,* meaning 'unseen' or 'blind'. We are blind when we worship the external at the expense of the vast riches of the internal. We are blind when we stop expanding. The kingdom of heaven is within. When you begin to put your sense of self in the external, you cut yourself off from your heart, focusing on the effect instead of the cause.

To put this 'loving money and using people' business into a current context, think for a moment about the classic image of a beautiful young woman who marries an older wealthy man. People around the couple whisper that she 'married him for his money', and 'He's taller when he's standing on his wallet.' Sure enough, after a few years of marriage, the woman leaves him, puts a fat wad of green stuff into the glove compartment of her new Mercedes, and speeds off. How about this one? Ever hear of the struggling medical student who weds a woman who dutifully supports him through college, holding down two jobs and paying the bills while raising their children? Once he's a fully fledged doctor making big money and living it up, he leaves his wife for a hot younger woman and starts a second family.

We've all seen these scenarios play out in real life or in the media. While not everyone marries for money or leaves a spouse for a younger model, the reality is that the stereotypes exist because people can be a means to an end. People can help pay your way through life. Some smell that good opportunity and jump at it. But they're acting on a false belief – the old chestnut that there isn't enough money to go around, so you'd better compete against every other hungry mouth on this crowded globe.

That's a tired old mind-set. Let's embrace a new reality based on expansion and integration. Let's create our heaven right here and now. When you expand your ability to receive more of everything you want, you not only live in harmony, but you release that harmony into the world – supporting the emotional, mental, physical, and spiritual wealth of the greater whole.

So if you, like me, were that kid who wondered why God made all the cool stuff imaginable – designer clothes, sports cars, mansions, *and* family holidays – but somehow didn't want us to enjoy them with all the enthusiasm of a kid on Christmas morning, you're in the right place. If you, like me, have always had a sense deep down that you could be rich as hell and still get into heaven, welcome home. I'm here to inform you that the days of faulty logic are wearing thin. They're being banished as we speak to scavenge on their own in the desert. *Don't let the camel myth dump its load of crap on you.* Still, some people will try and make you jump into a white robe with both feet and subsist on vegetables and rice while burning sage in the quest for true spirituality. That can work. I've been there and done that, and still have the gong ringing in my ears. But if you'd prefer to wear Armani and rock to U2 from the front row in Berlin, go right ahead, my friend!

4

Money Is a Spiritual Tool

When it's a question of money, everybody is of the same religion.
–VOLTAIRE

Figuring It Out

After I left home and began taking spiritual quests around the world, Dad didn't lay a bunch of guilt in my lap for bucking the system, thank God. I think he trusted that my rebellion and seeking was, at its core, about strengthening my connection with the Almighty. Dad has always been surprisingly non-judgmental. His faith in me superseded everything and fuelled my own faith in my quests. 'Keep an open mind,' he'd say. 'You're a good man with good instincts.'

As I delved deeper into my passion for redefining spirituality and money, I read books like *Think and Grow Rich, The Science of Getting Rich,* and *Bible Mystery, Bible Meaning* – early-twentieth-century masterpieces that remain popular today. Not only did these books give me insight, they also provided me with information on discipline and the practice of success. After I had devoured them, I realised the opportunity to make my unique contribution. I had spent years studying the missing physics component that evolved in the decades since those authors were around, and I also saw how the *other key* areas of life – relational, mental, and physical – needed to be fortified for this God and money combo to live in harmony. For example, I realised that I couldn't meditate at all whenever

I had a headache or a stomach problem. Feeling emotionally down in the dumps didn't exactly inspire me to go for a workout. Interestingly, when I wasn't fit, I didn't have the same motivation for business or even meditation for that matter. I saw for the first time how the five key areas, which would evolve into the five pillars, are totally interdependent. It was clear to me that they needed to be in harmony for the money to stick around and for God to remain in the building.

As I began to play with the idea of the five pillars, I realised that I had at one time or another experienced challenges and hardship in each of them. Often more than once!

Consider the physical and relational pillars – man, did I bounce from extreme to extreme! I had an incredibly strict upbringing. I never had a drop of alcohol until I was probably twenty-eighty or twenty-nine years old. I was a virgin until I was twenty-five years old, then married my girlfriend because we'd had premarital sex and I felt so guilty – needless to say, that marriage didn't last. My brother and I started hanging out and things got pretty crazy. Me and tequila developed a pretty good relationship. We started clubbing every single weekend, notching our belts; I thought monogamy was a type of wood. A nerdy, skinny failed athlete as a kid (which must have disappointed my dad, Mr Golden Gloves), I took up competitive bodybuilding and made it my new religion.

As far as the spiritual pillar was concerned, I went from faithfully attending my dad's Protestant church to studying everything from Buddhism to the gods of ancient Egypt. I can't remember a time when I didn't think the most important thing was how the universe worked and how to figure it out. I was reading mysticism, Shirley MacLaine, Seth, and Ruth Montgomery. I was driven to this inner world and mysticism out of the pain of not being accepted in the world, yet I recognised there was this big incongruity between what I knew in my head and how I was acting in my life.

I learned that if there's chaos between your inner and outer worlds, you're going to attract chaos – great lesson. I don't think it was any accident when I had a major motorcycle accident in the late eighties. I got hit head on and spent months in recovery. I went from seventeen stone of hard-earned bodybuilding muscle to twelve stone just like that. But there was a great gift in all that pain. It made me take a look at my life, at who I was and what was truly important.

With the Financial Pillar, it seems I also had to swing from pole to pole, living with great material wealth, then with next to nothing, as if I had to road-test my parents' ideas on money against my own. You know what? I think I was right all along! If anything, God wants us to have more, to be bigger and better – reaching the potential He's given us, but only if we can handle it with humility and the right intention. I'm now convinced that being poor isn't the way – in fact, if anything, being even richer is the way. But what's different is your *relationship* with your riches!

While I still have my challenges (I am human!), travelling from extreme to extreme with all the poles has convinced me of the necessity of harmony among them if we're to grow and expand. When it comes to the financial pillar, I still have my challenges, but they're more of the 'my business is growing faster than I can keep up with' variety as opposed to the old 'I don't know if I can pay everyone this month.'

Think Bigger

People often say to me, 'James, money is my greatest challenge!' Or, 'If I had more money, then everything else would fall into place.'

'You and the rest of the planet!' I answer.

Money brings up our insecurities and fears like nothing else. Money is at the root of most arguments and insecurities, including wars – *especially* wars. While it's only one fifth of the equation for Harmonic Wealth, money is a very important tool and it affects all of the other pillars. You've probably heard it said that money will never make you happy. When I hear that I answer, 'No kidding! Your refrigerator won't drive you to the grocery store either.'

The point is that money is meant to make you happy, but it will never make you feel secure. In fact, according to Ervin Laszlo's book, *The Chaos Point,* a survey in 2000 by a US private bank found that 64 per cent of Americans who had an average wealth of $38 million or more still felt financially insecure! Being happy, fulfilled, and secure comes from within. Money will, on the other hand, make life more comfortable and give you more options. You need a certain amount of it in today's world to pursue other areas of your life.

Don't fall into the trap of thinking you can grow spiritually, be healthy and fit, emotionally stable, mentally sharp, and have harmonious relationships without a certain amount of money – you can't! It was Gandhi who stated, 'There are people in the world so hungry that God cannot appear to them except in the form of bread.'

Now, you might just be trying to figure out how to pay your bills and have enough left over to put more fun into your life, or you may have it pretty good financially and you're just ready to improve. Either way, I promise we'll delve into the practical stuff shortly. But this foundation-building information is a vital part of taking you where you want to go and beyond. You can always tell how tall a building will rise by looking at the depth of the foundation. Let's dig deep.

Remember how at the start of this pillar I said there's nothing as important as expanding your consciousness? Well, it takes a bigger person to make £100,000 per year than to make £10,000. Now please understand . . . not a *better* person, but a *bigger* person. There's not one of us who's 'better' than another – we've all been given gifts from our creator. But it takes a bigger thinker, a bigger risk taker, bigger action, a bigger grasp on how the universe and its laws work. Likewise, it takes a bigger person to make £1,000,000 per year than it takes to make £100,000 per year. So if you're ready to secure that foundation and go big, then you have the right book in your hands.

Quantum Creations – Reap the Bounty

Try this on for size: if you want to make more money, learn a little something about physics. Understanding how a certain subset of physics called quantum physics operates in your life can increase your capacity to attract and sustain wealth.

If you remember anything about physics from high school, it's probably good old Newtonian physics: what goes up must come down (gravity), every action has an equal and opposite reaction, and so on. It's the physics of the tangible world. Everything's observable and everything plays nicely by the rules. Quantum physics is a whole other game with a whole different set of rules. Stuff happens in all these different dimensions. You're dealing with particles/waves too tiny to see, so the conventional rules about space and time and observability (the notion that internal states can be known by external outputs) get thrown out the window. It's enough to blow your circuits. While Newtonian physics is the physics of the tangible, quantum physics is the science of the intangible. We could call Newtonian physics the physics of the physical world, while quantum physics is the physics of the spiritual world.

I know this sounds confusing and maybe even irrelevant. I mean, you don't need to know how aspirin works to make your headache go away, and few of us have any clue as to how electricity works, but that doesn't stop us from being able to turn on a light switch in the dark. So, do we really need to have an understanding of quantum physics to create material wealth?

No, it's not absolutely necessary, but it helps. It's helped me a lot. Particularly when everything appears to be going left in my life when I want it to go right. Understanding the physical basis underlying the creation of wealth has helped me gain confidence in the laws that govern the universe, and it has worked wonders for my own self-confidence. By being able to put wishful thinking to bed, my mind and body have been more attuned to receiving wealth on all fronts. All great minds, from modern science to the spiritual traditions, agree that everything physical and tangible comes forth from the non-physical, intangible spiritual domain.

Newton vs Quantum

I've had no formal training in science, and even though I hated physics in school (couldn't stay awake for a simple half-hour class), once I started learning about quantum physics and how it relates to wealth, I just couldn't get enough of it. In fact, I've had my nose in quantum physics books for well over a decade. I can remember sitting on planes reading books like *Wholeness and the Implicate Order*, *The Tao of Physics*, and *The Self-Aware Universe*, and the guy sitting next to me would say, 'What are you reading?' and I'd say, 'I haven't got a clue!' Many times I found myself reading and rereading the same page ten, twelve times. I just knew that there was something valuable in there for me. One day it all came together in my mind and I could see how the different theories related to one another.

Believe it or not, most of the ideas in quantum physics were introduced in the 1950s, but they're just now reaching the greater population. As we discussed, I'm convinced that the quantum physicists, the chaos theorists, and the biologists of today are the mystics of the twenty-first century.

The world of Newtonian physics involves direct cause and effect, linear thinking, and a mechanistic approach in the familiar three-dimensional world we see around us. The quantum realm is non-linear, operating on subtle energies more often intuited than measured, in dimensions we can't detect with our five senses. To achieve true Harmonic Wealth, you've got to know how to operate in two realms simultaneously – to respect the linear, Newtonian results you can see with your eyes while acknowledging what's happening on a non-linear quantum level in the realm of spirit.

Believe me, straddling these two worlds is one of the most challenging things you'll ever do, and it's tempting to lean to one extreme or the other. Most people swing their pendulum in the Newtonian direction, thinking they have little or no effect on the world around them. Living by sight versus vision, they become consumed with a mechanistic worldview of physical cause and effect, doing, doing, doing, and trying to 'make it happen' so much so that they often block the natural, abundant flow coming right to them from the unseen world. Others swing too far into the quantum world and become what I call 'ceiling surfers'. I once had lunch with someone who announced he was going to transform the molecules of his pizza into a salad! That's taking a principle so far it becomes ridiculous. It will bring you nothing but disappointment.

Newtonian physics is the physics of the small mind of men. Now I'm not knocking the third dimension; I love it here. But we must access the true magnitude of our total power and ability, become masters of the quantum domain, while still thriving in the Newtonian world of action. When you master both of these worlds, you're unstoppable.

Everything, Including Money, Is Energy

We live in a vibrational universe. What appears to be empty space is the seat of unlimited energy. The money you want, the relationships you want, everything from a Porsche to a pine tree comes from what quantum physicists call the Zero Point Field. This label, first proposed by Albert Einstein and Otto Stern in 1913, has many names in science. It's also called the *subatomic field,* the *quantum hologram,* or the *plenum,* which means 'fullness'. A theologian calls it God – the source of everything. Some brave academics are even calling the Zero Point Field the *mind of God.* Whatever you call it, labels don't make much difference. The word water doesn't make you wet. So I encourage you to choose whatever label works best for you.

Everything that appears solid is comprised of 99.9999999 per cent light or energy. Every single thing in your world, from this book to your car to the clothing you're wearing is nothing more than stable light that's condensed in the Zero Point Field. So says quantum physics. Point one: everything you want – the cash, the lover, the body, the intellect – is all 99.99999999 per cent light. Point two: light (or energy) vibrates; it has a resonance or a frequency. Understanding this is *the key* to achieving anything and everything you want. If you think you're just running around as a personality trapped in a meat suit, think again. You're a field of energy operating in a larger field of energy, and your energy field is vibrating. Point three (and this is a big one): you'll never attract high-energy vibrations – known as results – from a low-energy vessel.

The Zero Point Field interconnects all time and space from the finite to the infinite like a vast invisible web. Look around you right now – go ahead, I'm serious – look around you. What may appear to be empty space is in fact pregnant with unlimited potential and possibility. That's where you come from – unlimited and infinite. That's who you are. All the energy you need exists in the Zero Point Field around you right now. It is you. Do you get that? According to some scientists, there's enough energy in one cubic metre of the Zero Point Field to boil every single ocean on the planet. Everything in your universe is comprised of this same energetic source, and yet you think you don't have any energy? *Well, James, I just can't get started in the morning without my coffee.* Come on! You come from this field! You *are* energy!

Let's assume you choose to call this field God. Now, keep an open mind. If you come from this field and are made of the same energy, wouldn't it mean that you and God are the same thing? What do you think the Christian prophet meant when he said, 'I and my Father are one' (John 10:30)? The only difference is that one of you is in form and the other is not. Quantum physics tells us that every single thing comes from the Zero Point Field. Spiritual traditions tell us that every single thing comes from God. It's all the same stuff – including you. The only difference between your body and a BMW is the frequency of vibration.

Of course you aren't the totality of God or the Zero Point Field (neither is your BMW), but it's the height of arrogance to say you and God are different. The great Essene tradition stated that the greatest sin is to question your divinity. Let me give you an example.

I have a home on the island of Hawaii. If I take a cup and dip it into the Pacific Ocean in front of my place, I obviously have a cup of Pacific Ocean. I could fly with that cup miles and miles away, and by the time I got to Kansas City or even Shanghai, the contents of my cup would still be Pacific Ocean.

Imagine for a moment that this cup of water could think and talk (bear with me on this one). Wouldn't it be completely arrogant for this small cup of ocean to start to think, believe, and argue that it wasn't

Pacific Ocean? Wouldn't it be totally ignorant for it to actually believe that it was separate and different just because it was in a different container in a different location?

Ocean is ocean. Separateness is illusion. Get over the ignorant/arrogant thinking that you and God are different. Understand that you and everything are the same, literally. The only defining difference between you and anything else is the rate of vibration. That's it. Get this; if you want to attract a new result in any area . . . you're already it! All you must do is come into harmony with it. Ponder that one deeply.

You and I have barely scratched the surface of what we're capable of being, doing, and creating in our lives. This book is ultimately to remind you of your unlimited creative powers and to allow you to experience greater levels of your God-like abilities to create outrageous results in every area of your life – yes, including money.

5

It's Already Here

Empty pockets never held anyone back. Only empty heads and empty hearts can do that.

– NORMAN VINCENT PEALE

A Dualistic Universe

We really are living in the most exciting time in world history. As scientific minds, one by one, climb the mountain of truth, they find the mystic sitting there, eating a sandwich, saying, 'What the hell took you so long?' This is creating a visible release of confusion and guilt across the globe, and millions of fans are singing the praises of this new way of relating to life. Movies like What the Bleep Do We Know!? *and* The Secret *have awakened humanity to so many things, including the incredible news that science and religion no longer oppose one another. But because this is a dualistic universe, the ideas that attract passionate enthusiasm from some are the same ideas that elicit anger, fear, and criticism from others. I would expect nothing different. If anything is ever loved it will also be hated. Anything that creates wildly empowered enthusiasm will also create fear.*

Throughout history, any time a 'new' idea (or an old idea that's been newly discovered or packaged) goes against current mind-sets, three predictable phases play out. First, the new idea is ridiculed. Second, it's violently opposed. Third, it's accepted as fact, rendering it obvious or self-evident . . . usually after the opposition has died.

Even if you've heard this example, I believe it bears repeating as much as history repeats itself, so put your mind-set back in the sixteenth century for just a moment, a time primarily driven by reverence for religious institutions, with certain rigid ways of thinking. No judgment, that's just the way it was. At that time, Earth was the centre of our heliocentric universe. We considered ourselves to be God's greatest creation. Of course, as the be-all end-all, the Sun revolved around us. How could it not?

When Nicolaus Copernicus studied the heavens and realised that the Earth, in fact, revolved around the Sun, he knew his findings would be considered blasphemous, so he arranged for them to be published only upon his death, a superior marketing strategy that created quite a stir. Just in case he was already relaxing with his feet up in heaven, upon publication the Catholic Church promptly condemned him to hell. Whoops . . . marketing ploy backfired. A few decades later, a scientist named Giordano Bruno confirmed Copernicus' revelation and further stirred the pot by questioning the virgin birth. Bruno was promptly burnt at the stake. Nothing like arriving in hell already well done. When Galileo published an account in 1610 that was favourable to Copernicus, he was ordered imprisoned and spent the rest of his life under house arrest. Finally, in the seventeenth century, when Sir Isaac Newton categorically declared that the Earth revolves around the Sun, the idea was accepted as self-evident.

Here's the rest of the story:

The Vatican formally published an apology, officially letting Copernicus out of hell in 1992. I'll bet Copernicus is pissed off! Spending all that time dodging hot coals and pitchforks on a bum rap!

The latest in quantum physics and the power it puts in your head, heart, and hands is radical thinking compared to the traditional mind-set. As we discussed, anything new tends to create fear. When Edison invented the first telegraphic recording instrument in 1871, people who heard their voices played back to them considered it a hoax or black magic. When electricity was new, people thought it was so dangerous that lampshades were shielded with glass panels to keep people safe.

So when I tell you that some of the greatest physicists and minds of our era are postulating that you have infinite potential to create everything you desire within the Zero Point Field, that in this way you are in no way different from the Creator of the Universe you were raised to revere, that you and the Divine are one, keep an open mind. If your world view requires humility before the Creator, please understand that these new theories ask nothing different. Quantum physicists are simply using new tools and cutting-edge theories to give a scientific basis to what spiritual traditions and teachers have taught us since antiquity.

Radical shifts in thought are taking place at an accelerated speed and are already affecting every area of your life – from your physical health to your wallet to your relationship with Spirit. I want you to be up to speed.

Are all new ideas good ideas? Of course not. There are as many false beliefs in science as true ones. How on earth are we to become expert enough to separate the good ideas from the bad? As you work through this book, you'll gain skills for listening to your 'inner-tuition' and staying alert to universal intelligence on all levels without opening yourself up to every last weird idea, which can be just as dangerous as closing yourself off to everything. We all know people who change with the wind, blowing into the latest trends like a kite on a current. It's easy to see how foolhardy they are as they grab onto ideas just because they're new. But the cynics are equally stunted – they don't believe a single thing unless it's squarely placed on the tip of their nose.

It's Time for Expansion

Life is forever expanding . . . anything that's not growing is dying. Holding onto false beliefs or refusing to open yourself up to new perspectives gets in the way of your personal expansion. Having an open mind and a pioneering spirit are necessary components to living on the cutting edge – my favourite place to hang out. Think about it: Columbus benefited hugely from trusting that the earth was round. The fact that he didn't fall off the edge of the world and was able to make it back home when mass consciousness thought the world was flat made him a rich man greatly in favour with the queen, while opening up the world for everyone else – a major win-win. Columbus provided value to the world, and had an inspiring and great adventure . . . and he got rich in the process of making history. Those who hung onto flat Earth had unadventurous lives and kept sitting on their flat wallets!

No one who was normal ever made history.

So if you're running around with false ideas and outdated information, you risk being left behind as others embrace unlimited vistas. You'll end up with less to give others and fewer opportunities to be of service and value to the world.

Okay, now let's lay a solid foundation first before we lead into application.

The Science of the Law of Attraction

You've probably heard about the Law of Attraction, which I've been working with and teaching for over two decades. This law simply states that like vibrations are attracted to each other, and dissimilar vibrations repel. In other words, you'll never attract prosperity into your life if you're constantly sending out vibrational waves of poverty and lack. There's just no way around it. As I stated earlier, you'll never attract high-energy results from a low-energy vessel.

Media sound bites have a way of making our very real Law of Attraction sound like wishful, magical thinking. How easy it is to make fun of someone who says, 'Put your energy out and you get more of the same back.' But let me share with you evidence from the field that shows there's not only 'something' listening, but it's actively working in your favour. These theories of how the universe works might not be 100 per cent proven yet (although they haven't been disproved), but check out the people who are working on them! The guy who coined the terms black holes and worm holes, an originator of nuclear fission? John Wheeler. The fellow who discovered nanotechnology and won a Nobel Prize for his work in quantum electrodynamics? Richard P. Feynman.

Come on! These aren't slackers or fringe people. They are solid scientists doing amazing work.

Even though I've spent years working to understand the science of the unseen, I don't pretend to be an expert. But my semi-obsession with this stuff has allowed me to link some of these theories together in a way that makes me feel more excited than ever about living a richer, wealthier life. What could be better than discovering that we don't just have God on our side, but science as well?

Time Is On Your Side and Your Other Side and Your Other Side . . .

There's a concept in quantum physics called vertical time. Einstein said that time does not exist as we know it: 'For us believing physicists, the distinction between past, present, and future is only an illusion, even if a stubborn one.' Time, future, past, and present coexist simultaneously right now. We tend to think that time is horizontal: the past is behind us, the future is in front of us, and it goes onward in this sequential ever-unfolding way. If it were written as a line on a page, from left to right, we would say (in Western culture at least) that the past is on the left and the future is on the right.

But with vertical time, if you can imagine putting a line on a piece of paper that represents now, then right above writing 'now,' and above that another 'now' and so on in a vertical line. 'Now, now, now, now, now, now . . .' goes into all these different dimensions.

Some physicists have proposed the M-theory (M stands for membrane or magic), which says that there are at least eleven dimensions that exist simultaneously. In the context of vertical time, that means that all our 'nows' would go up and down through at least eleven different dimensions. ⓘ

One of the most fundamental laws of physics states that energy can never be created or destroyed; it merely passes from one form into another. Okay, now stick with me . . . first there's vertical time, then there's the Everett-Wheeler-Graham Multiple Worlds theory (Many-Worlds

Interpretation). A mouthful, right? Basically what this theory reemphasises is that there are multiple 'nows', universes, or existences coexisting all at the same time. Everything that ever existed or *can* exist is *already here*. Quantum physicist John Wheeler postulates that by deciding which universe (now) we choose to observe, we are essentially choosing our reality, deciding to 'participate' in the universe of our choice. In this theory, right now there could be a universe existing where you are a multimillionaire. Right now, there could exist a universe where you have the perfect body and the mate of your dreams. You're the one who chooses (or not) through your act of intention and attention. Energy flows where attention goes. Through choosing your intention, then locking your attention upon it, you've chosen (and continue to choose) to participate in whatever universe you're currently participating in. Which one are you choosing? More importantly which one *will you* choose?

Think of it. All these theories suggest that you exist simultaneously in many different forms, dimensions, times – you are everywhere and nowhere, exactly as you do and do not want to be. I know it's mind-boggling. The theory of multiple realities was exemplified in the movie *Sliding Doors* with Gwyneth Paltrow. In one reality, Helen, played by Gwyneth, catches a train at the last moment, meets a man named James, and arrives home to find her boyfriend cheating on her with his ex-girlfriend; she dumps the cheat and takes up with James. In the other reality, Helen misses the train, gets mugged, is hospitalised, and eventually arrives home to find her man alone in the shower, unaware of his infidelity and therefore tied to an unhappy relationship. In the movie the two realities then move forward in tandem, flashing from one to the other. What I like most about this parallel universe theory is that we're not creating anything at all. God created it. The Zero Point Field created it, and we choose to step into it.

What every theory in quantum physics has in common is you, observer and participant. With your clearly defined intention, and your unbending and consistent attention, you choose which world you're going to participate in.

You see, your desire properly understood isn't greed, not even close; it's your Higher Self, calling, prodding, challenging you to rise to a higher level of achievement.

Particles of Desire

The Wheeler–Feynman absorber theory (another mouthful from quantum physics) was originally proposed to explain the action of charged particles, such as photons. Let's apply this theory to the particles of your desire. ⓘ

Suppose that the particle gets emitted from a source (you) and can interact with one of two detectors (future possibilities). As the particle leaves the source, it sends a wave of probability from the source (called the *offer wave*) forward in time to the detector. We'll call that wave your *intention*. When the wave reaches one of the detectors, that detector sends a *confirmation* or *echo wave* back in time, basically stating, 'Hey, signal received!' These two waves going forwards and backwards in time can interact in several ways in the now: they can cancel each other out, build on each other, or do something in between in the space-time continuum. In other words, you've got waves of probability (thoughts, feelings, actions) going back and forth between now and the future, and the waves can intersect and interact anywhere along the way in what's called an *interference pattern*.

Remember we discussed that everything appearing solid is nothing more than stable light? Well, these wave interference patterns are what stabilise the light. Science literally tells us that the things we observe in our outer world are nothing more than a projection from our inner world. Okay, take a breath and let's break this down in practical terms.

Imagine your desire, your offer wave for the future is, 'I want to make £200,000!' Let's call your desire in the future your echo wave, which is your Higher Self, calling forth from the future, challenging you, and saying, 'This is what I want for you.' Those present and future desires can meet and interact to create an interference pattern, cancelling one another out or reinforcing one another. The key is the thoughts, feelings, and actions you're projecting right now.

If you're taking action based upon where you're going (£200K) – in other words, constantly thinking it, feeling it, acting upon it – then they reinforce each other and the money starts coming into form. Conversely, if you're putting out an intention of £200K but then worrying over your credit card bill, telling your friends how broke you are, and feeling generally pitiful, they cancel each other, the universe stating, 'Your wish is my command.' Guess what? Either way you become a prophet, but the choice is yours as to whether or not you truly profit.

Anytime you think, feel, or act broke, or practise the I-can't-afford-that syndrome, you're sending out an offer wave that is bound to cancel the higher-quality echo wave from your future.

Back in school when you studied how waves interact, you likely learned that two positive waves can interact and become twice as big, or that a positive and a negative wave can meet and cancel each other out, so that you end up with a big fat nothing. In other words, only waves that are in resonance with each other can harmonise. Our desires are the same way!

We can create our reality based upon where we choose to participate – our offer wave. This is where going 3 for 3 with thoughts, feelings, and actions is really critical. Suppose my desire, the confirmation wave coming from my Higher Self in the future, is saying, 'Okay. Let's do this. It's time to get on *Big Brother*, be a millionaire, and be physically fit.' But if the offer wave I'm giving out is, 'But I'm broke, I'm not talented, I'm fat,' then those waves are not going to harmonise. My present and future won't harmonise. They'll intersect but they'll cancel each other out. It's all energy, and those rates of vibrations aren't in sync.

This is the scientific underpinning of the Law of Attraction. Now you see how setting your desire (intention) in the present – that is, creating your offer wave – equates with how you're choosing to participate in the universe. But the most important thing is that you must stay locked onto it (your attention) no matter what! If what you're offering is out of resonance or harmony with what's coming back from the future, you won't be able to create it. You'll be your own worst enemy. You're Aladdin with the genie in your own bottle, and your personal genie always grants your wishes. Unfortunately in this case it's stating, 'Your wish of lack and limitation is my command.' You get to stay in your fat, lonely, and broke universe.

That's why making decisions based upon where you're going versus where you are is so critical. If you get what I call a future-pull, this high-level vibrational desire, then you *must* realise that you don't have to create it. *It's already created.* You just have to align with it. It's out there already, in that alternative universe in which you're already the star. You wouldn't even get the message if you didn't have the potential to be that person! So, get in harmony with it, start taking actions based upon that, versus where you currently are, and watch it unfold.

Desire vs Fantasy

If you look at the Latin root of the word desire it translates as 'de-sidere,' meaning 'of the stars or heavenly bodies'. As we've discussed, when you have a desire for something, it's your Higher Self speaking, prodding, wishing you to grow. Your Higher Self is the Creator, God, your Holy Guardian Angel (you choose the term that works best for you). Understand that your Creator doesn't want you to *have* toys and things. Your Creator doesn't want you to *do* certain things. Your Creator wants you to *become* the person necessary to *have* and *do* those things. In other words, your Creator wants you to grow – to continually reach for the stars.

I remember years ago hearing one of my mentors say, 'Decide to be a millionaire, not for the green slips of paper, but for who you'll have to *become* to get there.' That's what we're doing together – expanding who you are in all of the key areas of your life so that you'll grow into the person who can create all that you desire. It's really not the goal completion, but the growth that comes in the process that your spiritual self truly desires.

I promise, you'll never get a desire, a true desire for something you can't achieve. Never have, never will. When you get a real desire, it's your Higher Self saying, *Come on, this is what you're capable of; this is what I have in store for you.* It's the greater, grander you, echoing back through time. How cool is that? Now the only question is: will you heed the call? It was the great mythologist Joseph Campbell who stated, 'The big question is whether you are going to be able to say a hearty yes to your adventure.' Well, what will it be?

A lot of people will say to me, 'Well, that's not true, James, because I used to have a desire to be a professional footballer and I never achieved it.' I say, 'No, you didn't, you had a wish or a fantasy, and that's different.' If you truly have the desire to do something, there are only two reasons why you don't accomplish it: 1) You either haven't stuck with it long enough and you've quit, or 2) you didn't believe in yourself and therefore didn't even make the attempt . . . or gave it half effort. Anything else, and it wasn't a true desire.

We live simultaneously on three levels – spiritual, mental, and physical. Knowing this, what you must do is threefold: first, create a Spiritual Prototype, outlining your future pull, your desire from the future. The moment you have it outlined it *already* exists on the spiritual plane in another dimension – you just sent out an offer wave. It's not in the third dimension yet, but that doesn't matter, it's still real. Second, if you can write it down specifically and describe it either in written form or verbally, you have it on the mental plane. If you didn't have it on the mental plane you couldn't describe it. Now, think about it . . . you've already got it on two of the three planes in which you exist! The minute you can visualise it and specifically describe it, you're two thirds of the way there. Do you get this? That's exactly why I want you to do the exercise in the introduction – to start getting your deepest desires down on paper. Once you have them clearly defined, you've accepted the offer wave of your desire. All you're waiting for is a measly third of the equation – the physical. Finally (and this is the hardest part), you've got to think, feel, and act in accordance with that spiritual prototype – no matter what.

We tend to think, *If I take this action I'll get that effect,* but that's not accurate. Your action is nothing more than a confirmation of your future pull. That doesn't mean action's not important – it's critical. But it's not the action that's creating your results . . . the action is confirming the universe you've chosen to participate in. Do you follow me?

When we get the desire (our future-pull from our Higher Self that's already designed and chosen our highest outcome), our job is to act in accordance with that future pull by making ourselves ready to receive it. Let me repeat myself because it's that important. Action is critical, but it's not the action that's really creating the outcome – the action is just confirming that you're in the right universe, on the right track to your outcome. So as you think, feel, and act in accordance with your desire, it's just a matter of waiting for it to unfold through the sequence of events into the final third of the equation, the physical world.

Results: When the Waves Hit the Shore

Having the courage and patience to keep putting out those offer waves is the hardest thing you'll ever do, because your good old Newtonian world view will teach you to trust your physical senses and they'll often tell you that you're bonkers. I believe that's why Jesus said, 'Judge not according to the appearance' (John 7:24). Appearances only tell you who you *were*, not where you're going or who you're becoming.

Your current level of results, your appearances, are nothing more than the residual outcome of your past thoughts, feelings, and actions. The offer and echo wave patterns of your past. *This has nothing to do with what you're capable of or who you're becoming*, unless you judge by appearances and continue to make decisions based upon those results. If you do, you'll create nothing but more of the same.

Here's the real rub, and something we'll cover in depth in the mental pillar: a lot of the offer waves we're putting forth (which are currently creating our holographic universe in this moment) are *unconscious!* They originate from deep within our unconscious mind as unresolved emotional issues. But don't despair; I'll show you how to bring those unconscious thoughts into the light so you can send them surfing on positive offer waves!

I can spend fifteen minutes with you and tell what you've been up to for the last five years – what you've been thinking, feeling, and acting upon. I can look at your body, I can look at your bank account, I can look at your house, your car, your relationships, your joy, or lack thereof, and see what you've been offering because your results are nothing more than a biofeedback mechanism, a mirror for who you are. Think about a mirror for a moment. A mirror doesn't judge, doesn't say something's good or bad, doesn't edit or delete – a mirror just reflects back whatever's there. Do you follow the metaphor?

Your universal mirror is exciting because when you get what you've been wanting, you know you're on your game. When you have less than pleasing results, that's just the universe reflecting back to you where you have the opportunity to learn, love, and grow. Getting angry or upset at your results is counterproductive, because it's just a loving perfect universe saying, 'Hello? *This is your thirteenth marriage, are you going to wake up?'* or '*Hello? You're broke again, are you going to embrace a better way?'*

Have I ever got angry when I experienced less than pleasing results? You bet I have. The kid who grew up wanting bigger, faster, further away also wanted everything yesterday and done my way or no way. But humility is a powerful force that finds each of us in whatever mode will best get our attention – be it financial failure, a divorce, a motorbike accident, or all of the above! Humility brings us back to the heart.

There were also times in my life where I thought it was so spiritual to divorce myself from the desires of the physical plane. I bought that story hook, line, and sinker, and I was oh so spiritual. The reality, though, was that when I denied the riches of the material world, I was no earthly good. *A Course in Miracles* says, 'All things are echoes of the Voice for God.' When you truly understand this you find the good and God in all, including money. There's a rhythm you fall into, an elegant dance, and the entire experience becomes harmonious and meaningful. Once and for all you find yourself in a place of such awe, wonder, and joy that you finally know what it means to be wealthy. That, my friend, is Harmonic Wealth.

Please believe me when I say that you and your desires are the echo waves of God calling you into a future of unlimited capability. *Now let's take those desires, the offer waves, from your heart soul, and give them wings.* Like a magnificent eagle rising on an upward spiralling thermal, the time has come for you to soar.

6

Your Results Are a Reflection of You

A feast is made for laughter, and wine maketh merry:
but money answereth all things.
– ECCLESIASTES 10:19

Where Credit Is Due

Are you living month to month? Spending your entire salary on rent? Paying the minimum on your credit card balance each month? You're not alone. Many people don't have any cash left over after they meet their most basic necessities. You want off this treadmill. You want financial success, don't you? I guarantee if you don't do something radically different than you're currently doing, you're going to be in the same place one year from today as you are now with two exceptions: you'll be one year older and twice as frustrated. So open your mind and be open to changing a few ways of doing things. You can grow great wealth – and more importantly, you can grow to become someone ready to handle great wealth. This chapter will show you how.

Create Your Own Lottery

Why is it that many people who win the lottery are flat broke and unhappy within a few short years? Why is it that winning huge sums of money often leads to bankruptcy, divorce, family feuds, and even early death? Why do so many footballers squander their wealth? Is it because they're careless spendthrifts? Soft touches? Of course not. It's because they aren't yet the type of people they need to be to live at the level of financial wealth. They're still living with the lottery mentality. They see the creation of wealth as a passive act; they were just lucky to hit the jackpot. Deep down, they don't feel deserving of the good hand they were dealt by fate, so they usually end up getting what they feel they deserve – nothing. They haven't become the creators they must be to make and sustain wealth.

Anything that's gifted to you in this universe that you don't have the capability to create for yourself will always be taken away.

One of my clients had an uncle who won $1,000,000 at a casino and was homeless and living in his car with his wife and kids a year later. The money didn't change who he was inside one iota. It only magnified his fears, his belief that he wasn't worthy, that he couldn't possibly deserve the kind of freedom guys have with that kind of cash. He felt an overwhelming compulsion to act in accordance with how he felt about himself, and couldn't squander the cash fast enough. God wasn't punishing him; he just couldn't keep anything that wasn't within him. Your results are only and always a reflection of you.

Have you ever noticed that wealthy people who lose their fortunes more often than not make them back, and then some, in staggeringly short periods of time? Things that are self-created are more readily self-sustained and rapidly (if necessary) re-created. But if you don't know how to generate it in the first place, you won't know how to keep it, even when it falls in your lap. If you can't create it, you can't keep it. It's that simple.

You may think you want a huge inheritance, but unless you develop the capability to create that kind of money on your own, believe me, it'll be a nightmare. It'll turn your life upside down like a tornado hitting a shack. I recently told my parents that I want them to spend their very last penny a moment before they transition from this plane because I'm creating my own wealth.

Don't wish or wait for anything or anyone to create wealth for you.

Decide right now that you're going to go out and do it for yourself. Remember, not for the slips of paper – no way, but for the person you'll need to become to create that level of financial abundance.

A good friend of mine, Patricia Fripp, once told me, 'Ever since I was a little girl my mother always told me to grow up and marry a millionaire.' After a brief pause she stated, 'I always thought it made so much more sense to just become one myself.'

Create your own lottery. Tap into the great sea of money flowing around this planet. Only then will you stop worrying about scratching off the paint from some cheesy little card.

Money Is a Magnifier

If you're going to attract more money into your life you must realise that money is a magnifier, that it will highlight your traits – positive and negative, good and bad. If you're anxious about money matters, you'll stew endlessly over your newfound cash. If you're pessimistic, you'll find yourself surrounded by people who resent your wealth instead of those who applaud it. If you're generous, you'll see wealth as an opportunity to give more. You've got to be strong enough to stand under that magnifying glass or you'll get fried in the rays.

People say, 'I want to become a millionaire.' Has that been your mantra? If so, ask yourself if you're prepared to handle a millionaire's challenges. There's always a price for the prize, my friend.

It takes a bigger – not better – person to make £100,000 per year than £10,000. If you're not sure about that, let's use Donald Trump as an example. I was in New York City recently and in this particular area about every third building has Trump's name on it. I thought, *Wouldn't it be awesome to own a third of New York City?* Well, yes and no. Like everything in this plane, we can't escape the Law of Polarity or duality. There cannot be light without dark, and there is no money without responsibility. Think about it: who do you think has more real estate problems – you or Donald Trump? Who do you think has more tax issues, more employee concerns, more governmental challenges – you or Bill Gates?

Many believe that success is a result of chance or luck. Wrong again . . . thanks for playing. Creating and maintaining financial wealth means that you've got to be willing to stretch yourself, eradicate your demons, take risks, take massive action, and chase down every last detail. It takes tenacity and responsibility to do all that, and not everyone's up for the challenge. You also have to have tremendous courage because money always brings up issues – always.

When your mind says, *But where's the money coming from?* wisdom and courage say, *From wherever it is.* But that doesn't mean you can sit on your bum all day with your head in the clouds. You have to take bold action to reinforce to yourself and to the universe that you're in the universe of your choosing. Out of all the options, you've chosen your specific offer wave and come hell or high water you're riding it. Fortune favours the bold.

You Must Grow to Gain

We often have lopsided perceptions in our society. We think financial wealth should be all rosy. When we get there, we'll spend our leisurely mornings sleeping in, planning our day as we choose. That's just not reality. Will that happen some days? Sure. But as you play a bigger and bigger game, you'll also have bigger and bigger challenges. I know a multitude of multimillionaires, and without exception they're all busy. Any other idea is illusion. You'll have more headaches, more emergencies, more things to protect, more things to lose. In fact, the more money you make, the more opportunities you'll have . . . to lose it. Your lawyer may become the highest-paid person in your life. What do you think takes more energy to maintain – one home or two, a Skoda or a Porsche? But take heart, that doesn't mean your life won't be fantastic. I just want to prepare you with a good reality pill.

Success is messy. But so is life. Deal with it. Poverty is messier.

As you break old limiting patterns and clean up your pillars, some days you're going to make great headway, only to find yourself slipping back. You'll feel like hell and want to give up on your dreams. That happens to everyone. But rather than resisting the challenges of growth, your job is to develop greater capacity and capability to ease elegantly through the bumps and blocks in life. That's called evolution. It brings harmony and joy and success.

Just be realistic and know that if you're currently challenged by the challenges of a thousandaire, you'll go into nuclear meltdown as a millionaire. Seriously. But you can shift that, starting now. You can grow, and your results will reflect your growth.

In becoming bigger, you'll notice that you grow most when you're on the border of chaos and order. This is proven by all studies in science as well as psychology. Back to living on that edge I like so much.

I recently toured the California wine country, and was fascinated to learn that in winemaking the grapes are purposely stressed. Growers take care not to give the grapes much water, even though they raise them in full sunshine, purposely keeping shade to a minimum. The stress is intentional; it keeps grapes right on the border between survival and almost dying because the grapes that survive the test make the finest wine. There's a metaphor here: don't wish for an easier life. Wish to be at your finest. Just as the finest, most expensive wine comes from the grape that can stand the greatest stress, you too will grow in direct proportion to the stress you can sustain.

My intent is to get you right on the border of chaos and order by showing you what we now know in the study of the brain, psychology, biology, even metaphysics.

Are you ready to grow?

It's your nature to grow. In fact, it's the nature of the universe. Our universe is expanding as we sit here. Galaxies are spreading out, growing faster than ever in world history. On a smaller scale, think of a flower. It's either growing or dying, blooming into its own colourful expression of nature, or wilting in on itself, surrendering to the earth. There's a law in our universe that states, 'If you're not growing you're dying.' Nothing stays the same. You might tell me that you're satisfied with the way things are. I won't believe it. If you are, you're dead. There's a big difference between being grateful for your current state and being stuck in the death of complacency.

What Chaos Can Do

The Belgian physicist Ilya Prigogine won the Nobel Prize for chemistry in 1977. Through his work in dissipative structures, he taught us that we grow in direct proportion to the amount of chaos we can sustain and dissipate. What that means is the grandest systems are the ones that can sustain the influx or the greatest amount of chaos and not go into nuclear meltdown. This explains why we shouldn't fear chaos. In fact, we must embrace chaos and even be grateful for it (yes, I'm serious) because the more chaos we have, the more it proves to us we're growing. Any system, human or otherwise, that's alive and thriving is dynamic – rigidity and predictability is death.

It's really easy to be the Buddha sitting in your living room all by yourself. All of these old, catchy phrases you've heard before, 'Be careful what you wish for,' 'God punishes us by answering our prayers' – are true.

When you develop a level of mastery and understanding, you move into a state of profound gratitude, even for the shit (an acronym for spiritual harmony integrating totally). Do you get it? When you get it, you'll have it.

The chaos tells you, 'I'm accomplishing what I set in motion.' That's why in the Eastern tradition the thousand-petal lotus, which represents enlightenment, grows out of the muck and mire. In the esoteric tradition, the philosopher's stone (another term for enlightenment) is always found in a pile of dung.

Consider what Prigogine said, that there's constantly new energy coming into any system and there's constantly worn-out, old energy exiting the system – call it a human being, call it a relationship, call it a business. The system stays in a state of harmony as long as the influx and the outflow are in equilibrium. When there's more influx of new energy coming in and/or less outflow of old energy, then the system goes into disharmony and chaos. In this defining moment it has two choices: it either disintegrates and dies or jumps to a new level of capability and capacity – breakdown or breakthrough.

Let me give you a practical example. In my business right now, for instance, we have leaped to a new level. Phones are going mad. The server won't handle the level of traffic. Don't have enough staff. Don't have enough desks, or space to put them even if we did. There's this tremendous influx of new energy. I've got to slough off or let go (or let die) the things that are outworn and have outstayed their welcome. To the degree that I'm willing to do that, I move to a new level of capacity and capability. What gets me going about Prigogine's work is that if any system going through that chaotic time doesn't die, it always leaps to a new level of capacity and capability. It never goes backwards, never. It dies or literally makes a quantum leap.

Here's another example: a pot boiling on a stove. Put the pot on a high flame and it will boil and bubble and splash over and make a mess. That's death and chaos. However, put that same pot on a low flame and it'll simmer, and the transmutation to a new level – steam – will take place with a natural elegance.

Bees Won't Sting Me Anymore

I believe the stress of growing is the very reason why so many of us don't reach our fullest potential. What we must keep in mind is that the master embraces pain and pleasure in the pursuit of his or her vision and intention. An easier life is a fantasy. When we create our dreams, there's always going to be some part of the creation that isn't quite what we prefer. That's part of the game. We're always going to have challenges, self-doubt, uncertainty, screwups, pain, and pleasure. Truthfully, if we ever 'got there' in every area, we'd be bored stiff.

A friend once asked me, 'James, do you ever have a bad day?'

I quickly answered, 'I don't have bad days. I do have challenges because challenges are a part of life and growth, but I don't define them as "bad". They're opportunities. They make life more interesting.' The person of low awareness sees everything in life in a dualistic perspective, either as a blessing or a curse. The master of life sees all things as opportunities.

Even enlightenment doesn't promise the absence of challenge. Far from it. We have this lopsided perception that there's going to be this grand end state of achievement called enlightenment where 'Bees don't sting me anymore,' 'Broken glass can't cut me,' 'My hair will never fall out,' 'My teeth don't stain,' and 'My crap doesn't stink.' Pardon the pun, but that's just bullshit. True enlightenment is about mastering life to such a degree that no matter what's going on around you, you're in a state of harmony or equilibrium.

The this-life-is-supposed-to-be-easy mentality is a modern-day illusion, a lie that's hurt a lot of people (maybe you too), stopping them in their tracks before they'd even had a chance to begin. Don't buy into that bull for another minute. It's time to take your power back and take charge of your life. It's time to embrace the duality, no longer running from challenges, pain, or chaos. The things you're accomplishing will only be easy to the degree you've outgrown them. Read that again. Larry King said to me, 'Boy, this sounds hard, James . . . This is a lot of hard work isn't it?'

I said, 'It is hard work, Larry . . . but being broke and miserable is hard too.'

Look, you're going to invest your life in something, so you might as well invest your life in something that lights you up. The master always keeps his or her eye on the prize, knowing that pressure creates abilities. Pressure promotes growth. Growth leads to what?

Money.

We Grow from the Inside Out

Wealthy people, and I mean people who are truly wealthy in all areas, don't allow others to determine the quality of their lives. They never allow circumstances or others to determine how much income they earn or their level of harmony with regard to their spiritual life, their health, their relationships – anything.

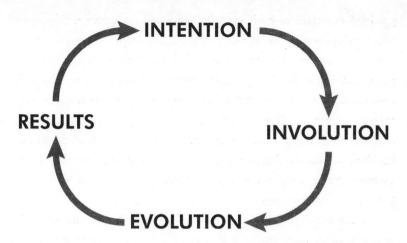

To have more you must *be* more. If your intention is big enough, then you must grow to meet the size of that idea. Similarly, if you have an idea that doesn't cause you to grow, it isn't the right idea. In other words, the right intention and the right desire have to make you stretch.

Growing is an inside job. Once you begin to go inside – involution – and grow, your results on the outside – evolution – must happen. Going within leads you to take different actions; your goal begins to take form and ultimately becomes a result in your life.

When you achieve the desired result, what happens? 'What's next?' happens, doesn't it? The basic principle of life, of spirit, is fuller expression and expansion. Your results become the springboard for fuller expression, which then brings grander, more exciting ideas and goals into view. Are you with me?

Once you get that next idea or desire – the intention – you again have to grow to meet the size of that new idea, so involution kicks in all over again. New actions begin to happen and your new bigger idea starts coming into form. You get new results, and so on. This is really simple, but it's how the creative process works: inside out, involution always preceding evolution.

Think back on any goal you've achieved, and you'll see that this cycle occurred. You had an idea, a desire, and you had to grow to reach it. Perhaps it was when you got your first car loan or first mortgage. Now, if that payment was a stretch for you, you had to expand your vision of yourself, didn't you? You had to see yourself being able to reach for more than you had been getting. You had to realign your possibilities to meet the size of the idea.

What you need isn't more money but more growth. We all do. Money is nothing more than a measuring stick of our growth.

Now pay attention because this is big: your results will always level out to the degree of your growth. Think hard about that truth. Your results will always level out to the degree of your growth. Every change in our universe first comes from a shift in consciousness, and your thoughts, feelings, and actions all have to be bigger to receive more.

That puts a whole other kind of urgency on going within, doesn't it? We're not just talking about good old philosophical ideas. No. We're talking about your ability to realize your goals in the here and now. Truly wealthy people understand that their business, relationships, and finances improve in direct proportion to how much *they* improve.

How much is it worth to you to grow?

Be the Success You Seek

Your life, your business, your bank account, your net worth is an outcome of who you are. Your world is a direct reflection of you – of what's on your inside. That's why I challenge you to become bigger – an example of the behaviour you want to observe in the world around you. To do this, you must take full responsibility for your own life and stand accountable for your results. Your results are the direct outcomes of your thoughts, feelings, and consistent behaviors. To take control of your destiny, you must begin to take full responsibility and accountability for everything in your life. It's not the government, the economy, your parents, or your Uncle Freddy that's responsible – it's you! Plain and simple.

It may seem simplistic – and you may have heard it before. But I promise that if everyone in the world took total and complete responsibility for their lives and their results, the world would change. And change dramatically.

No matter who you are or what you've been taught, you're wired for this process of wanting more and fulfilling that want in spite of anything you've been programmed to believe to the contrary. Just remember that a legitimate goal, one that'll drive you and be worthy of you, must be a stretch. Pick something big and bold and you'll become big and bold. Be the success you seek. Embody it with every thought and word. The universe won't pour energy into a vessel that's not giving it off, so make decisions based on where you're going, not where you've been. That's how you control your destiny.

So, when I say, 'Decide to be a millionaire, not for the green slips of paper, but for who you'll have to become to get there,' does it make you nervous or get you excited? Does the idea of expanding freak you out, or make you want to take on the challenge? When one of my mentors challenged me to decide to let financial wealth into my life so I could see what I was capable of, I decided to follow his challenge. Now I'm challenging you.

'But James, I'm not smart enough, rich enough, connected enough, or young enough to do what I want to do.' Oh, really? Tell that to Colonel Sanders. This guy was in his seventies before selling what would become the world's most popular chicken recipe. I've made a fortune the last few years, and I was nearly bankrupt as a forty-one-year-old. Was I just supposed to roll over and give up then because I hadn't 'made it' in time? Who's the timekeeper anyway? I want you to play by your own clock, one set to your personal time zone.

It's imperative at this juncture that you're really honest with yourself, that you face the facts as they are in this moment not to beat yourself up but to empower you. Think of this next section as a fun little wake-up call.

I Want it All – Now! Pleasing Activities vs Pleasing Results

Some of us make our growth a whole lot harder than it needs to be. You know these people, right? Their self-destructive habits or bad luck sets them wobbling back just as soon as they get a little momentum. Usually, when you look closely, a lack of willingness to do what it takes figures somewhere in the equation. Laziness and the desire for instant gratification are a danger in our society, much like drugs and alcohol. In fact, they're often tied, but that's a story for the mental pillar. Enemies of wealth come in many forms. Few of us are willing to see how imprisoned we are by our time-wasting habits. But not you, right?

'I want it now!' How many times have you heard children say that? 'I don't want to wait, I want it now!' Have you ever come up with an idea for something, found yourself becoming impatient almost immediately, and not investing the necessary time to see it through?

A friend of mine used to wake up with screenplays in his head – whole detailed plotlines, incredible stuff. Despite the fact that he had always wanted to get into the movie business, he never took the time to write his dreams down. He was too busy doing the fun stuff – going to the gym with his pals before going in late to work, mucking around at weekends, and watching sports on TV every free moment. Eventually those intricate plotlines escaped him. They vanished from his mind. Then guess what happened? Surprise, surprise: his movie idea dreams stopped coming altogether. Perhaps they were downloaded to someone else? Someone who would record them? The universe said, 'Next! No more "future-pull" for this guy. He's asleep.' I don't know. I also don't know if his ideas would have become hit movies. But he'll never know either.

I frequently have people come up to me in my seminars or at the end of special appearances and say, 'James, I want to do what you do.'

'Great,' I say.

'Do you have any recommendations for me?' they ask.

'Yes, I do. Buy my systems, study them, attend my live events, study everything I do, every move I make, or do the same with anyone else you respect in this business. Find someone who can mentor you, read four or five books a month, invest in yourself for the next three to five years minimum, join a speaking club, and get in a situation where you can teach someone else's materials until you develop yourself to the degree that you can write your own. Then it'll begin to happen for you.'

Their enthusiasm drains from their faces. *But I want it now!* They don't like my answer because they have a desire for instant gratification, for following the path of least resistance. With the least amount of pain, they want the most amount of gain. Yes, a good number of them want to grow, but they want to wake up with full understanding and the ability to communicate everything in one fell swoop. Sounds familiar? We live in a world that's addicted to the concept of maximum return for minimum investment – it's an epidemic. Let that not be you.

Look, I'm not condemning anyone because I fell into that trap a few times myself in earlier years. How do you think I know it doesn't work?

The universe wants for you exactly what you want. Remember your Higher Self is always calling and challenging you forward – that's your echo wave from your future. All you have to do to harmonise with the future-pull is lock in and lock on. It must happen – it's just a matter of time.

Now I know we discussed vertical time and parallel dimensions earlier. We also discussed that when you have something spiritually and mentally you're two thirds of the way there. You're on the offer wave and you just have to ride it. Well, that remaining one third is the physical plane and in the third dimension there's a little thing called gestation. It's actually part of the Law of Gender, which states that everything has a gestation period, a time period that must pass before things will come into form. If you plant a carrot seed, it takes about seven weeks for the sprout to make its above-ground entrance. Bamboo, which can grow up to thirteen feet in as little as one week, takes up to seven years to break through the surface of the ground. But for seven long years it looks like absolutely nothing's happening. Now that takes some commitment.

We all know that a baby takes nine months, which makes perfect sense when we see how much has to happen while the baby's growing inside its mother. No one in his or her right mind would argue that we should mess with that system by shortening it. We have to look at our desires with the same wisdom and understanding. We often have a tendency to overestimate what we can do in a year and underestimate what we can do in a decade. There's always a reason for the period of time it takes for you to reach your goal. The reason might be to give you time to grow into the person who's ready to receive it.

How long will it take to create the financial wealth you desire? I'm not sure. But one thing I promise is that the bigger the intention you have, the greater the commitment it'll take. Be certain that your desires will come to you in the right time, in the right way.

It's easier to have courage and trust the process when you feel you're making headway. Mastery is not persistence when you see a light at the end of the tunnel. True mastery is persistence when you don't yet see the light. Soon, we'll talk about how to take your big ideas and goals and break them down into smaller, bite-size pieces. But before we can do that, we first have to figure out how you spend or invest your time.

Are You a 'Now' or 'Later' Person?

If I asked you what kind of person you are – a 'now' or 'later' person – which would you choose? I'll give you the breakdown. The 'now' folks are consistently drawn towards pleasing activities, spending their time getting lost in TV, sex, food, laziness – you know, all the fun-in-the-moment stuff. The 'later' group, on the other hand, is drawn towards pleasing results, often engaging in less-than-pleasing activities in the moment. They invest their time in things like going to the gym, working long hours, reading good books, attending personal transformation events, hanging out with people who stretch their thinking, following through, risking, becoming comfortable with being uncomfortable. Which of these two groups of people do you think experiences real freedom? Which category do you fall into? Be honest.

Just for the record, we're never comfortable when we're setting records. Comfort zones can lull you into complacency like a sinkhole full of quicksand. Mastery comes from accomplishing less-than-pleasing activities necessary to fuel the attainment of our long-term goals. Beware of getting seduced by what I call the Follow Your Bliss trap, or the I-just-want-to-do-the-things-that-bring-me-joy mentality. While bliss is important – we'll get to that – find bliss and joy doing the things that create the life you deserve.

'It's Sunday,' a friend and fellow author said to me recently. 'I don't want to write my online course today.' I know how he feels. But when these thoughts enter my mind, I've learned to place my attention elsewhere. If I can see myself lounging in Hawaii drinking a cool drink or relaxing on a beach while the outcome of this present-moment work generates the income to fuel that freedom, I'm more engaged. Or I stop for a moment and think about all the people this particular project will help, and then I get inspired.

Come up with whatever ideas inspire you to make taking action more exciting. You'll find your true joy in fulfilling your potential versus selling out and falling short.

Winners take the action that others won't. Most people get seduced by whatever's happening around them and are unwilling to do the hard work. They're fragmented or in conflict; their words and actions are at odds. Integrity (from the same roots as the word integrated) comes when a person's words and actions match.

True integrity – the true test of character – is to live what you say is important to you – even when you don't feel like it – to live your values above and beyond your moods.

TV, 'the plug-in drug', doesn't hook me. But other things have. Spending money lavishly on expensive trips and toys, as you know, has been a vice. Just because you're thinking prosperity doesn't mean you should go out and buy three Armani suits tomorrow. If it's a decision that accelerates the accomplishment of your vision, the risk might be wise; that's called investment. But if it's just something to feed your ego or appetite, then forget about it.

Think about it this way: if you heard me teach one thing but then saw me consistently doing the opposite, wouldn't it be hard to take me seriously? Take yourself and your desires seriously and live your values. In the long term, you're the one who gains.

Following Your Bliss – What Does that Really Mean?

Richard Branson has become one of the richest men in the world because he followed his bliss. He and I recently spoke at the same conference and he said, 'You know what? I've never done anything thinking I was going to make money. My criterion has always been: "Is it going to be fun?"'

I couldn't agree more. But again, I know better than to think Richard Branson didn't work his arse off creating his recording and airline empires. I'd bet my net worth on the fact that he does some things that aren't his favorite activities – probably even daily. But the bigger picture is that his work is fun for him. Your work should be your joy and love made manifest through action.

The warning I have for you is to be careful not to turn having fun into a cop-out. 'I just can't do it if it's not fun. It's not fun for me to have to be up until midnight studying.'

I've never been a big sports fan, but the athletes I've met understand the concept of following their bliss in connection with hard work. No one can train for you. No one can lift your weights for you. Top athletes didn't waste their childhood hours playing endless hours of video games. On the contrary, they were outside practising, giving 100 per cent of themselves to their sport well after the sun had gone, long after their peers had gone home for dinner. Do you think it was fun for them to wake up at 6.00 a.m. on weekend mornings to travel to the neighbouring town to train? Or dunk themselves in ice baths when painful injuries required it? Hardly.

Years ago I heard Dan Millman, author and ex-Olympian gymnast, talk about getting up at 4.00 a.m. as a kid to work out before school. He had a great saying: 'Discipline brings excellence and excellence brings freedom.' It would have been easy for people in his life back then to have seen his seven-year-old self as a slave to his workout regime. But that discipline brought a level of notoriety and discipline that would lead to a lifetime of success, wealth, and creative freedom. Does that sound like slavery to you? Well, let me assure you, there's only one place in the universe where you get the reward before paying for it: a restaurant. Everywhere else you have to pay first.

Be honest with yourself when assessing whether you're a 'now' or 'later' person. If you're willing to pay the price in advance of your future-pull, to hold your intention and keep moving forward, your days will be full of good, and lots of it. You can change if necessary. It may just be that you've never been inspired. This book can help with that. If you're currently a 'now' person, you may get the happiness you're reaching for for a moment or two, but you'll never find true harmony and joy. The 'later' people know that doing whatever it takes now brings the wealth they seek and the masters find wealth in the journey. They have a respect for time, for how long things take to gestate. The irony, of course, is that there's true joy in the disciplined path. It may not feel as good from time to time, and the inner rewards may seem immeasurable in the short term, but check out the glint of peace and joy on a 'later' person's face. Their mighty outer rewards speak for themselves.

By the time you're done with this pillar, I hope you'll have a new respect for third-dimensional time. It's marching onward for us all, you know. There are only two things you can do with time: spend it or invest it. If you spend it, it's gone forever. When you invest your time, you'll create a lifetime residual. I wonder if you've ever considered time like this.

The $200,000-a-Year Reality Check Exercise

Here's a creative way to gauge how you're spending your time *and* money, quite literally.

A client named Bob came to me wanting to catapult his yearly income from $50,000 to $200,000. After a few initial questions regarding his schedule and daily habits, his main financial obstacle was staring me in the face like a neon sign. The culprit? A nasty five-hour-a-day TV habit, an addiction Bob vehemently defended in creative but pointless ways.

'My friends and I all watch the same stuff. It bonds us.'

'After a long day at work, this is how I unwind.'

'I learn a lot from TV; it helps me see the world since I can't afford to travel.'

'My golfing buddies are all sports freaks. If I don't know the scores of the latest games, I can't keep up with the conversation.'

'Everyone's doing it. Don't tell me you don't watch *American Idol!*'

And on and on he blathered.

'You have exactly as much success as you really want,' I told him. 'How you spend your time tells me everything.'

Bob started to defend his position until I blew him away with the following exercise. I'll start by showing you how we applied it to his yearly goal of earning $200,000. Afterwards, I urge you to go ahead and plug in your own numbers.

Bob took out a piece of paper and wrote down his yearly goal of making $200,000 at the top of the page. We took out a calendar and a calculator and calculated the following statistics beneath this financial goal.

First, I showed him how, by subtracting two weeks for vacation from the 365 days in a year, Bob was left with 351 days to earn that $200,000.

Next, I knew that he didn't want to work weekends any longer, so we took Saturdays and Sundays out of Bob's equation. Bob was surprised to see that keeping his work weeks to five days would mean that 100 days were suddenly removed from his total. Now we were looking at 251 paid days left from the original 365.

Finally, we took his goal of $200,000 and divided it by the remaining 251 days. Here's the reality check: in order for Bob to earn $200,000 in 251 days, he'd have to earn about $810 a day. That means never getting sick or taking weekdays off.

'How much does that come to at an hourly rate?' I asked Bob, telling him to account for eight-hour workdays. He was quiet for a minute after working the calculator.

'Oh my God,' he exclaimed. 'That's over $100 an hour!'

'Yep. More than you expected, isn't it?' I asked. He nodded. 'Now, from this perspective, can you really afford to watch five hours of TV a day? That's over $500 you're spending on your favorite programmes every single day – $2500 per week, not including weekends.'

'God, no! James, I never thought of it like that before,' he said. 'I knew I was wasting time, but I had no idea how much.' I could see something in him click just as I'd seen happen for hundreds of clients before him. 'Five hours of TV time is like throwing $500 out the window,' he said.

'Exactly,' I said. 'How much more productive could you be if you unplugged?' I asked.

'I get it,' he said, shaking his head.

Think about your own life. I don't know what you want to earn, but a large percentage of the people who attend my seminars have a fantasy income goal of £500,000 a year. That comes to £2,000 a day, my friend, or £250 an hour! Are you investing your time worthy of a person who earns that kind of cash?

Even if you just want to make £40,000 a year in a peak year, which is admirable, that still comes to £160 a day. Do you currently have the habits of someone who can sustain that day after day after day?

TO MAKE THIS MUCH PER YEAR, YOU'D HAVE TO EARN	PER DAY	PER HOUR
£100,000	£405	£50
£200,000	£810	£101
£500,000	£2024	£253
£1,000,000	£4048	£506

Back to Bob.

He, like many people – maybe you – was not only losing precious earning time through his time-wasting habits, but any free time he had left was being eaten up by mindless chores. A single dad to a teenage daughter, Bob spent five hours a week cleaning, doing the laundry, and taking care of his garden. I asked him about getting a cleaner once a week and a gardener.

'I can't afford a cleaner and a gardener,' he said. 'I'm not made of money!'

'You never will be with that mind-set,' I said. 'Your bank account is not who you are; it's who you were. Look at your goal sheet. You're currently making over $200 a day, with a goal to be making $800 a day. Both now and in the future, can you really afford not to get at least limited help for $10 an hour?'

Wealthy people understand that as £50+-an-hour people they absolutely cannot afford NOT to hire a £10-an-hour cleaner, gardener, or assistant. They understand that they'll never get wealthy doing all of their own mundane tasks. There's only so much time allotted to each of us and we have to be smart when planning how to make the most of what we've got. If you're spending your time on £10-an-hour activities thinking you're going to get to £500,000, think again.

Wealthy people also know their limits and don't waste precious time trying to become proficient at something that someone else could do twice as fast and more effectively. Wealthy people have figured out that if they want to have a major impact on their life and the world, which everybody from a schoolteacher to a world leader can accomplish, they have to ask themselves, 'How can I invest my time and energies most wisely?'

Many times when I go through this exercise with someone they say, 'Well, it's easy for you, James, you make a lot more money than I do.' That might be true, but how do you think I got here? I then respond, 'The reason I do now is because I put this principle into play when I didn't.' If you wait until you think you can afford it, you never will.

We need to think in new ways for this new time. In today's world you and I are being asked to do things differently, more and more rapidly. What may have brought you success in the past may not guarantee success today. The things that may have worked really well in the past may be your greatest failure today. Embrace change and get support so you can stay on that cutting edge.

In my first year in business, I made almost $200,000, putting me in that $800-a-day category. Taking an hour to mow my lawn – at $100 an hour of my work time – seemed in the way of my goal to earn $1,000,000 a year back then. I could have thought, *Well, I can't afford to hire employees yet,* but I sensed that I couldn't afford not to. So, while the high school kid cut the grass for relative pennies, I was building a foundation for millions.

That's how I've built a multimillion-dollar business, by constantly hiring great people who 1) do the jobs I know are not worth me doing and/or 2) are better at those things than I am anyway.

Individuals I work with give me two consistent reasons why they're not yet ready to hire help. The first one is full of hot air. The second needs to be weighed carefully.

The hot air argument goes like this: 'It doesn't feel right to ask someone else to clean for me or get my shopping. I should be able to do it all myself.'

Oh, really? How's that working for you? How is it making less money than you want or need? How is it being knackered at the end of the day when you'd like to be available for your friends and family? How much personal time are you investing in yourself these days?

I'm not going to justify someone's guilt long enough to explain why they're engaging in pointless, outdated, and faulty thinking. Let's just cut to the chase. Give up the guilt or financial wealth will always be just outside your reach. Sorry, but that's the truth.

Second, if you're a secretary, a teacher, or somebody who makes less than £30,000 a year, I can already see your stress about employing help. Or maybe you make more than that, but you spend more than you make, dipping into your savings every month. Perhaps you and your husband are dealing with credit card debt and although you keep saying, 'I need a cleaner, I need a cleaner,' he's not budging. Relax.

Each situation is different, and it all boils down to what kind of person you are. Thoughts are energy, and what you focus on expands, so you never want to take action that's going to make you feel more desperate.

Some people are motivated by expansion, and getting the cleaner will allow them to use that eight to ten hours they'd otherwise be spending on housework to build their businesses and get out of the hole. Others will get so stressed that they'll knock themselves out of the flow. Remember the 3 for 3 formula. You must constantly monitor your thoughts, feelings, and actions and keep them in check and alignment.

If you're in debt, get a debt-repayment programme in place so that you know it's getting handled. Figure out how much you can pay towards it each month and set up a standing order. Forget about the debt – it's handled. Now, focus your entire energy and effort into creating the wealth you desire and deserve.

You always have to monitor how things affect you emotionally. Ultimately, if you get that cleaner when you're still financially strapped, you need to make the most of the new time freed up and invest in the creation of new sources of income, which we'll cover soon. You have to be willing to be flexible. If you try one way and it doesn't create harmony within your family or makes you an emotional wreck, you need to be able to alter your approach. If you determine that you're not quite ready yet for outside help, make it a goal to look forward to. Then you'll have a plan of action. But always be willing to stretch and don't just procrastinate because it makes you feel a little uncomfortable. Remember, discomfort is a part of growth – no matter what rung of the ladder you happen to be on.

7

Money Is an Inside Job

Success is the child of audacity.

– BENJAMIN DISRAELI

Moving-Towards or Away-From Strategies

It's time to stop reacting and start creating. If all you ever do is react – How am I going to pay that bill? How will I get out of this dead-end job? – you don't give yourself the energy or freedom to build the wealth you want. You're too busy driving while looking in the rear-view mirror.

There are two distinct strategies that determine why you do what you do, and the comprehensive harmony (or lack thereof) in your life will tell you very quickly which one you're employing. You're either moving towards your goal for financial freedom, or you're moving away from something that's causing you pain.

The moving-away strategy goes something like this: 'I'm going to prove something to you and the world.' This approach is often coming from an insecure childhood or background, perhaps as the skinny kid everyone else picked on, or the one who never fit in, or the person who could never be good enough for his or her parents. This person has lots to prove. I know this because that used to be me. I remember walking into the gym in my early twenties and telling the gym owner, a big body-builder, 'I'm going to compete in bodybuilding one of these days.'

'You'll never compete in bodybuilding. Your body is not right; you don't have the genetics,' he said.

I'll show you, I thought as I walked away. I did. I pumped a ton of iron, entered a load of competitions, and won them. But that's not an elegant way to live – not even close. I was moving away from my fear of failure. There's very little joy in this strategy.

Unfortunately, in one way, shape, or fashion most of society is motivated by the away-from strategy. People rarely, if ever, change until they experience enough pain or have an extreme life-changing event. Social psychologist Morris Massey's research found that very few people make significant life changes after the age of thirteen. By this point in life, according to Massey, a person's core level values and strategies are locked in and they rarely if ever change unless the person experiences what Massey terms a 'significant emotional event'. This type of event causes the individual to step back, take an inventory of his or her life, and potentially choose a new direction or strategy. In my case, a motorbike accident forced me to step back and stop running from the ten-stone nobody I thought myself to be and move towards healing, and the discovery that I was more than this body. I would speculate that in Richard Branson's case, at least at this point in his life, he's moving towards his mission to find alternative fuel sources. Acting from a place of a fullness versus lack, his work is touching the whole world.

Abraham Maslow talked about two types of needs: *deficiency needs* and *growth needs*. Deficiency needs come from lack – you know, I've got to make more money because I don't have enough. I've got to have a relationship because my life sucks. Deficiency needs are an away-from strategy. Growth needs come from fullness, the place where life is so full and so grand that I have to express it because I'm an example of the potential within the entire human race. I am an example to others of their own potential, of the potential of the human species, and I've got to act because my cup is so full it's overflowing. That's a very elegant place to be. On the surface, it may even appear as if the deficiency (away) and the growth (towards) individuals are doing the same thing. Perhaps they're both very active in the world. But internally, one is in a state of disharmony and the other, harmony.

University or Bust? Growing Through Learning

Did you know that 85 per cent of the self-made millionaires in our world don't have a university degree? Eighty-five per cent, including Bill Gates! I don't have a degree either, and Bill and I are both doing okay.

For a long time, I had a belief that because I didn't have a degree, I couldn't be successful. Do you think that hindered me? You bet. It hindered me for a long, long time. But then I realised that there are plenty of PhDs running around who can't rub two pence together, so I got over it. I also began to notice that many A and B students I met were working for C student owners. Check it out for yourself – you'll find the same thing. Most people who do radically new things in the world don't fit into the common mould. That *really* helped me get over it. Remember, no one who was normal ever made history.

Howard Gardner, a professor at the Harvard University Graduate School of Education, says that our school systems are dysfunctional; unless you want to be a really good maths or English teacher, you're not going to learn a whole lot of valuable things for your day-to-day life in school. There are always exceptions, but people whose minds are on the cutting edge (often becoming our greatest entrepreneurs) seem to understand this, at least unconsciously, as they're going through the school system. Biding their time before going out to make their mark, they learn not to let poor marks define them. Many use school as a way to learn how to get along well with others – an invaluable trait for making money. In case you haven't noticed, God doesn't knock on your door and hand you your wages. Inspiration may have got you the job, but it's still people who sign the cheques.

Philosopher and social pioneer Eric Hoffer wrote, 'In times of change, learners inherit the earth, while the learned find themselves beautifully equipped to deal with a world that no longer exists.' In short, get out of the past and get yourself on that cutting, leading edge. Get yourself between chaos and order.

Sure, if you're one of those individuals who's earned a lofty degree you can certainly become outrageously wealthy as well. You just may have a different set of challenges to overcome. For instance, you may possibly have to work harder to overcome the social programming you bought into.

We all have our challenges.

No matter on which side of the fence you fall, there's no way you can lessen the value of lifelong learning. Anyone who knows me knows that I'm always reading about five books and hanging out with brilliant minds, asking countless questions. I want to learn everything about everything, even though logically I know that's totally impossible.

In these rapidly changing times, how we learn is often synonymous with how we succeed. Do you learn by continually looking back to compare and analyze the results of others or the results of your past? Or do you continually act boldly (following your intuition) and adjust as needed? While both strategies have their value, please remember that in a rapidly expanding universe the old answers may not bring you new results. In fact, most people rarely think. As we'll discuss in the mental pillar, true thinking is instantaneous. All deliberation and analysis are grounded in social conditioning. Read that again. It was Einstein who so wisely stated that we can't find the solutions to our problems with the same level of thinking that created the problem. Do you drive results or do results drive you? Taking charge of your destiny starts with taking charge of how you grow even if you're currently feeling stuck. Always remember your results are a reflection, a biofeedback mechanism, of you. Change the inside and you change the outside.

Again, it's about a shift in consciousness. Society programmes you to look for change from the outside in. But you'll see in each pillar I'm going to hammer home that all wealth and achievement is an inside job.

Help! I'm Stuck in a Dead-End Job

Don't like your job? You'll have more to love when you start loving what you have. Once again, it's about focus and where you're placing your attention. Remember, everything is energy, including you. Are you concentrating on the blessings of your job, or on the curse of it? Thoughts are directional; they lead you to a specific destination. Energy flows where attention goes. Like a radio, all you must do is turn to the right station and tune in. What station are you tuned to, head-banging hard rock making you uptight and tense, or something that makes you want to dance?

Here's a thought: money is an idea. A good idea. I give you permission to direct yourself towards lots of it. That's right – as of today you have complete permission.

It's also a measure of consciousness. If you're not making huge amounts of money right now, one of two things is happening. First, you're holding yourself back, making yourself small. Or second, you're not providing enough value to the world.

People constantly come up to me and say, 'I want to create a new job, I need a different career,' but they're on half throttle in their current job, thinking, *I'm out of here shortly.* I wish you good luck with that mentality because you're going to need it.

You're never going to be blessed in this universe by being less than your current position demands. You're never going to be blessed by putting out inferior energy or product and expecting a high rate of return for your 'efforts'.

To leap forward in life you have to outgrow your current position. You accomplish this by loving what you do and being at the top of your game; and when you've mastered your job thoroughly, you'll have no choice but to burst out of it. How many times have you seen someone putting in a little bit, thinking they're going to get a lot back? It doesn't work that way. There's a law in our universe that says the more you give, the more you receive. Is this true in your finances? Absolutely. It's true in your relationships, your fitness, health, and everything else. (Just in case the distinction isn't clear, I'm not talking about giving from an empty emotional cup like the guy at the start who blew all his casino winnings!)

When I left the AT&T School of Business, I left at the top of my game. I was the number one producer year after year. I knew I was leaving someday to do something bigger, but I gave it my all while I was there. I left at the top – my very best.

When you outgrow your current position, the universe (that future-pull we discussed) will kick you out of your nest so you can fly.

If you find yourself working in a job you don't want, another thing to do is to focus on the skills or tools or networking connections you're making at your B job that will help you once you land your A job. At AT&T I learned how to train groups of people without a clue that one day I'd be using those skills to speak before stadiums of people. Those years have been invaluable. Never see a single step of your journey as a waste of time.

Remember, everything is energy and energy vibrates. In an energetic universe it's all about your vibration. You can't vibrate at your peak when you're stuck, so it's time to give up the lies you're still holding onto about wealth. My goal is to help you shatter tenacious ideas that have festered into facts in your mind. For instance, if you grew up with a limiting belief about your capabilities, it's time to erase those tapes right here. Many of us carry the belief that we're stupid or incapable because of negative events, even silly things from our past – like the time we fell asleep on our desk. Or the time we got caught passing a flirtatious note to the babe across the room when we were supposed to be reading. It might help you to list the things in your past that still play havoc with your mind, masquerading as facts. Get them out of you and into the light of day.

Success is an inner game. It's not what you do that determines your success, wealth, and achievement – it's how you do it. Look at any two people working side by side. One is hitting their objectives and the other is barely making ends meet. Yet they appear to be doing the same thing in the physical world, but looks are deceiving. People have said to me, 'My God, James, if I could just spend a week with you I'd know how to do it.' Well, I hate to disappoint you, but if you spent a week with me, you'd see me answering emails, developing new programmes, taking conference calls, dealing with my business issues, and talking to lawyers –

with lunch, a workout, and a meditation thrown in there somewhere –
nothing too groundbreaking. But the difference is the internal game.

Success Isn't About Hard Work, Your Product, or Service

There's a little lie floating around the planet that success has very little to
do with fulfilment and is mostly about hard work. Do you know anyone
who works incredibly hard, working long hours? He or she might even
have multiple jobs, and yet they're barely making ends meet. If success were
about hard work, we'd have millionaires living on every corner. There are
many, many people who are really good in the world of action – work,
work, work, work, work, work, harder, harder, harder, harder, harder – and
they never get anywhere, except to frustration and a living hell.

Another lie is that success and fulfilment in your work have everything
to do with your product or service. Actually, on a larger scale, these
things have very little to do with the results you produce. I meet people
everywhere in the world with amazing products and services who aren't
producing amazing results, and I find people with okay products and services who are making a fortune.

Success Isn't About Skills

If you study a person who's doing extremely well – let's say they're earning £250,000 a year – and compare them to someone who's doing not
quite as well – let's say £25,000 a year – is the £250,000-a-year individual ten times more skilled than the £25,000-a-year person? No way. If
you compare their skills, you may find a razor's edge difference. However,
if you compare people by the way they think, feel, and act on a consistent basis, is there a big difference? You bet there is. If you look at the way
they invest and use their time, is there a big difference? No question.

Many times, if you're not careful, you can convince yourself that certain things cannot be accomplished because you weren't born with those
skills. That type of thinking is dangerous. Many people throughout history have achieved what seemed to be the unachievable with the

necessary desire and determination, the necessary commitment to become outstanding. When the intention is clear, the method will appear.

It's a funny thing about a clear and unbending intention; it constantly seems to create its own opportunities as well as its own capabilities. I'm not suggesting that hard work, skills, and good products and services aren't important – they're just not the primary driving factor. Your unique gifts are there for you to build on and to use, never to limit you. The fact is, the more unique you are, the less likely you are to fit the common mould.

Thomas Edison flunked out of school. Beethoven created some of his most incredible compositions after he was deaf. It was reported that he handled the violin awkwardly in school and preferred playing his own compositions instead of improving his technique. His teacher called him hopeless as a composer.

We could give countless examples of people who have overcome adversity. You probably have your own. So a word of caution: understand and utilise your unique talents but never ever limit yourself by your uniqueness. Improve upon your talents, utilise them to the fullest, and continually focus on providing more and more and more value.

If you don't believe me, that having the right mind-set is more important than having the right skills, complete this powerful exercise:

Write down three of your top successes or accomplishments so far. 🌐 While some of the exercises we'll be doing can be done in your head, this one is far more poignant on paper. This is huge, so really do this.

Your success could be finishing school or university, landing a job in a competitive industry, or marrying the man or woman of your dreams. Even if you don't think your accomplishments are that impressive compared to what someone else might put down, this is only about you.

Did you come up with three things? Please finish this before you go on. It's okay to reach back to your childhood as well. Like the time you won the painting contest or the cup for your school team. Maybe it was the day you helped your grandmother move out of her house, cleaning forty years of rubbish out of her garage.

Once you have three, I want you to look at your list and choose the one event that brings up the strongest feelings of accomplishment, the one that really made you feel as if you'd tackled and conquered something worthwhile.

Now, I want you to brainstorm a list of the qualities and characteristics that led you to achieve this win. How were you thinking? What were you feeling? What were you doing or not doing? Qualities like determination, passion, focus, trust, and confidence might come up. Or vision, persistence, kindness, patience, honesty, or enthusiasm. Come up with as many qualities and characteristics as you can. Do that now before continuing.

Now that you're done, it's time for the fun part. Go back through your list and beside each quality write down if it's more mind-set related or more skill related.

Notice anything interesting here? I'm betting that most, if not all, of the qualities you wrote in your list were mind-sets, not skills. Do you see where I'm going with this? Success, wealth, and even fulfilment have very little to do with skill, intelligence, or even your product. Every Olympic athlete has the skills, yet few win the gold. It's all about the mental game. This is why sometimes the most unlikely people succeed while you scratch your head wondering why. It's because they understand how to use the power of their mind-sets. I guess you could say that doing so is their greatest skill.

I learned this early in my career, when I was a national sales trainer for a Fortune 500 company. I would travel all around the country to teach groups of people the latest and greatest sales skills. Do you know what I observed? Only a very few of those people would go out and literally change their lives with what I'd taught them, boosting their results and their finances. What do you guess the majority of the people did? You guessed it: absolutely nothing. They went back to their offices and did the same old things they'd always done, with the same lacklustre results.

Success Is About Service: Give More to Get More

You cannot give what you don't have – if you want to give more, you have to become more. Continuously invest in yourself.

Next, I suggest that if you focus on making your first or your next million, you ultimately won't live a harmonious and fulfilled life. Instead focus on providing a million dollars worth of service – ten times more value than what you ask for in return – then you'll have the life of your dreams. Truly wealthy people always give ten times more value than what they ask for in return. In fact, in many cases when an individual interacts with them, they'll feel they have underpaid for the services, the product, or the idea they acquire. Truly wealthy people are great givers, and that's true in any field. They're continually focused on providing more and more, giving more and more value. How can you do that in your area of expertise?

Henry Ford told us several years ago, 'Wealth, like happiness, is never attained when sought after directly. It comes as a by-product of providing a useful service.'

I just want to make a really simple point. When you're considering providing more value, it doesn't have to be something that's really complicated. People often think that to provide more value, they have to spend a lot of money or do something grandiose. But I want you to remember this principle: small things done consistently in strategic places create major impact.

Consequently, as you think about providing value, just ask yourself, what are those small things you can do that will be perceived as high value? What are the things you can do to build relationships so that when your product or service comes to mind, you come to mind?

It's not the enormous things you do that create high value in many cases, it's those small things done consistently in strategic places that create major impact. This is true in all areas of life, personal or professional. In your personal life, it's not the huge vacations you go on or the great gifts you purchase for each other, it's those small I love yous, those small thank yous, those small ways of supporting each other that make a major difference, isn't it?

Psychic Income vs Material Income

People ask me, 'Does the Law of Attraction work?' Of course it works. But that's asking the wrong question. The right question is: what's my unique purpose, and how can I use the Law of Attraction to give value to the world? When you've defined your true life direction and followed it, you're living the real secret.

One of the most brilliant minds who ever lived, Albert Einstein, said, 'Not everything that can be counted counts, and not everything that counts can be counted.' I'd like you to count income in a different way from here on. There are two types: psychic and material income.

How many times have you been involved in a community activity, volunteering, or, if you have children, at the school? Maybe you've donated your time to worthy causes and you've received absolutely no monetary or material income. Let me ask you, why did you invest any of your precious time without financial reward? You know the answer: you did this because you received something in return that told you that you were part of something meaningful. You were contributing, giving at a higher level. That's psychic income, and it's the most important income you'll ever receive.

Every single one of us has a deep need to contribute, to give something back, to be part of something meaningful, and that's how you and I are going to define our psychic income. Your psychic income is the most important income you will ever, ever receive.

Money is nothing more than a neutral tool. It's like a knife; you can use it to cut bread or turn it into a weapon. The tool is neither good nor bad; it just is. It's only defined by the intention of the user. For this reason, let's talk about how we can actually create a monetary income that allows our psychic income to flourish. I'm going to suggest that you create enough money in your life so you don't have to worry about it. When money becomes a non-issue, you're able to put your primary focus on the other key areas of life – your relationships, your intellect, your health, and your spiritual life. Sound good?

Why Am I Here? What's My Purpose?

People ask me all the time, 'How do I find my purpose in life?' or 'How do I get inspired?' You begin by paying attention. My teacher in the

Huna tradition (the original spiritual tradition of the South Pacific) taught me, 'For everything in life you must pay attention. To the degree you do not pay attention you pay with pain.'

Think back to your childhood – the clues were there from the start. There've been many times in my life where I'd hear a certain piece of music and be moved to tears. I learned to pay attention to those times when I was so moved emotionally, either while reading a book, watching a movie, or listening to music. When that happens, I stop and ask myself, *What's going on here? Why am I getting so hooked emotionally?*

During the movie *Braveheart*, when I saw Mel Gibson's character yell 'Freedom!' at the top of his lungs right before he dies, I was a mess. I'm getting emotional just thinking about it. Why? Because part of my purpose in this lifetime is to help people unlock that part of themselves to remember who they are and to truly be free, abundant, and joyous. Seeing him, I could barely contain myself. That told me something about myself.

Those are times when your purpose, your inspiration is speaking to you. Yours will be different from mine and mine is different from the next person's. But that's where you need to start paying attention.

How to Never Work a Day in Your Life

I once asked myself, *Is there a magic formula for making money while having fun and being free? How can I do what I love and be paid handsomely for it?* I looked to those who were already doing it for clues.

When they are interviewed, we often hear celebrities say, 'I've never worked a day in my life.' While that sounds like an exaggeration, I've come to understand the mind-set. When you make money doing what you love to do – something that isn't someone else's dream for you – it's easier to see the necessary grind as part of the package. Understanding that no one gets off scot-free enables you to embrace hassles as part of the game. But sometimes people have to be reminded of this perspective.

A fairly well-known client of mine would get angry when people began stopping her in public when she was in a hurry or didn't have her make-up on. I reminded her that she always wished to have a greater span of influence and had had that intention for years. Everything comes with a price, and having people come up to her out of the blue was a price for the success she'd sought.

Frankly, I could empathise with her. *The Secret* had just come out around this time, and I found myself getting impatient with several people who stopped me on my way out of the gym when I was already late for an appointment one afternoon. But I told my client that mastery in the moment requires that we stop, take a breath, and realise that challenges are the proof we're creating the lives we asked for. All those nights we lost sleep studying and preparing for this, all those parties we missed while our friends were out dancing without us was all paying off. Our intentions had become reality.

In shifting her focus towards gratitude, my client was able to see that the challenging aspects of her work were nothing other than a continuous, beautiful, divine unfolding of how she was manifesting and expressing herself in the world. That's the outlook of someone who's never worked a day in her life despite often working round the clock. I travel over 200 days per year currently. Often someone asks me where I'm going next week. After I answer them, they frequently say, 'Business or pleasure?' My response is always, 'Yes.' Mark Twain nailed it when he stated, 'The secret of success is to make your vocation your vacation.'

This mind-set, joyful in nature, is contagious. You can see it in our greatest philanthropists. By doing the work that gives them passion, they uplift the world. Think Richard Branson, Bill Gates – we can't take our eyes off them.

On the flip side, you can look at someone for ten seconds and see if he or she is happy with the way he's earning his livelihood. We won't name names here, but it's not hard to spot the guy who made his fortune from an ego place, lugging around a wounded, competitive, repulsive energy for all the world to see, still moving away, and away, and away. 'They might as well take out a billboard for their fears,' life coach Rhonda

Britten says. Do you have a billboard over your head? If so, what does it say about you in big capital letters?

A certain amount of financial wealth can help you grow to your spiritual capacity as well. It'll enable you to visit the sacred sites, read the books, attend the events, and sample the beauty the world has to offer – all more challenging without the benefits of time and money. In growing spiritually, spirit requires one thing and one thing only: fuller expression and expansion of consciousness. That means immersing yourself in the right kind of energy and information.

No matter what you've believed in the past, no matter how financially stuck you may think you are, you can turn it around. Your current results are a direct reflection of the person you have become up to this point. But that's not a fraction of who you truly are. No matter how poor or amazing your current financial situation may seem, it's not even close to your capability. Not by a long shot.

As you read through this book, I want you to hold the intention of growing, finding your unique identity, and living a life of Harmonic Wealth by sharing that new person with the world. Who are you, what is your unique mission, and how will you share your beauty through the services you provide?

Again, we're back to the fundamental philosophy that wealth is not the result of making money. Making money is the result of wealth: wealth of relationships, wealth of knowledge, wealth of health, wealth of spirit. When you become a harmonically wealthy individual, money comes as a by-product of who you are in the world. What could be freer than that?

8

Getting Real

Happiness lies not in the mere possession of money;
it lies in the joy of achievement, in the thrill of creative effort.

– FRANKLIN D. ROOSEVELT

Setting Goals and Intentions

Okay, I'm going to tell you some things you've probably heard before, but guess what? Studies show that it often takes hearing something fifty times before you get it. Repetition is the second law of learning and transformation. Recognition is the first. You'll never transform and grow until you recognise you need to.

If at any time in this chapter you find yourself thinking, *I know this,* follow up with an immediate question: 'But am I doing it?' If you're not, then you know about it but you don't *know* it. Knowing about something is just intellectual fodder. Knowing it moves it from your head to your heart and ultimately your feet (as in get moving). The reason so many authors are talking about the same stuff – setting goals, creating vision boards, establishing good habits, managing the use of your time – is because these things work. I'm a big lover of one-stop shopping. I don't want to send you scurrying to other books to find out how to do these things. I want this book to give you every tool you need to create Harmonic Wealth. That's efficiency.

I promise I'll give you new twists on what may be familiar topics –

things you haven't heard before. These strategies will not only make these everyday ideas more exciting, but will take your results deeper.

Stay with me.

Setting goals is nearly as automatic as breathing. You can't help yourself from making them even if you wanted to. I had a friend once tell me, 'James, I've never set a goal in my entire life.' This is ignorance of a fundamental truth. Think about it. Anytime you've ever changed, improved, or achieved anything, you started by setting some kind of goal, didn't you? You wanted three A levels, so you got yourself to school every day and passed the exams. You wanted to make money, so you applied for your first job and started clocking in. You wanted to be in a relationship, so you put yourself out there and started dating. You can't even get out of bed in the morning without setting the intention to do so. Whether consciously or unconsciously, you make decisions every day about what you intend to do. When you create a strong enough reason within you to achieve your intention, you get it done, don't you?

Many people talk and write about setting goals. I prefer setting intentions. Intending to create something is much more powerful than just setting a goal. Intention has resolve, discipline, and commitment. Goals are finish lines, but intention is the process of achievement.

Setting a clear intention is important because it gives direction to your unconscious mind. Remember, you form your world with your intention and you hold it together with your attention. Your intention is the direction you choose, the directional system for your attention. Understanding this gives you the edge – applying it makes you wealthy.

All Goals Are Spiritual Goals

Set the intentions you truly want and deserve – not the ones that sound good to others, are solely self-effacing, or fulfil your parents' dreams for you. You don't have to justify what you want to anybody. When somebody looks at you with a scowl on his or her face and says, 'Why do you want that?' your only answer needs to be, 'Because I do.' Some people will call you selfish or greedy for wanting things for yourself, that's their business. Yours is yours, but don't let that stop you for a moment. They'll either learn by your example or they won't.

But let's acknowledge that there is a dark side, a secret side to goals. Lots of people go for their goals to prove something, to beat someone out of something, even to screw somebody. If that's where you are, acknowledge that. Having a negative motivator can actually be really powerful in getting you started. It's valid, but there's a higher way, a better way to go. Isn't doing something that makes your heart sing a little more attractive than running from pain? Think about it.

Although much of the time you'll be after the tangible physical goals – the new car, house, or computer – recognise that it's not really the tangible that's driving you. It's the spiritual being inside you wanting to unfold and express itself so you can become the person you need to become to create that intention. Your Higher Self and the universe both know what they're doing. Trust that.

The bottom line is that time is finite, but energy is not. I don't care if you've had two hours of sleep or eight. I don't care if you've had your coffee or not. The only reason you're not totally vibrant, vital, and alive is because you're doing something to cut yourself off from your source and the future-pull of your destiny.

So isn't it time to align with your spirit and plug back in?

The Power of Your Anti-Intention

When some of my advanced graduates are setting down their intentions, I also have them define their anti-intention.

An anti-intention is the polar opposite (often seeming like the downside), the fallout that occurs when I stay focused on my intention and goals. If my goal is 'I'm excited and grateful earning an extra £2,000 a month,' my anti-intention is 'I'm embracing the challenge of growing my business, I have less time to waste, and I'm putting more effort into financial planning.'

On 1 January 2007, I said, 'I want to have more influence and get on television a minimum of twelve times this year.' In thinking of my anti-intention, I had to ask what's the price I'm going to pay to make this happen? The price, as we discussed previously, is extensive: I'm on the road more; I have less quiet time; I'm dealing with venues much larger than my team is used to; there are more people and things vying for space on my calendar. But knowing my anti-intention keeps me from getting ambushed by the effects of my intentions, and (this is the big one) when they happen I'm grateful for them instead of being frustrated by them. Anti-intentions are the indicators that my intention is moving into form.

Looking to quantum physics and the Law of Polarity, negative events are proof positive of the good we're creating. The good news is: I'm rich. The bad news is: I'm rich.

If lots of money is what you intend to create, your anti-intention would be that with bigger cheques come bigger delays or complications, more debt and responsibilities. When you accept the often grander complications and stay in gratitude for your abundance, signing bigger cheques and dealing with bigger challenges won't faze you. It's a sign you've stepped into the big time.

Brainstorm

Let's supercharge the power of anti-intention. Let's look at your anti-intention and take it all the way to the end by asking what is the downside of the downside? So often we stop ourselves from getting what we want because we fear that the price will be horrible. But what if our fears are blowing small concerns out of proportion?

A client of mine was afraid of success because she thought her older sister would be jealous and her husband might feel threatened. But after pushing through the fear and making more money than each of them, her sister was excited – they celebrated in Bali – and her husband was elated, finding a lower-paying but more enjoyable job. Her fears, it turns out, were nothing but bullshit.

If you've got bullshit fears, tell yourself that it's time to let them go and that you're done giving them airtime. Change the channel.

If they still seem valid, however, ask yourself, 'How can I handle this challenge creatively?' Give your marvellous unconscious mind the task of coming up with a solution.

Here's a great tool I've used for years to kick the unconscious into creative gear. Brainstorm all the ways you consciously know how to deal with something. Write down everything, from the most simple to the complex – the most ridiculous to realistic. Then just set your list aside and allow your unconscious mind to go to work. That's right; forget about it, but pay attention when answers start appearing. Trust that when you give your mind a job, your unconscious mind never stops working to bring you the answer. To illustrate, when you forget a person's name and try as hard as you can to remember it, it usually escapes you, right? But ten minutes later, when you've let it go, the name pops into your head. Brainstorming works in much the same way. Once you start this process, be prepared to get insights anywhere and everywhere. I recommend carrying a pad of paper with you in your purse, in the car, by your bed so that you're ready to capture your new insights. You'll be surprised by how creative alternatives just pop up out of nowhere.

Putting Your Intentions on the Fast Track

When I ask my clients, 'Do you know what your intentions are?' they usually say, 'Yes!' Then I say, 'Show me your list.' 'Oh, they're all in my head,' they answer. And that's exactly where they'll stay until you write them down. They'll never have meat on them. You already understand that you don't randomly get a desire unless you also have the ability to make it happen. Making it happen begins with writing it down, concretising your intention, mobilising the energy in the Zero Point Field to help you achieve it. So how do you write down intentions effectively?

A Goal Is Accountable When It's Countable

First off, your goals should be both specific and measurable. Only then will your mind know what to do to make them real.

Now let's wax scientific again for a minute.

We already know that everything is made of energy and energy vibrates – we call that a frequency. Right? Well there are a myriad of frequencies or vibrations in this universe from super-fast to super-slow. For example, ultraviolet waves have a frequency of 10^{14} cycles per second while cosmic waves have a frequency of 10^{24} cycles per second. So what? Well, by contrast your kitchen table has a frequency of only a few cycles per second, and so does your car. Point? To bring things from the non-physical realm of spirit into the physical realm of form you have to slow them down – right down. You do this by making them ultra-specific and measurable.

Realistically, if they're not specific, how will you know if you've achieved them anyway? If you say, 'I want to have a better relationship with my kids,' how do you measure that? How will you know when 'better' is achieved? 'I want to make more money and work less.' What does that mean – an extra dollar and one less hour? But if you write down something like, 'I'll go to Disneyland with my kids in the next twenty-one days' or, 'I will raise my hourly rate by five pounds and cut my workday by one hour in the next two weeks,' that's specific and measurable, isn't it?

No Time Like the Present . . . Tense

There's an even better way to record your specific, measurable goal: put it in the present tense.

Write this: 'I am so happy and grateful to be spending this amazing day at Disneyland riding on the canoe ride and getting myself and my kids wet.' Can't you just see yourself there? Can you feel the joy and the wetness? Need a towel? Each time you read or say these words, you'll find yourself imagining all the many things you'll do after the canoe ride: dropping down the elevator of the haunted house, seeing the fireflies and listening to the drunken pirates sing as your boat carries you through the Pirates of the Caribbean ride, eating ice cream in a cone and loving every bite.

'I want to lose ten pounds' tells your unconscious mind that you need to lose it and you'll end up continuously needing to lose it. Always wanting and never having, your wish is my command. Instead write 'I am so happy that I'm healthy and energised, weighing nine stone, and wearing size 8 jeans' (assuming that nine stone is ten pounds lighter than your current weight). Do you notice and feel the difference, writing as if you already have your intention right now? The genie is impartial and always says, 'Your wish is my command,' so make your statements specific, positive, and present tense. Define it like you have it.

Emotion Is Energy in Motion

As you begin to write, start with 'I am so happy and grateful that . . .' 'I am' puts your goal in the now. ('I will become . . .' keeps it in the future and 'I want . . .' keeps you longing and never having.) All wanting affirms not having. Think about that one long and hard.

Here are some powerful examples to get you started. Take out your notebook and script ten unique intentions just for you. ⓘ

'I am so happy and grateful that I've made an extra £2,000 this month.'

'I am so happy and grateful that I'm the owner of the most profitable law practice in the area – providing tons of value and helping hundreds of people.'

'My family and I love living in our seaside dream home.'

'My wife and I enjoy driving our new Mercedes with the top down and the wind in our hair. We're like kids again.'

Using words like *happy, excited,* and *love* pulls in the emotional element that's so crucial. Emotion is nothing more than energy in motion. Emotion is the gateway to motivation. One of the most powerful creative emotions is gratitude. When you're grateful you're sending out the message, 'Thank you, send me more.' Anyone can be grateful after the fact; the master is grateful in advance. Make your intention something that turns you on and fires you up, not just something you think you can get. There's a fine line between stretching yourself and being wimpy. A good test is to read your intentions out loud. You'll be able to tell in an instant if your voice lacks passion; it's harder to fake speaking than writing. Choose courage – set intentions that'll cause you to stretch and grow, make you feel strong, empowered, and attractive. The human spirit will not invest itself in mediocrity.

Aim High . . . But Be Real

Aim high enough to inspire yourself to grow into your new life, but pick something that's believable. A stretch, but believable nonetheless. You don't want to set yourself up for failure.

For instance, I know a woman who cut out a magazine photo of a young lovely about thirty years her junior in a bikini and put it on her refrigerator. Extreme words or images that seem far-fetched will make you think, 'Yeah, right, that'll never happen to me.' If you can't stretch your imagination to believe you'll obtain the image, find a more believable one.

You have to set tangible, believable goals. Bear in mind that even though we're dealing with the financial pillar here, it's not really money you want – it's what you think money will bring you. How do you visualise a million pounds? How many stacks of notes is that? A million-pound home or a million-pound body, on the other hand, will bring up a clear image in your mind. Visualising it clearly is the key to living it.

Oh, and let me let you in on a little secret (well, not that little): many people who watch *The Secret* or study the Law of Attraction hear that the universe doesn't distinguish between goals that are large or small. While this is true, what they don't take into consideration is the Law of Gender, which states that everything has an incubation or gestation period. It takes longer to grow a mighty oak than a willow. So if you're growing oaks, prepare to stay the course through thick and thin. Your 3 for 3 has to lock onto a target, and stay locked on. The locking on is where most people lose it. They set a huge intention and control their attention for a time, but when it doesn't happen overnight they say, 'This doesn't work!' As always, the genie responds, 'Your wish is my command.'

Again, we often overestimate what we can do in a year and underestimate what we can do in a decade. I remember several years ago my business was dodgy – I mean, *really* wobbly – and as a result I was too, just barely making it from month to month financially. My girlfriend at the time said, in a moment of frustration, 'When are your ideas going to hit? We've been at this for eighteen months!' I only chuckled and assured her that it was on the way and reminded her that I was growing oaks, not willows.

See It, Feel It, Do It

Every morning when you get up, when your unconscious mind is most receptive, picture your intention before you even get out of bed. If you can see it and feel it, so can your unconscious mind. Your unconscious mind runs the body; therefore you'll get up and take action on it.

Walk out onto the balcony of your new home; see the ducks gliding on the surface of the lake, the deer grazing in the tall grass off to your left. Smell the dew in the air as you walk down to have your morning juice in the hammock overlooking the water where the kids' tyre swing hangs from a tall oak. Hear the birds singing in the trees and feel the breeze upon your skin. Your children wake up and run out with the golden retriever to greet you with their tight, warm hugs, blurting out the words you never tire of hearing: 'Mum, Dad's got breakfast ready!' Well, okay, maybe that last part's a stretch, but you get the idea.

At night, relive your vision, planting the picture in your unconscious mind as you drift off to sleep. This will begin to set up an active and magnetic force unlike anything you can believe. Here's a critical principle: the last thing you think of before you go to sleep is what your unconscious mind has to work with all night long. Whatever your unconscious mind consistently has to work with, you consistently move towards. By the Law of Attraction, it moves towards you.

Too hard, you say? Look, you're already thinking and feeling something, I assure you. Just train yourself to make it something you actually desire and deserve.

Financial guru Chellie Campbell says that many people 'set' goals but few 'get' goals. Do yourself a favour by putting your heart and soul into this. She suggests you add playful affirmations like 'Money flows to me easily and effortlessly' and 'People love to give me money' to your intentions. I've never been a proponent of affirmations on their own, but I stand behind decrees and proclamations used in conjunction with action. Here's one I've used for years: 'Endless oceans of money flow to me, in ever-increasing quantities and avalanches of abundance, for I am one with God and God is everything.' Make up a few of your own.

9

Unstoppable Steps – Unstoppable You

Action without thought is mindlessness,
and thought without action is hypocritical.

– AYN RAND

The Universe Loves Speed

You have over a trillion cells in your body, each with a capacity of 1.17 volts of elec-
trical power. Think about it – that's over a trillion volts of electric power at your
disposal. When you listen to and act upon your future-pull, over a trillion soldiers
with a trillion volts are saying, 'You got it.' That's why it can feel next to impossible
succeeding at something you don't love because every single cell in your body is saying
'No' or 'Whatever.' I know a guy who does handyman work but can't stand his job,
so he keeps attracting 'no' experiences. Bad clients come out of the woodwork; so many
haven't paid him or have contested his work that it's gotten to be a joke. Some joke.

Personally, I love big intentions. Teetering-edge, I call them, the kind that
makes me feel as if I'm standing on the edge of a 150-foot cliff.

I wasn't always so courageous.

My teacher and I were sitting in silence on the side of a mountain in
Cutimbo, the burial grounds of all great Peruvian shamans, when I asked,
'How do I know when a path is the right path, don José?'

'When you don't feel prepared to take it,' he said.

Bingo.

That's what I needed to hear. His words gave me permission to jump when I was terrified, to move on without guarantee. Allow them to do the same for you.

If trusting a shaman halfway around the world seems barmy to you, let my certainty overcome your doubt. If you read biographies of wealthy and famous people, you'll see that most of them were walking in the dark just like you throughout much of their journey to the top. They'd get glimpses of what they were supposed to do, and could often see their destination, but the daily steps were mysterious and only revealed one by one as they stepped forward in courage. Did they feel 100 per cent prepared to create or receive the things they were going after? Rarely. Climb one peak and you'll be high enough to see the next. If you're waiting for the perfect time to act, within the perfect parameter of circumstances . . . Oh, please don't make me finish this sentence.

No one's perfectly ready for big success. I promise; no matter how perfectly you think you've planned, it won't unfold according to plan. Big success gets you ready for big success. It doesn't matter if you're not prepared because you're going to figure it out along the way. People and circumstances will show up and come to your aid just by virtue of the fact that you're in motion. So if your heart is saying, 'Move,' just get moving – one step at a time – even if they're baby steps, even if you have to crawl.

One of my favourite lines from *The Secret* is 'The universe loves speed.' How very true. The downside is that if you don't take fast action, you probably never will, meaning that your future echo wave and offer waves won't harmonise. It's important to take action within twenty-four hours of setting a new intention. 🌓 Fail to do this and you'll fail to realise your potential. Most people do. It's not that the universe doesn't want to help you – far from it. What you want wants you. What you're seeking is also seeking you. Simply put, if you don't take fast action, and if the universe were a train, you'd be getting to the station five minutes too late, expecting it to be waiting for you on the tracks, the conductor waving you aboard with a hearty smile.

Six a Day: The Formula for Practical Magic

The following amazing story is well known in some circles; perhaps you've heard it. It's worth hearing again if you have, and if you haven't, it might well change your life. Believe me.

I'll keep the dialogue short since I wasn't there (thank God, because I'd be *really* old), but the gist of the tale goes like this.

At the turn of the last century, a man named Ivy Lee met Charles M. Schwab, president of Bethlehem Steel. His objective was to sell his services to Schwab and help Bethlehem become more efficient. Schwab's reaction was that his people already knew what they should be doing – his problem was just getting them to do it. As a result, Schwab wasn't buying.

'Just suppose I could give you a tool, an action that would guarantee you'd become more efficient, you'd be interested, wouldn't you?' Lee asked. 'Better yet,' he continued, sensing Schwab's resistance, 'how about if I just give you the idea – let you use it for twenty-one days; if it works, share it with your employees. Then send me a cheque for whatever you think it's worth.'

'Well, okay, what is it?' Schwab asked.

'At the beginning of every single day, or better yet, at the end of the day before the following day, take out a piece of paper and write down the six most important things you need to do to achieve your objectives on that particular day,' Lee said. 'In fact, go ahead and do that right now for tomorrow.' Schwab thought about it, and wrote down six action items.

'Now put them in order of importance, one being the most important, two being the second most important, and so on,' Lee continued. So Schwab did that.

'Starting tomorrow first thing, start on item number one. Do not go onto item number two until you have fully completed item number one.

Then continue in succession with each number. If you get to the end of the day and have not completed your full list of action items, then roll over your actions to the next day. If five and six are left one day, they automatically become items one and two for the next. Use this for as long as you like, and then if you think it's worth something send me a cheque for that amount.'

Less than a month later, Ivy Lee got a cheque in the post for the then princely sum of $25,000. Attached was a note signed by Charles M. Schwab: 'That's the most powerful tool for achievement that anyone has ever taught me, and here's a fraction of what it's worth.'

Bethlehem Steel was relatively unknown at the time, but would go on to become the world's largest steel producer in the world within five years. Schwab would earn $100,000,000 on his own, making him the most powerful and famous steel man alive. The $25,000 investment turned into many millions at a time when the average income in the American workforce was around $2 a day.

Since then, many powerful businesspeople have attributed their success to this technique. So, if it's good enough for them, guess what I'm going to ask you to do every day, starting today? That's right. Do what I call your Critical Six. But only if you want to skyrocket your results.

If not, don't bother.

Stay Focused

Too many people quit right before their dreams take physical form. What if you were the guy watering the ground for six years with no sign of bamboo, but because your neighbours laughed at you — What the hell are you doing? — you stopped? Define your action items, your Critical Six each day in connection with your intentions and values, put them in order of priority, and have the courage and commitment to stick with them. 🟡 Roll the uncompleted actions to the top of next day's list. The only exception to the rollover is if — and only if — something more urgent arises for the next day.

Be honest with yourself and truly committed and again stick with it even when it looks like nothing's happening. You're going to face distractions – the phone, e-mails, friends, co-workers, and family members bombarding you with their emergencies. Activity does not equal accomplishment, so no matter how many things scream in your ear for attention, stay focused. Unless they're getting you closer to your intention, ignore the distractions.

Flag this page and come back to it in a week and ask yourself: am I writing down my Critical Six daily action steps in priority order? Am I really doing them? Are there parts of my list that I could delegate or pays others to do? Don't fall into the trap of getting distracted with mundane goals. Going to the post office and supermarket may give you a break in the day and a change of scenery, but is that the most effective use of your time?

Get in the habit of asking yourself before you do anything: could someone else do this for me? If someone else can, even if you're not yet in a position to hire anyone, just know that it's not a top activity and make a commitment to yourself to engage in fewer of these actions.

The good news is that you've already got the skills to do most of what you need to do to realise your ultimate goals. Learning is often remembering what you already know. I mean, really, haven't you known the actions you've needed to take for a long time anyway?

The attitude I want you to have is that achieving your intention is fun and adventurous, and you're going to be good at this. What if you come up with more than six action items? That's likely. Trim them down to six maximum. Actions that are not in alignment with your intentions don't make the cut. Yes, I know the washing-up has to be done and the dogs have to be walked, but these things should not be done during your primary creation time.

How Can It Be Done?

When taking action, focus your intention and keep your attention upon what you choose to create. Each time doubt arises, ask yourself, 'How can it be done?' As long as you keep your focus on what you can do, your mind will stay in the creative zone. Being innovative and creative sets the Law of Attraction in motion.

You've got to unleash your marvellous mind – remove all limitations. Thoughts are powerful things. Remember the carrot seed in the ground – if you don't expect it, you won't feed it. Expectation plus action will attract whatever's necessary to fulfil your goal: more time, talent, money, assistance, education. Your expectation will be rewarded. Providence will move and things will work in your favour.

Will the universe give you feedback? Absolutely. Be forewarned that it may look and feel like rejection. It may look like you're not good enough. You may feel like a failure, but that's an illusion. There is no failure, only feedback and learning. You're only given what you can handle, and the only time you fail is when you make the same mistake over and over again, expecting different results each time.

Old programming will try and keep you in your comfort zone. But disconnect from the past. The past tells lies about your future. Even your present tells lies. When you look at your current results to define your future, you're thinking in reverse. You're backing into your future, looking to the past, defining life by the view in the rear-view mirror instead of looking forward through the windscreen. But I know you're thinking more clearly now. No more driving in reverse for you.

Here's one to consider: people who want to be perfect right out of the gate (or ever, for that matter) have the lowest standards for achievement. Why? Because perfect is impossible. Think about it; if you always want to be perfect you've got a great excuse for doing nothing, haven't you? You'll just tell yourself that you'll never get there, so why even try? Easy, right?

Whatever you do and no matter how things may look, *don't change your intention*. Refine it, clarify it, improve it – do whatever you have to do to brighten it and make sure that your passion for it is stronger than ever. Be the dedicated gardener who continually waters his seeds.

Intention Cards

I want you to buy a deck of sturdy index cards and cut them into a size that fits easily into your wallet or pocket. These are your 'intention triggers', and this simple practice is powerful.

Each morning, I want you to write down your main goal or goals on one side of a card. You might want to put it in the form of a purpose statement, keeping it in the present tense; make it something you look forward to writing and reading. Make it something that you can create a clear mental picture around and continually focus on. That's why it has to be tangible. Remember, you can't visualise a million dollars – neither can I – but you can visualise what a million dollars will give you. Get it?

On the other side of your intention card, list your six most important action items for the day. Carry this card with you everywhere. Never leave home without it because it'll keep you on track. When you go to the bathroom, read your card. Feel it in your pocket at regular intervals. When you come to a traffic light, get on the train, or get into an elevator, pull out your card and read it. Out loud is even better. It doesn't matter what other people think. Verbalising your goal ramps up your emotions and gets you more involved. Remember, energy flows where attention goes. These cards and activities are what I call 'attention grabbers' and they keep you focused.

I put my card by the lamp next to my bed each night, making it the last thing I see before I fall asleep and the first thing I see when I wake up. Do the same. You'll thank me, I swear.

Visualise Without Ceasing

Remember how we talked about the power of a person's mental game? It may appear as if a person's doing regular activities when in fact they're busy internally creating a wealthy empire in their heart and mind.

People in my industry used to say to me, 'You'll never be on *Oprah*, you're too far out – not mainstream enough.' Yet, being on *Oprah* and *Larry King Live* were two of my biggest intentions and I let no one or nothing knock me off my game.

'I'm the new mainstream,' I'd answer as they sniggered, taken aback by my certainty. I knew that world consciousness was expanding and that my message was being embraced by more and more people; big media was the natural evolution of my work.

For six years I visualised being a guest on both the *Larry King Live* and *Oprah* shows, feeling the feelings of already being there. I'd watch Larry asking people questions, and pretend that he was looking at me to answer them, and I did. I would sit on Oprah's couch, laughing and interacting with her. I felt the excitement in my stomach as well as the feeling of touching millions of lives.

I was using my thoughts and feelings – two out of three. To go 3 for 3, I had to add the action piece. Did I pick up the phone and call CNN or Harpo Productions saying, 'Have me on the show'? No, and I didn't send cards or letters either. The old model of nagging someone until they give you what you want is dead. When it works, which is rare, you make too many enemies anyway. It's much more powerful to attract what you want. Attractive marketing is the most powerful. In my case all I knew to do was work on making myself more skilled, knowledgeable, and attractive. I continued moving forward towards my intention by reading, studying, growing, expanding, travelling, providing value, giving more, becoming a better me, all the while visualising and knowing that a universe existed where I was already there. All I had to do was get there and allow it to unfold.

Guess what? In November 2006 Larry King's office called, and I was on his show twice. He'd throw out a question from a caller or someone in the audience and I'd answer it, just as I had done in my mind. In January 2007 Harpo Productions called and I was on *Oprah* – twice. She and I laughed together and shared some fantastic moments on her couch, just as I had seen in my visualisations.

Visualising Is the Key to Realising

Used by all high achievers – either naturally or through conscious discipline – visualising is the key to realizing. Your unconscious mind drives behaviour, and it doesn't know the difference between something that's vividly imagined and something that's happened on the physical plane. In short, your thoughts and feelings make it real.

Time and time again people tell me that they see themselves in their visualisations but they aren't getting results. There are only two reasons for this: they're either not taking action – make-believe without action might be fun for a child, but it's childish for an adult – or they're not visualising correctly. (They're seeing themselves as though projected on a distant movie screen rather than seeing what they want through their own eyes, smelling the smells, feeling the feelings, hearing the sounds.) Let's say your goal is getting an MBA. Don't merely view yourself receiving your diploma; hear and feel your shoes march across the wooden planks of the stage as the dean passes the diploma into your hands. Look out into the audience from centre stage, catch your dad taking pictures and give him your proudest smile. See how you can tell, even at this distance, that Mum is crying. Feel the difference?

A friend of mine had fallen on hard times and took a job working at an upmarket lingerie boutique waiting on wealthy patrons – a painful experience until she began passing the time visualising. As she hung the shop's cashmere bathrobes, she'd imagine the feeling of being enveloped in one after a long leisurely bath in her (future, although she imagined it in the present) sunken jet-pool bath. She'd sashay across the store after customers left, holding up the Turkish cotton nightgowns against her body in the mirror, slipping her feet into a pair of plush chenille slippers, imagining frequenting this expensive boutique as a paying customer.

Frequently her mind would race to Paris, where she'd be having coffee with her boyfriend just before going shopping. Within a few years she indeed owned the big bath, had a maid who washed her silk lingerie, and had booked her first flight to Europe.

Intention Triggers and Attention Grabbers: If You Can See It, You Can Be It

Let's revisit something we already know. Quantum physics tells us that we hold our world together with our attention. In fact, the most widely accepted principle in quantum physics is called the observer effect. Without going into complicated detail, the observer effect basically tells you that you get what you're looking for.

Think about it. If you want proofs in your world that people are mean, nasty, and selfish, can you find them? Of course you can. Conversely, if you want proofs that people are loving, caring, and kind, can you find those as well? You bet. It's all there and the bottom line is you get what you're looking for. That's the observer effect.

Now, I'm assuming that you've chosen your intention. So the most difficult second step is to direct and control where to place your attention. That's why you need intention triggers and attention grabbers to lock you on track. These keep your inner vision more powerful than mere outer observations.

When is the best time to visualise? All the time. Every chance you get. The mind thinks in pictures. Period. I don't care what you've been told – your mind thinks in pictures.

Some schools of thought state that there are people who are more auditory, others who are more feeling-based, and those who are primarily visual. This is true; yet no matter what, we all, every one of us, think in pictures. So make your goals even more believable by surrounding yourself with magnetising images. The picture of your goal plants a seed in the garden of your unconscious mind and your unconscious then does two things: 1) sends out the offer wave to the future, and 2) moves your body into action.

We've already talked about one intention trigger – the intention card. This little card grabs your attention and is a constant visual reminder of where you're going and who you're becoming. Let's talk about another that will help focus your intention and control your attention.

Vision Boards

You've probably heard of vision boards by now; most people have. I've been teaching this concept, and even had my seminar participants make them in my live events, since the mid-nineties. But have you made one yet? Now is the time and I've got a few tricks and twists I bet you haven't heard of yet. 🔵

You'll need a big piece of thick paper or corkboard. Now collect images of everything you want to attract into your life. Use photographs, artwork, magazine photos, or printed Internet images. Make it a fun project – like being a kid back in nursery art class. If you've got kids, make it a family project – get them to cut out images and paste them on their own boards. Or even make one for the entire family. Money and the toys it brings don't have to be so heavy and serious! Blast loud music that inspires you, maybe even makes you want to dance. Label it MY TREASURE MAP or whatever makes it exciting for you. But it has to be fun. Remember, your feelings are vibrations and send powerful attractive forces out into the universe.

What if you're embarrassed about people seeing these boards? Do they seem too trite to display out in the open? What if you don't want to expose something so personal around the still negative people in your environment? Make small ones and put them inside your wardrobe or cabinets that you open frequently. In some ways this is even better than a big one. Hang one inside the door of your bathroom cabinet so it catches you by pleasant surprise each night and morning. Energy flows where attention goes and you need constantly and consistently to control your attention. That's why attention grabbers are key. You need to have them everywhere so you'll see them all day long in a variety of places.

Here's how to take a common idea and ramp it up a notch. Make your board 3-D. Cut out coloured copies of your face and the faces of people you love (even your dogs), and paste them on top of people doing the things you want to do. There's your head on a person skiing. There you are lying on a beach, hugging your partner in front of the Eiffel Tower, playing golf at St Andrews, standing with your family and your dogs in front of your second home – you get the idea. Then paste on the stuff from your life: a menu from the restaurant you wish to frequent more often, the brochure from the bed-and-breakfast you dream of visiting or owning, dried flowers from your wedding bouquet (to help strengthen your marriage) – not just magazine pieces, but things that mean something to you from your physical world.

Then – this is key – when you look at these images in multiple places every day, several times a day, imagine that you've already had these experiences and that these boards are merely your photo albums. Close your eyes and relive those moments through your own eyes again. If you can see it and feel it, you're on a high-speed path to achieving it. As always, get busy!

Intention Triggers

You can also create intention triggers to carry in your purse or put by your bed to flip through before you fall asleep. Personally, I love having powerful images that emit high vibrations in my line of sight. One of my friends has hers beautifully framed. They grab her attention during a phonecall, or when she needs to take a break from the computer and focus elsewhere for a minute.

Take photos of your larger board or photos that make you feel abundant, and post them everywhere. I've had clients make collapsible boards that are portable. Go to the showroom, sit in your dream car, and have someone take a picture of you in it or of the view you see sitting in the driver's seat, looking over the dashboard, with your hands on the steering wheel. Do you understand what we're doing here?

Quotes and sayings inspire too. My friend Linda walked dogs in her neighbourhood each morning with her neighbour, Brooke, who was pregnant with her second child. Brooke was having a terrible time with morning sickness. She felt ugly, fat, and guilty for not having an ounce of energy for romance with her husband. To lighten Brooke's load, Linda used her label-making machine to create inspirational stickers for Brooke's bathroom mirror. In her eye line while she brushed her teeth, washed her face, or brushed her hair, Brooke saw these words: 'This is a blip in my long and beautiful life.' 'Our baby is happy and healthy – the perfect addition to our loving family.' 'My body is fit and strong. I am beautiful and my husband's hot!'

Those stickers made Brooke smile every day, helping her feel good and focus on what she wanted during a challenging time in her life. That painful time truly was a blip. The pain was real – Brooke's daughter was born ten weeks premature – but she's now strong and healthy and into everything, the perfect whirlwind addition to their family. Brooke signed up for Pilates, got in great shape, and she and her husband just returned from a second honeymoon together, where they fell in love all over again.

The idea is that each time you glance at your dream images, they grab your attention and focus you on your greater goal of wealth, health, and fulfilment, and also keep you in harmony internally and externally. The idea of stepping into that reality becomes closer each time you do.

Experiencing the sensory details and feeling the feelings as if you were there right now taps into one of the mind's most powerful tools. A reporter once turned to Walt Disney's nephew at the opening of the EPCOT Center and said, 'It's too bad your Uncle Walt didn't get to see this, isn't it?'

Roy Disney immediately replied, 'Oh, Uncle Walt did see this, and that's why you see it now.'

Doing What Wealthy People Do Right Now

Here's another trigger and grabber that I promise works.

Years ago I heard a speaker state that I should keep a $100 bill in my pocket at all times. This was in my early twenties, back when $100 was a lot of money. I went to the bank, took out the cash, put it in my wallet on top of a wad of one-dollar bills, and immediately felt like a high roller.

I never spent that hundred, always just the other notes. This gave me a constant visual of having money in my pocket. Later I began carrying more, going back to the idea that if I'm an $800-or-more-per-day person, I should carry at least a day's worth of money in my pocket at all times.

As my wad grew, I'd walk into my favourite store, look at something expensive, and know that I could pay cash for it that minute. Not that I did, mind you, but I'd go into the vibration of financial abundance just knowing that I could. That felt great! Can you feel the power of that versus having a few crumpled fivers in your pocket that you squeak out every once in a while. I see people shopping with that tight, vice-grip look on their faces and I want to say, 'Loosen up, my friend. You're scaring money away.'

Every time you reach in your pocket and feel cash, it sends a powerful message to your unconscious – 'Hey, I've got money.' Here's a weekend project. Walk into nice stores with the 'job' of spending that cash in your pocket . . . but only in your mind. You don't even have to do it, just know and feel that you can. Try on the £2,000 Armani suits, imagining that you've got the cash to buy them now. Try on Rolex watches, Tiffany wedding rings, and designer dresses with the expectation of owning them. This raises your energy.

Shift Your Mind-set and Prepare Your Intention

Sit under a shady tree in a beautiful park and feel the well-being rise up inside you. That's a great way to shift your mind-set without involving money. If your park is too crowded or distracting, drive out of town and sit where you can watch children playing with nothing but time and love on their side. Tour a rambling museum and appreciate fine art, or sit in a large airy library surrounding yourself with the wisdom of the ages, or visit a luxurious hotel lobby.

Read autobiographies by famous people; they often have riveting rags-to-riches stories. Read theirs and use your imagination while scripting your own story. If it's convenient, visit a castle as I did. There are infinite possibilities – get creative. The trick is to embrace the royalty within you wherever you are, even if all you do is stay at home cutting pictures out of *Hello* magazine.

Another thing I suggest is to prepare for your intention in advance. If you need a personal assistant, get her desk ready. Get her phone connected. Ask around about possible candidates, even if you think you can't afford her yet. Start the interviewing process. Call local colleges and see if you might be able to get someone to do work experience for you for free or a nominal wage – a win/win for each of you.

10

Your Wealth-Building Routine

Once you learn to quit, it becomes a habit.

–VINCE LOMBARDI

Harmonic Habits

Habits are the things we do naturally and automatically without thinking. They've been conditioned into us and come directly from our unconscious mind. Changing our lives starts with changing our habits, our automatic responses.

Behavioural scientists tell us that we can recondition or form a new habit within about twenty-one days. Success isn't by chance, luck, or some capricious God who rolls the big success dice and selects favourites at random. (Lucky is a good name for a dog but a poor excuse for success.) Success is about healthy habits, little things done correctly over time, that become big realised goals. The absence of strong, positive habits can topple even the strongest pillar.

Make a commitment to develop good habits no matter what's happening around you – even when you're faced with tragedy.

Letting Go

In the period following 11 September 2001, many industries were in chaos. As a public speaker dependent on travel, my business took a hit in October, and I lost about $60,000 worth of bookings in the weeks that followed. Many people found themselves in a similar position, and I remember hearing several colleagues speaking about how awful things were, how they'd surely continue to go downhill. A handful of people were insistent, though, that this kind of thinking was going to get us nowhere.

A friend of mine, Bill Bachrach, who coaches top producers in the financial services industry, started spouting off about how the whiners needed to shut up and get back to business. He may not have had the Law of Attraction in mind, but he and I were advocating the same approach: stay intent on creating the results you want, do the job you know you must, knowing that it'll pay off in time.

I was rocked by 9/11 as we all were, and I consciously chose to work on the spiritual, intangible side of the equation. Yes, the loss of money was a setback for my business, but I chose to see it as temporary. I also began to look for the higher awareness in the tragedy. I mean, come on – New Yorkers helping each other? What a concept! The shocking destruction didn't have to be senseless.

Subatomic scientists have learned that every interaction consists of the destruction of original particles and the creation of new particles. Positrons and electrons colliding annihilate each other, but from the annihilation come more positrons and electrons – more than existed before. This teaches us that the creative process is the process of destroying (letting go of) the old more quickly.

I have found in my own life that the more I let go – stop controlling and start trusting – in relationships, business, money, and the like, the more quickly I leap forward. In my world (and remember, my world is not everyone's reality), the tragedy of 9/11 came to signal a change. I viewed it as part of a greater plan. I expected people to be more open to stepping back, observing their lives, making changes, and realising that maybe it's not all about money and materialism. We'd had this hot train of consumerism, and then this horrible event occurred that really took everyone's breath away. It caused most of us to re-evaluate. It was symbolic, of course, that an icon of our economic prowess lay in rubble.

I came to think of these events as a wake-up call – not that people should live in fear, but that economic power, while important, is not all there is to life. As a result, I figured, people would be more open to the message I was already delivering. While they still would (and do) want financial wealth, they would take a more harmonic and comprehensive approach. Because I put my intention and attention on building my business from that platform, it boomed that year. Believe it or not, my six-figure revenues rocketed to over seven. You know, the greatest gift wasn't even the money – it was hearing the stories and seeing the faces of all the people as they finally understood and achieved Harmonic Wealth.

Be wary of buying into collective thinking. Sometimes the collective isn't thinking clearly. Sometimes it's not thinking at all. Don José Luis once said to me, 'You can play the game – just don't buy in.' Good advice.

You've Got the Time

Almost all my clients have the same complaint when they start trying to achieve their goals: 'How can I ever do this? I don't have the time!'

Here's a fact. When your intention is great enough, you will *always* find the necessary time and energy to accomplish your desires. You can state excuses to the contrary, but holding onto your stories is just another way of wasting precious time.

'James, I'm aching to write!' a woman told me at one of my seminars. 'But I have two small children at home and I'm a single working mother.'

'If your intention was great enough, you'd find a way to make it happen,' I said. 'Write at the edges of the day.'

'There are no edges in my day!' she said, folding her arms across her chest.

It's not that I don't empathise with people and their very real challenges. But the question remains: what are you going to do to move beyond them?

'Writing at the edges of the day' was a direct quote from Toni

Morrison. As a single mum with two little kids, Toni would write whenever she could – in the middle of the night, the next morning at the breakfast table, spilling cereal on the pages, in line at the supermarket – wherever snippets of time could be had. Truth is, she found more than snippets and edges – nooks and crannies are everywhere too when you're looking for them. The results speak for themselves: Toni went on to win a Pulitzer Prize for fiction and the Nobel Prize in literature. Would J. K. Rowling, a single mother on the dole, ever have created Harry Potter if she hadn't had such a powerful belief in her creative abilities and intention to bring them to light?

History is filled with unbelievable characters who, in the days before TV (a theme perhaps?), would raise nine children, run a farm, take care of a dying parent, volunteer during wartime, and write twenty volumes of a book. They didn't have the time, support, money, or right environment to accomplish what they did, but they did it anyway because that's what mattered to them.

Eighty per cent of Americans polled say they want to write a book one day, and yet only 2 per cent do. As I told the woman at my seminar, Toni Morrison was willing to pay the price for the prize because she was passionate about her goal. Knowing what she wanted, setting the daily goals to make it happen was as natural as breathing. Forty-plus years later, she's not sitting on a pile of empty excuses, but standing atop a writing legacy built one page at a time.

Your God-Given Energy Supply

Inspiration and enthusiasm are paramount. Are you really going to stay up in the middle of the night to accomplish something if it doesn't inspire you? Sleep is too powerful a drug – and it's often overrated. But when you're inspired, you're beyond time and space. When you're inspired, your inspiration feeds your body. Time is gravity bound. Inspiration and spirit are not. When you remember that your goals and desires are spiritual, you'll get past your limitations and step into your God-given energy supply.

In the East yoga means 'union', becoming one with the entire universe, to literally become God in human form. One form of yoga, called *bhakti* yoga, is falling so fully in love with the object of your desire that you and your object merge. In these moments you move into a timeless state of inspiration, and you realise the divinity of all things. Here's an example.

A friend of mine rarely gets seven hours of sleep and often exists for weeks on end sleeping between two and five hours, even staying up for twenty-four or forty-eight hours straight at least once a month in order to finish her art. She's so in love with her work that it supercharges her results and makes her high. She can sit for five hours straight without looking up. Because of her ability to power through the night and often sleep at the edges of the day, she's totally available for her family much of the time. Does she look haggard and weary? Sometimes, but not often.

People usually think she's in her early thirties when in fact she's a decade older.

You know how when you're falling in love you don't need to eat or sleep? That's because you're running on your body's own dopamine. My friend's work creates a kind of dopamine for her. Wouldn't it be great if your work did that for you?

Time, Precious Time

Good habits and time are inseparable, aren't they? If you have an antagonistic relationship to time (you resent its laws), it only stands to reason that your habits will be erratic.

Time is a sacred, precious commodity that we've all needed, wasted, argued, and tried to bargain with. Napoleon Hill said that time will not tolerate indecision. In short, it's our greatest ally or worst enemy.

First, let's get one thing straight. Managing time is never going to happen. All you can do is manage the way you relate to time.

I hear a lot of people say, 'Time flies when I'm having fun.' Not true. 'I just don't have time.' Again, not true. Time is time. A day is a day. It's twenty-four hours. A week is a week, a month is a month, a year is a year.

Time is nothing if not consistent. You cannot save time; you can only spend it or invest it. Tick, tick, tick.

The fact is, you have all the time there is. We all do, so stop fighting against it. When you say you don't have time to work out, for instance, what you're really telling me is that working out is currently not important enough given everything else you've got on your plate. How you spend your time, like how you spend your money, tells me what you value most.

If you're truly passionate about your intention, you'll focus your time on it, often to the exclusion of other activities. If you're spending thirty minutes daily checking your voicemail, sixty on e-mail, and 120 driving to and from work, does that get you closer to your goals? Only you know, but you might want to start paying attention . . . or risk paying with pain.

If you're one of those people who has to answer the phone every time it rings or talk to every person who walks past your office, once you start working with your six action items, you'll notice that the less you deviate from your list, the quicker you'll realise your goals. Suddenly (and hopefully) those lesser activities will have less and less fascination for you because you'll see that they steal your dreams moment by precious moment.

Time Thieves

Try this on for size. I often have clients keep a written log of every minute they spend in a twelve-hour period. ⬤ Most hate doing this, whining all the way through it. But they're amazed to see how much time they spend on the phone, in the mirror, looking for stuff, watching movies, going through junk mail, and so on. Get real and identify your personal time thieves. Remember how much you're worth per hour? How much money are you wasting on these things? I find that many might as well just drive along with the window down and throw fifty-pound notes out in fistfuls. At least someone who needs them more than you do might get them.

If your argument is, 'But I need to relax; I need to have fun,' no one's saying you can't relax. But ask yourself, are you really relaxing when your to-do list is hanging over your head? No one's saying you can't have fun. I have tons of fun. But are you really having fun when you're putting your feet up while the details of your dreams are being pawned off for tomorrow, or the next day, or the next? Learn to have fun doing the things that bring your intention into reality.

The Alchemy of Time

Let's talk about alchemy. Alchemy is the transmutation of one thing into another, moving something from one state of evolution into the next. That's what we're going to do with your time. Contrary to popular belief, a disciplined and organised life is actually a liberated life. With your discipline you're transmuting what was once chaotic and random into something organised and directed. This new directed energy can be focused like a laser into creating what you want.

As we discussed earlier, most people fool themselves into thinking they can grow oaks in willow time. Did you know that if you got up one hour earlier and got started an hour before you usually do every day, you'd have NINE more forty-hour weeks per year? Isn't that fantastic? Talk about a present – I just gave you one with wrapping and a bow. If you're in sales, what if you made five more calls a day or took one extra meeting a day? If you're a writer, what if you wrote one more page a day? In a year that's 365 pages – a whole book. Do you see how small changes bring about large returns?

One of the simplest ways to increase your effectiveness is to allocate your critical six action steps into blocks of time: one-, two-, maybe even four-hour blocks. Begin by focusing on things that are most important to you and not allowing yourself to be interrupted. I do this by allocating the first two hours of my morning to my most important tasks, the list of my action items. What would happen if you returned all your phone calls from 11.00 a.m. to noon, and didn't answer your e-mails but once or twice a day? Do you think you'd have more time and energy to focus on your action items?

Be ready for a mind shift because the most important aspects of our life are rarely urgent and yet urgency steals our time and life away, doesn't it? We become slaves to minutiae, while the vital things slip away. Let this not be you.

Four Questions to Build Momentum

Keep pushing. Keep moving. You're growing and expanding, as your results are. Yet it's a good bet that you'll be hitting some common roadblocks and stalling.

'But James, I'll get tired of writing this stuff down.' Yes, I'm sure you will. I do too. It seems redundant. But you need to grab your attention by the scruff of the neck. Besides, what could be more important right now than developing new habits – new ways of thinking and acting? Wealthy people have the ability to give themselves a command and then follow it. It's a true test of personal integrity and self-worth. The greatest promise you'll ever keep is a promise to yourself. How much self-worth can you have if you're not honest with yourself? If you can't count on yourself, how much can you expect others to respect and value you? How can you expect to control universal energies if you can't even control your own energy?

If you're still unsure when to move forward, ask yourself these four questions:

1. Do I feel totally prepared? (Remember that 'no' is the right answer here.)

2. Is this decision/action in alignment with my vision?

3. Will making this decision accelerate the achievement of my intention/vision/goal?

4. If money were no issue, would I make this decision?

When I find myself saying no to the first and yes to the other three, I act boldly. Fate favours the bold. Another way to check myself is to ask, 'What would the person I choose to become do in this situation?'

When taken together, these four questions create an unbeatable formula, marshalling unlimited energies of power. You're going 3 for 3 – your thoughts, feelings, and actions create a powerful, undeniable magnetic field.

Wealthy people – and I'm talking about those with Harmonic Wealth – don't waste time knowing what they want one minute and then allowing themselves to sink back into fear or doubt the next. That only attracts confusion and anxiety. Great achievers focus only on their visions and fire those visions with wisdom, courage, and commitment, regardless of their current circumstances. They know it's only a matter of time before their visions come into physical form. They know that the stronger their belief, the faster they'll attract the results they desire and replace their old programming.

The path will present itself. Don't get caught up in next week. Don't even get caught up in tomorrow. Get totally immersed in today. You have your vision; you have your picture. Now give it 100 per cent of your focus right now. Get in the flow and go for it.

By understanding universal laws, you don't have to trust. You don't have to believe. You know. Let your salary be your report card. Like Richard Branson says, 'Money is just a convenient way of keeping score.' Let me tell you something: belief and trust are a great starting point, but *knowing* beats everything.

'And all things, whatsoever ye shall ask in prayer, believing, ye shall receive and ye shall have' (Matthew 21:22). See? I'm not just making this stuff up.

To recap, in going 3 for 3 you'll:

1. Get crystal clear about what you want – see it in 3-D. See it, feel it, smell it, taste it, hear it, and make it specific and measurable.

2. Ramp up those feelings – think about why you want the thing. What does it feel like to have it? Who have you become?

3. Take action every day, based upon where you're going, not where you are. Know that what you want also wants you.

Welcome to the Promised Land

Let's suppose you've begun to achieve some of your intentions. You're continuing to set new ones that are specific and measurable. You visualise and reflect on your inner vision. You've got your intention triggers and attention grabbers all over the place. You make up intention cards every day to maintain focus. You practise time alchemy, placing activities in efficient time blocks. You practise impeccable wealth habits to stay on track. In other words, let's say you've arrived at the promised land and fully secured your financial pillar. What should you do now to maintain it while you work on the other four pillars of Harmonic Wealth?

Ditch the Diving Board – Put Up the Parthenon

Look, I know there's something you do unlike anyone else. You have unique gifts, and the question I want you to start thinking about is, 'How can I provide value above and beyond my presence? How can I package that, bottle that, put it in a book or DVD, wrap it in some way, shape, fashion, or form so that it gets to the most people?'

Wealthy people have multiple sources of income – let's call them MSIs for short. When I was at AT&T, I had a single source of income, what I call a diving board. A diving board has one point of contact. If that contact point breaks, what happens to the board? It falls into the drink and you could end up gasping for air. Consequently, with my diving board I had a lot of insecurity and self-doubt.

I didn't like living with financial uncertainty, so I modelled my finances after the Parthenon. Nowadays, if any one (or two or even a few more) of my pillars collapses, the structure – meaning my finances – still stands.

You want to step off that rickety diving board and build yourself a financially secure dwelling. How? The first step is to open your mind to the possibilities.

I once read a study of wealth in North America that said the top 3 per cent earn 315 times what the bottom 97 per cent earn. Do you really think the top 3 per cent are 315 times more talented or smart? Of course not. Let me ask you, is that gap getting closer or further apart? The reason it's getting further apart is because that 3 per cent are using their time, creating the foundation from which they can then go and put more of their focus on their psychic income. You only have a finite amount of time to earn your life's savings. When your earning potential is tied to trading time for money, you're always capped at a certain level. I don't care how much money you make, you're capped in the diving board model.

Let's look at the average way people trade time for money. No matter what salary you earn – £30,000 or £100,000 a year or more – aren't you trading 40, 50, 60 hours a week for that money? The vast majority of the population does that. Regardless of how hard you work, regardless of how brilliant you are, how creative you might become in the future, as it stands, aren't you still only 'worth' £30,000, £50,000, or £100,000 per year?

I'm saying that you're worth much more than that. Human worth is not tied to net worth. Read that time and time again.

Trading time for money as a sole strategy is the worst plan of action in the world; in fact, it's almost next to impossible to amass wealth this way with only one source of income.

There are only three things you can sell in life: your skill, your knowledge, or your product. Skill is the worst, because it takes time. Knowledge and product take initial time, but when you set up residual income, you earn money while you sleep with little management. When you have enough of those, you can do whatever you love to do whether you get paid or not. Do you get it? Are you thinking?

MSIs are not another job. They ultimately cannot take a tremendous amount of your time because then you're still trading time for money. It took initial focus and work, but I now sell online courses, learning systems, books, DVDs, and CDs – products that don't require my presence to generate income. I get cards, letters, and e-mails from all over the world, places I've never physically been, from people who tell me they've been touched and affected by my programmes. There's not a day goes by that we don't get some kind of cheque in the mail at the office. 'Mailbox money' rules. I want you to start thinking about how you might create your own mailbox money, no matter what your field is.

I also own income properties, which I have other people manage. Otherwise, the money I earn requires my physical presence, which can be a nightmare with lost rent and late-night phone calls: 'Oh, my tap is leaking' or 'My refrigerator is broken.' No, thank you. Not a chance.

Think creatively about what you can do. A teacher, for example, could write a book. A massage therapist or beautician could create creams, oils, and lotions. A businessperson could tape his or her coaching programmes. A gardener could sell seeds. A cook could market different pasta sauces or recipe cards. Instead of getting tripped up right now on the actual product or service you could sell, the bigger and better question is, what unique service and value do I have within me that I can provide to the world above and beyond my presence? Focus on the question and the answers will appear.

If you look out your window down the road, it's quite possible that not one of your neighbours is doing this. Like many of the things I teach, this isn't necessarily for the average person. I'm asking people to go beyond average. Remember, no one normal ever made history.

Celebrate Your Wins

Do you get so busy that at the end of the day you feel like you haven't got anything done? That's because you're focusing on things that are broken and need fixing. When you begin celebrating your successes, you start to see how much you are really accomplishing.

The June 2007 issue of O: The Oprah Magazine contained an article entitled 'Better to Celebrate Than Commiserate' in which author Shelly L. Gable, PhD writes that couples who celebrate each other's happy events (like promotions or raises) report greater satisfaction in their relationship and are less likely to break up than those who offer support only during rough times.

We all have 'now' needs within us. We all have our impatient side. I encourage my clients to celebrate their successes, both individually and with others. You've heard it before: enjoying the process is the name of the game. This is true wealth. How many times have you heard about people who toiled in tough jobs for forty years only to die right before retirement? I hope they had some fun along the way.

Jump up and down and show genuine emotion when your spouse gets a big win. Make him laugh with a silly chicken dance across the living-room floor. Treat yourself and a loved one to a great dinner when you hit a milestone. Purchase something nice for yourself as a reward. Have a stroll in the park or a walk on the beach. I have friends in LA who almost never see the ocean; what's that about? They're so busy working that they consistently put off things they love for a time when they'll be less busy.

Treat yourself well by satisfying your need for instant gratification in a harmonic way. Are you with me?

Practise Gratitude

In a vibrational universe, as we discussed before, one of the most powerful magnetic forces you can employ is gratitude. You want your dreams to come true? Try sucking them towards you by becoming a Hoover of gratitude. Gratitude ramps up your energy, makes you feel good, and makes what you want rush towards you with greater intensity.

Do you compare your life to some higher standard and focus on what yours is lacking? That's showing ingratitude. It's relative, isn't it? Your income may feel like nothing compared to a lawyer or doctor, but what about against the average income in Bangladesh – £900 a year? You may not have a world-class physique, but do your lungs pump air? Do your kidneys function properly? People on dialysis would tell you that your physical vitality is priceless.

Since everything has a vibrational correspondence and like vibrations attract like, to lack gratitude is to ensure poor results. Recent studies prove that doctors and nurses spend more time with patients who show gratitude, thus increasing the quality of the care they receive. A friend had jaw surgery and couldn't speak, but wrote enthusiastic words of praise to his doctors and nurses in the hospital on a large yellow pad. His daughters were amazed to see that somehow all the busy doctors and nurses always seemed to have time to come into his room for extra visits, to sit for hours with his family in the waiting area or in their offices talking about his prognosis, but also about their own hopes, dreams, fears, and families. This, despite being swamped with full wards at one of the nation's most prestigious hospitals.

Appreciation gets you better customer service. It gets you freebies and discounts. Your hairdresser will cancel what she's doing when you have that last-minute special event you have to look great for. The service department at your computer shop will put you at the front of the line or work late making sure you're satisfied. You get better attention from friends and family. Gratitude doesn't just make the universe respond, it makes the people in your life respond.

There are two levels of gratitude: the things you're grateful for now (things currently in your life) and the things you're grateful for in the future (echo wave coming your way). Remember, anyone can be grateful after the fact. It takes mastery to be grateful in advance. Both are equally important. Practise them both.

Gratitude is a great attention grabber. It works to focus your attention on the best. It begins as a point of focus and becomes a way of life.

Truly wealthy people expect to receive their dreams in advance. As you continually think, feel, and act on all the goodness you currently have, the vibrational universe orders more. Be grateful for your desires, for how they inspire you to grow. Then as you write your six action items every day, be grateful for your ability to achieve them.

You've Arrived! Giving Back

We make a living by what we get, but we make a life by what we give.

— WINSTON CHURCHILL

There's an old story about a man who dies and says to God, 'Wow, it's a mess down there. Why didn't you send someone to do something about it?'

God says, 'I did. I sent you.'

Oops.

Life is like a boomerang. As you give, so shall you receive. You've heard it called the Law of Cause and Effect, or karma. What goes around comes around. What you sow, so you shall reap. Get the picture?

Money changes everything, but it doesn't fix everything. That's why you must continue giving energy to all of your pillars, never neglecting any of them totally, and why you must focus on giving. Give the best of yourself to yourself and to the world.

Money is energy, to be healthy energy must flow. Remember that. Remember, too, that we live amidst endless resources, that we need to keep the big picture in mind. The ultimate objective is Harmonic Wealth — a state of harmony and well-being in all areas of life. Money and its trimmings alone will not create this for you.

Doubt me?

A survey of forty-three countries by Ronald Inglehart indicated that human happiness shows a strong correlation with economic development. However, once a country's GNP reaches about £5000 per person, a further increase in financial wealth alone won't result in a further increase in the sense of well-being experienced by its inhabitants.

I just want you to keep the overall objective in mind. As long as you keep your head on straight, you can obtain money and things while still living a harmonic life.

Suppose you become extremely wealthy, a king or queen. What is your obligation in that role? No one works alone in this world. Assisting people in their cause uplifts your own. As we covered in Chapter One, I hope you see that if your wealth is made on the backs of others, you're living backwards. You have to love people and use money, not the other way round. There's enough money out there – make it from doing work that uplifts you and others, expanding your vibration and your gifts of value to the world. Then your entire life will become a beacon of inspiration – a rich and royal example of what the human spirit is capable of achieving.

PILLAR II

Relational

Relationships. In the Western world we equate relationships with romance, something comprising candlelit dinners, long walks on the beach, and lovemaking until dawn. We consider every other relationship – with friends, relatives, clergy, colleagues, employees, nature, you name it – as a lesser, more watered-down version of that ideal. Given how we devalue those relationships, is it any wonder many of us are deficient when it comes to relating to the people and challenges life brings?

You can have a truckload of cash, and if you're not effectively relating to others and the world around you, you'll be emotionally bankrupt. That's why we need a new mind-set here, one that realises the inherent value and equal worth of each and every one of our relationships, one that realises a relationship is really just the act of relating.

If someone comes to me and says, 'I'm having problems with my relationship,' I immediately ask, 'How long have you had problems relating?' Notice the verb. A relationship isn't a thing; it's a process. My intention is to help you master the process of relating to yourself, then to romantic partners, your family, your team, and ultimately the entire world around you. Because when you have loving, sustaining relationships – friends to laugh with, a romantic partner to share with, co-workers who motivate you, people in your community to inspire you – you wake up every morning feeling wealthy beyond measure.

ELEVEN

Know Yourself

Knowing others is intelligence; knowing yourself is true wisdom.
– TAO TE CHING

Three Key Relationships

We each have three key relationships: relationship with self, which is how we value, see, talk to, and believe in ourselves; relationship with others, which is how we communicate, value, and act with others; and relationship with the world at large, which is how we see, value, and act on behalf of our communities and nature, great and small. Which one do you think is more important? You guessed right if you said self.

It's more important to *be* the right person than to find the right person, to be in harmony with yourself before you try to harmonise with anyone else. So you must first heal and empower your relationship with your self, and then move on to building deeper relationships with others and your community. You'll never find the perfect relationship external to you unless and until you perfect your internal relationship.

The universe is a constant biofeedback mechanism telling you by way of your exterior results who you are on the interior. When the quality of your relationship with others improves, it's an indication you've done the necessary work to fix the relationship to self. If you can do that, when you build a strong relationship with yourself, then all of your relationships will mirror that healing and strength.

Learning from Experience

I'm far from an expert on love. I'm more of an expert on studying and exploring love than living the idealised love poets write about. And yet, when people tell me their stories of how they've failed in love, I get very uncomfortable. You see, I just don't think the words *failed* and *relationship* should be used together, because every single 'failure' can bring with it success as long as you're open to learning and growing.

Instead, learn from your experiences – the good, the bad, and the embarrassing. Don't think of them as mistakes; look at them as experiences that'll bring you closer to what you truly desire and deserve. Learn how to love yourself without the wasted energy and drama of placing your love on the wrong person. Learn how to respect yourself so you can respect others.

The Secrets of the Self

The inscription over the Oracle of Delphi in ancient Greece once read: 'Know thyself.' Obliterated by time and known only to a select few was the rest of that inscription: 'and you will possess the keys to the Universe and the secrets of the gods'. Simply put, as you go inward, you start to grow. This involution causes you to take new actions, which bring about your evolution. As you continue to evolve and take more action, you produce new results. Involution always precedes evolution.

How well we know and cherish ourselves affects every dimension of our lives.

I was coaching a husband and wife once who were having a difficult time. They wanted to move to a new city and get a fresh start. 'The problem is that you and your troubles will still be there,' I said. They both held to the illusion that if they just had a better environment, nicer friends, and different places to eat, their life together would be different. Not so. We have what we have because of who we are.

Unless you're locked up in solitary confinement, the state of your relationships affects every area of your life. In order to conquer your demons and have a healthy spiritual life, for instance, you've got to heal your relationship with yourself and the world. Peace, joy, and wealth on the outside only come from the same qualities inside. You can't be flipping the finger to someone on the motorway and then run off to chant *om* for an hour and quote the seventh sutra of the Buddha. Part of the reason people become ceiling surfers and hide out in ashrams isn't necessarily because of their undying devotion to God. Sometimes it's because they can't deal with people – or themselves. This is spiritual escapism.

Three Levels of Vibration – The Three Notes of Your Song

Remember, everything is energy and vibration: like vibrations attract while dissimilar vibrations repel. Remember also that energy can never be created or destroyed. All that ever was or will be is here right now. What this means from a scientific perspective is that the love you think you seek is already present. The only reason you aren't observing the physical evidence right now is because you've been thinking, feeling, and acting otherwise.

To build a healthy relationship with yourself and others, you need to raise and bring into alignment the three levels of vibration that create the field of intention and attraction:

1. Self-image ('I think')
2. Self-esteem ('I feel')
3. Self-confidence ('I act')

It's important to understand how these three levels work together. Feeling good about yourself is vital, but if that's all you've got going for you, feeling good about yourself is no more effective than just sitting around visualising 'Feel good, feel good, feel good.' Likewise, focusing too much on self-confidence, following those teachers who advise you to achieve a 'peak state' by 'acting as if ' – well, if you haven't the self-image and self-esteem to support it, your 'acting as if ' will quickly become 'acting as idiot'. That's why you've got to go 3 for 3. 🛈 You've got to constantly work to align your self-image, self-esteem, and self-confidence. Only then will you have congruence in thought, feelings, and action, and only then will you attract the life you want.

Self-Image

Self-image is the way you think about yourself and your world. Most people attract characteristics they don't want because the majority of their thoughts are centred on the things they don't want. Say you don't want to be unhappy and what will you be? Unhappy. That's the Law of Attraction at work. This is one of the many reasons that surrounding yourself with abundance and prosperity is so important. It's the same with people.

If you're constantly thinking and feeling about the way things currently appear, you'll in turn attract more of what currently exists instead of what you choose to create. As difficult as it may seem, you must turn away from current appearances and focus your thoughts on where you're going instead of where you are.

Focus on the high-quality people in your life. Feed those relationships. If your self-image tells you that you're unworthy – a belief, perhaps, handed down to you by your parents – or you've been programmed with thoughts of guilt regarding opulence, abundance, and joy in your life, then you may attract people who treat you well for a while, but your underlying self-image will eventually repel their kindness and inspire bad behaviour. Conversely, when you repair and build a healthy self-image, you'll attract people who respect and honour your highest self and support your highest aspirations.

Self-Esteem

The heart is the locus of self-esteem. The feeling centre of the body, it tells us how we feel about ourselves and our lives.

As a man thinks in his heart, so is he.

– Proverbs 23:7

As we've learned from researchers at the HeartMath® Institute, the heart literally has cognitive capacity, so consider the quote from Proverbs no mere metaphor but the literal truth. Your feelings or heart thoughts literally change your reality, your relationships.

Now consider this. Recent findings from quantum physics suggest that your consistent feelings create an energy field surrounding your entire body, called a tube taurus, which attracts all with which it's in resonance. This field emanates from five to eight feet beyond the body and many forward thinkers believe it to extend several miles on the quantum plane. Bear that in mind when you attempt to change your life and your results. You may not have such a long way to go after all. Look within.

We often feel discouraged because we judge our world by its physical appearance when we should pay attention to the many great teachers and traditions that have told us not to!

The most important distance you must travel is the feeling.

Read that again.

In reality, the distance you must travel is not so much in the physical realm as it is in the feeling realm. If you choose to have healthy relationships, you must measure the distance between how you currently feel in relation to where you want to be. If, for example, you're a man who doesn't trust women, you can't attract a loving, giving partner. It just won't happen. So your first order of business is to focus on the feelings you want to live in. Cultivate them, even if they're foreign. As you wear them and walk around in them, they'll become second nature. The first and most important step is to travel in the realm of vibration to the feeling of joy, appreciation, and gratitude. As you do this you'll attract more of those feelings of abundance into your life and hence your results will change.

Please know this in no way implies that you need not take action – you do – but your emotions drive all actions. In other words, you may not be completely where you want to be with your current relationship, but you absolutely *cannot* feel disgruntled, dejected, or dissatisfied. Energy flows where attention goes. What has to happen for you to feel totally loved and loving right now?

Sit down and travel the distance right now. Know beyond a shadow of a doubt, and feel the deep feelings of gratitude, appreciation, and certainty that you're already in your primary loving relationship or surrounded by uplifting people. Make sure to love yourself first.

Self-Confidence

Self-confidence is the final and often most frightening step to creating relationship wealth. You must reach out. You must stretch yourself. You must act and act boldly; your actions must be completely congruent with who you're becoming and where you're going, not based on your current appearances. Emerson stated, 'If I have lost confidence in myself, I have the universe against me.' You must take action as a self-confident co-creator of your own reality whose results are never in doubt. Remember, we discussed previously that your actions affirm the universe you're choosing to participate in. To do this, recognise that your current results are nothing more than the outcomes of your past thoughts, feelings, and actions and while they may appear in your reality, they have nothing to do with your tomorrow unless you do nothing different.

Focus your intention and keep your attention upon what you want, no matter what your current physical appearances may suggest. Choose your offer wave and ride it for all it's worth. Then constantly think and feel a profound sense of gratitude, knowing that the good relations you seek, by the laws of this universe, are also echoing back to you.

Like Attracts Like

Think back to a time when you met someone so similar to yourself that you felt an immediate bond. You were laughing and smiling freely, giddy even. Isn't that an amazing experience? That's energy, my friend.

The best relationships are between people with similar energy. Think about how much you and your best friend or spouse or partner are alike. These people represent the seeds we nurture in ourselves, now brought to full flower through careful, loving tending. They reflect us – the good, the bad, and the indifferent.

Whenever relationships don't work out, no matter how complicated the reasons, at the base level it's because of a dissimilarity in energies. The vibe just isn't right. No wonder people often use the word chemistry when discussing this very issue. If you're attracting low-vibration partners, then something about *your* vibration is low.

Essentially, we're all looking for people who feel like idealised versions of ourselves. Decide to raise your own frequency and you'll be amazed to see how the quality of the people you attract rises.

What Can You Do for Yourself Today?

Harmonic Wealth is about learning how to attract everything you want into your life by raising your vibration. Once again, it's an inside job. Consider this: how you treat yourself is an example to the world of how the world should treat you. People cannot and will not treat you any better than you treat yourself. If you don't treat yourself well, others won't treat you well either. So, what can you do for yourself today?

Just as you have to grow to receive greater amounts of money, you have to grow to receive greater amounts of love. If you want to attract the right mate, you've got to take control of your own destiny, embrace the inside/out approach, and grow to meet the size of that new intention so you can attract the person who has that similar vibration.

If you've taken the actions outlined in the financial pillar, you're already raising your vibrational energy. Are you constantly studying, understanding, and immersing yourself in that which brings you value and power, and avoiding at all costs anything that weakens you? Are you setting your goals, making your intention cards, working your daily critical six action steps, and managing your use of time? All of those things are part of taking care of yourself and raising your energy.

But what do you do if the key people in your life weaken you? What if your dad is critical, or your sister drains you, or your husband is angry or depressed and your energy deflates around him? Does that mean you're supposed to sever ties? Maybe, maybe not. I've seen incredibly difficult relationships become whole and healed, where both people become strengthened.

In most cases, unless your situation is violent or dangerous, before you can even look at what's best for you, you've got to heal your relationship with yourself first. Every relationship starts with the individual. You may know that it takes two to tango, but did you know that your dance partner is a mirror reflection of you?

Solitary Enlightenment: The Self-Love Test

Here's a test to help you see if you have a great relationship with yourself or not. Schedule an hour where you can sit alone in your living room by yourself with no television, no music, no magazines, no books, no computer, no mobile, no pets, no alcohol, no food, no conversation, no distraction whatsoever. And no sleeping.

Can you do it?

'I'd go insane,' my friend Dan told me.

'Then you don't like yourself very much,' I said. He was disgruntled; I could tell by the way he lowered his gaze and grumbled something under his breath. 'Hey, sorry,' I continued, 'but how can you expect other people to want to be around you if you don't enjoy your own company?'

Do you enjoy your own company? Get yourself to that secluded space and sit with these questions:

- Do I enjoy spending time alone with me?
- What kinds of people do I consistently surround myself with?
- What do my ideal partnerships look like? In love, work, and life?
- Do I enjoy the time I spend with loved ones? Do they seem to enjoy it too?
- Is my sex life satisfying? Is my sexual partner satisfied?
- Am I able to resolve conflicts without residual resentment?
- Looking back at my love relationships, do I see similar traits or trends?

- What do I need to change about me to attract the kind of love I want?
- Am I willing to make those changes . . . *really*?

Ask yourself some of these probing questions and you'll get a sense of where you stand and where chaos may be brewing. Forget ideas of not being good enough, and zero in on what areas may require more of your time and attention. I'm asking you to get critical in the most noble sense. Forego judging yourself; that's counterproductive. Instead, observe what areas of neglect may be causing you to experience disharmony and use them as tools for growth. For example, if being alone freaks you out, it's time to ask yourself:

- Do I know my innermost thoughts, feelings, and values? Can I articulate them clearly?
- Am I really honest about who I am? Do I take time to reflect?
- Do I feel as if I can tell people the truth and not just say what they want to hear?
- What would happen if I regularly took time out from the mental chatter and clutter of my everyday life?
- What about sitting with myself is refreshing or distressing?
- When was the last time I took some personal space – had some high-quality 'me' time?
- When was the last time I celebrated who I am or something I've accomplished?
- If I'm nothing more than what I do and what I have, then who am I when I don't do anything and have anything?

Remove yourself from external noise and busyness. Take time to be, to enjoy quiet and introspection. Go where you can hear yourself think, where you can be creative, and tap into guidance. This is self-love. This is self-care.

Commit to your relationship with your self to build a deeper, more profound, more connected, more understanding, more aware relationship with your self. Your unique path for doing that will appear when you make it a priority. Put it on your intention card, and I guarantee that your relationships with others – your family, romantic relationships, business relationships, and siblings – will make your life rich.

You must also commit to embracing an unbending belief in yourself. If you don't, you'll never take the action necessary to make your goals a reality. You'll never even become a fraction of what you're capable of. Unless you're highly unusual, you have some limiting beliefs about yourself, gifted to you from an outside source at a very early age. You must be willing to do your inner work, the kind we're doing here, chapter by chapter, to see the results you want. The Law of Attraction is fuelled by expansion and self-love.

Self-Love vs Being Selfish

There's a big difference between being self-centred and being selfish. Being self-centred is taking care of yourself first and foremost, doing what's best for you, and living the life you choose. This is healthy. Being selfish is you trying to get *me* to live the life you choose. This is not healthy.

I've come to realise that if I make decisions that are best for me, then they are ultimately best for my relationships as well. This doesn't mean that I don't care for and think about others. Far from it. I love my relationships, I love people, and I want continually to be able to give more. But I also realise that to give more, I have to be more, and that comes from being honest about what I need and caring for myself. You cannot give what you don't have.

12

Become Your Higher Self

Don't ask what the world needs. Ask what makes you come alive, and go do it.
Because what the world needs is people who have come alive.

– HOWARD THURMAN

Attention Equals Love

Are you giving your higher self and ideals attention? Or are you in love with your misery, attending to it all the time like it's a bonfire that needs fanning?

Consider this: every time you whine and moan because you're alone and not in a relationship, you're actually telling yourself that you love being alone and lonely. Now you can disagree, you can protest all you like, but the fact is, giving your misery more energy and attention than you give anything else is a way not just to keep it alive, but to give it a pre-eminent place in your life. Energy flows where attention goes, right?

So ask yourself this: have you consciously chosen to create this misery in your life, or is it just a bad habit, an old story that's holding you back?

If you don't love yourself, you'll never attract people who truly love you – not ever. When you think of yourself as unlovable in any way, you're actually in love with that unlovable version of yourself, and your relationships can only reflect that. Maybe you're in love with your misery because it's that familiar friend who's all you've ever known. Perhaps, perversely, you've let your misery validate your worthlessness. I understand the desire to dwell in the familiar, to stay with the devil you know. Sometimes the fear of the unknown is greater than the misery of the known; but you'll never grow that way. That worn out story is long dead. It's time for you to learn you have other choices and act on them.

Be Responsible and Move Forward

When we discover something wrong, we have two choices: we can complain and blame, or we can change. I've learned not to beat myself up because that's a very low vibration, and by giving those mistakes attention, I pull more of the same towards me with a magnetic force. It's much more productive to ask, 'What did I learn? How can I apply it? What will I do differently next time?' Then move on.

Now, that doesn't mean I don't apologise and adjust my behaviour when I do something that hurts someone else. That's just part of being responsible for your actions. It seems so simple, and yet it's not the norm for people to take personal responsibility for their results and their actions. If it were, the world would change, not just on the personal level, but on all levels, including governmental. Everyone is always putting blame on something or someone else. If every single person across the globe would practise taking responsibility for his or her actions – being totally accountable for the results he or she achieves – the world would be transformed.

Remember, if you think your life problems are out there, that very thought is the problem because you're giving your power away. You're saying, 'It's my husband, it's my wife, it's my boss, it's my environment, it's my salary, it's my government.' It's endless. Being fully accountable is not a popular mentality. Too many times the easy road, the victim road, is the popular choice. It's always easier to place blame outside yourself. At least short term. In the long term playing the victim is disempowering and gets you nowhere in the world of results. Remember that attention equals love. When you play the victim, you feed the victim and the universe sends you more opportunities to be one.

Author Wayne Dyer once said, 'If our problems were caused by other people, we would spend a fortune sending them to a psychiatrist.' Kind of silly, isn't it? Another simple example of this is when you hear someone complain about someone else. Who are they defining? The other person? I don't think so.

It takes courage to be accountable. It takes courage to take responsibility for the things that happen around you. Let's take accountability one notch higher. Let's talk about being fully accountable for every single thing in our lives. Yes, you read that right – everything – even when it's not your fault. Because you should know by now that life isn't about fault, is it? It's about results. You'll always experience the greatest results when you become fully accountable. Only when you become accountable for everything in your life can you be responsible for changing anything. Everything is your responsibility; nothing is your fault.

Unresolved Issues Deplete Your Energy

Holding grudges is one way of blaming others, and it's a huge energy drain. Imagine getting into an argument with someone and not coming to a resolution. You go away and think about it, and the problem gets bigger and bigger and bigger; it takes up a lot of your energy. Science calls this an attractor field and the greater the mass, the greater the attractor.

An argument is like a fifteen-pound dumbbell. Imagine taking that fifteen-pound dumbbell, putting it in your pocket, and going to work. You try to ignore it, but you can't. You go down the corridor and it clanks into the wall. You sit down and it crashes onto your chair. You get up and you feel it pulling at your skirt or your trousers. There's no way you can get away from that damn dumbbell as long as it's in your pocket. It demands energy and holds your attention captive.

Some of us need to take the dumbbells out of our pockets, don't we? Could that be you? If you know someone with whom you have a broken relationship, apologise to them, even if you think you're right. For your own sake, let that energy go and forgive. There's a misconception that forgiveness is a gift you give the other person. Really, it's a gift you give yourself, the freedom from carrying and burning all that energy. An unwillingness to forgive is like drinking poison and expecting the other person to die. So, do whatever it takes for your own sake, because forgiveness does not let someone else off the hook. It lets you off the hook you put yourself on.

Forgiveness can occur in a single shift of mind, a single commitment to letting go of the past. Start by finding the blessing in whatever transpired. Truly forgiving is having the ability in your heart and mind to say, 'Thank you for giving me that experience.' If you can no longer communicate with the person directly, send out a prayer vibration or write a letter of forgiveness that you don't even have to mail. This practice will free you like nothing else. Too difficult, you say? Imagine that everyone you meet has been autographed by God, that they're all doing the best they can with what they know. We're all unique thumbprints of the Divine — God in human form. See if that helps.

To err is human, to forgive divine.

                                            – ALEXANDER POPE

Also, if you have guilt, let it go, because guilt is an emotion of the past. You absolutely cannot feel guilty about something in the present or the future; you can only feel guilty about the past. That's dead and gone. There's no way you can change it, so just let it go. Learn from it, apply the lesson in your life, and move on. Be grateful for the chance to learn the lesson, let it propel you to right action, then forget it; anything more is self-indulgence. Some of us need to get rid of the things that steal our energy or the things that we give energy to emotionally. Drop the dumbbell right now.

Soul Retrieval

In Elizabeth Gilbert's memoir *Eat, Pray, Love* there's a powerful scene on the roof of an ashram in India where Elizabeth makes her peace with her ex-husband, saying goodbye to him, forgiving him and herself, and reclaiming her joy. He's not present and there are no long processes, just Elizabeth's inner resolve to leave the past behind and move forward, which leads to a profound moment of personal empowerment.

Ask yourself what's holding you back. Is there someone or something you need to let go of? Perhaps you can't forgive a parent for your lousy upbringing, or you're still bitter about an abusive ex-boss who sidelined your career. Your willingness to release your grip will help you retrieve that lost part of your soul and allow you to move forward.

Part of the reason we get stuck pining for an old love or feeling bad about ourselves is that we don't often reclaim our full identity and harmony after a breakup or personal tragedy. We essentially get stuck in negative energy, putting our focus on someone else and giving him or her our power. Envision hanging onto a past situation as sending a stream of your personal energy consistently into the past. *I should have been more loving . . . I should have said what I felt . . . If I'd acted sooner, this wouldn't have happened . . . I could have put my foot down.* Obviously whatever energy you're expending is spent, leaving you less energy to live, create, and operate with now. It's time to take your energy back.

Every indigenous culture I've studied believes that when you go through an emotional trauma – abuse, a breakup, or the loss of a loved one – a part of your soul splinters or breaks off, staying with the person who hurt you, left your relationship, or died. When people say things like, 'I lost my innocence,' 'I lost my trust,' or 'The child in me died that day,' they are speaking perhaps more literally than they even know.

While this might seem bizarre to the modern mind, it's wiser than you might think. Physicist J. S. Bell has recently documented what is arguably the most profound finding in modern physics, called Bell's Theorem. Bell's Theorem asserts that things once connected mysteriously stay connected across all time and space; if two particles have interacted and are then separated, they are nonetheless entangled, and the actions of one instantaneously affect the other. There's absolutely no time lag. This is most true of things that are deeply linked by strong and intense vibrations – we could call them feelings and emotions. If this were a man and woman, regardless of how far apart they were to move – from England to Australia, for instance – they'd continue to have an immediate impact on one another. Change the energy of one and you simultaneously change the other. This has profound implications for your life and relationships. How many exes do you have that you're still connected to?

What's so incredible is that indigenous peoples the world over who've had no contact with one another often have this same belief, with similar remedies. For instance, a shaman helps people find and reconnect with those fragmented pieces of self. While I've studied and been initiated into many shamanic traditions, I definitely don't limit the idea of spirit strictly to shamanism. I believe there are many paths to healing, and when the student is ready, the way will appear.

If you feel splintered, start by being clear that you choose to be whole and healed. That sounds like a no-brainer, but plenty of people try hobbling along with one foot in this world and one elsewhere, which may sound like science fiction if you haven't felt the intense pull of wanting to leave this time and place. But if you have, you know how tempting it can be to disconnect your energy from this life, particularly when you're in intense pain.

Not long after her father died, a friend of mine was driving and blew a tyre at 70 mph. Making it to the side of the road to safety wasn't easy, but when she did, she suddenly realised that part of her had been wanting to join her father and hadn't been fully present. Her near miss made her fully aware of how very much she wanted to stay on earth, and she pulled her energy back immediately.

If you meditate – which I recommend – hold the intention to call back any part of yourself that may have broken off. Say, 'Thank you for giving me that experience,' find the lesson and the gift, and let go. A shaman can help you achieve an altered state in which your consciousness can leave the confines of your body. A good therapist, healer, or bodyworker may help you reclaim your wholeness. An LA-based healer, Guru Singh, conducts soul retrieval work in his office for everyone from taxi drivers to A-list celebrities, but believe me, we all have the God-given power to heal ourselves. Sure, you can seek out a healer or skilled therapist and this is helpful, or you can do it on your own if you're up to it. Bottom line, do whatever works for you to reclaim your full energy and vitality.

Be open to whatever process comes to aid your integration back into this body. Prayer and/or meditation may be enough for you. In essence, that's what a shaman helps you with anyway. I can't emphasise enough the importance of doing this for yourself.

Reframing History

Think about a time you desperately wished something had gone differently – whether it was when your dad walked out, the love of your life dumped you, or you had a terrible accident. Whatever it was, if you feel your soul and energy splintered, here are some other powerful techniques for self-healing.

First, since according to Einstein time is an illusion and the past, present, and future are all happening now, you can send energy to the person you were back when you were hurt. This might sound bonkers, I know, but you'll truly benefit by sending your past self some loving energy. Go back in your mind and see the scene, visualise what happened, feel the feelings, and then have yourself in this present time be there for your past self to do what no one did back then. That might mean wrapping your arms around your own shoulders, rocking yourself, saying the right words of reassurance, and so on.

The next thing you can do is visualise the experience the way you wish it had gone – not in a fantasy, where you try to convince yourself that the event never happened, but in a transformative way. For instance, if you go back to a time when you were five and your father walked out on your family, rather than having him stay, which you know didn't happen, have him say, 'I love you. This is not because of you. I will always love you.' Or go back to your greatest heartbreak and hear that person say, 'I'm just not ready; it has nothing to do with you. Someone better is coming for you. I'm not your destiny. Thank you for loving me and being part of my journey.' You're not rewriting history; you're reframing history.

Give yourself the healing by giving yourself the comfort you wish had been given to you.

Nothing is good or bad; it's the value we place on things that hurts or empowers us. You only lose a piece of your soul when you've decided that something is merely tragic, without the hope of a lesson or the possibility of grace. But think about it. No matter how horrific the event, there's always something good, some piece of grace within it that's yours to find. This is a harmonic perspective that brings true wealth. In going back, you might see that something you thought was really horrible might have actually been good. What did it teach you? Did you become more self-reliant? Did you build determination? Did it give you empathy for others? Maybe that accident led to your life's work. Maybe that breakup freed you to be with a better person. Maybe your dad's leaving forced you to be incredibly self-sufficient and now you're a first-rate parent to your own kids. From the vantage point of our small ego selves, we often can't see the bigger picture until years later. Some, in fact, never see it at all. A harmonic perspective doesn't make a situation any less challenging; it just allows you to realise how it served you. Everything does. The only question is whether or not you're open to exploring and realising it.

13

Become the Person You'd Like to Fall in Love With

I've learned that people will forget what you said, people will forget what you did,
but people will never forget how you made them feel.

– MAYA ANGELOU

Soul Mates: Heaven Sent or Hype?

'I want to meet my soul mate!'

It doesn't matter where I travel in the world; this is the one thing people consistently ask me to help them with. They're always surprised when I tell them that this concept is a load of nonsense. I apologise if my opinion sticks a hatpin in your romantic balloon. But mark my words: you'll never ever attract a perfect relationship with another human being into your life until you first and foremost have a perfect relationship with yourself. Because you'll continually attract your incompleteness.

I'm as romantic as they come – often too much for my own good. I also know there's nothing outside that doesn't come from inside, that in all reality there is no 'out there' out there. The whole concept of soul mates says that your completion resides in another person, your 'other' or 'better half'. 'You complete me' doesn't sound very romantic to me. On the contrary, I'd rather complete myself and attract my desired match who's already completed herself. If I don't attract her, I'm still happy on my own. Either way, I win.

Carol Allen, Vedic astrologer and author of *Love Is in the Stars,* writes about how identifying someone as your 'soul mate' often leads people to think, *This is the person God wants me to be with,* before they truly get to know someone. Being spiritually starry-eyed – being oh so sure the angels have sent you your 'destiny' – takes you right out of the moment so that you don't let things unfold or see your partner for who they are. Whatever you do, you'd better not mess it up because soul mates don't come along every day, do they? With this mentality you tolerate bad behaviour and knock yourself out for too long, then beat yourself up for 'blowing your chance', worrying that you've created all sorts of new bad karma. Sound familiar? I hope not.

Relationships require hard work, and big relationships bring up all of your unresolved stuff. But I assure you that you can't miss out on meeting your soul mate. As you raise your vibration, you'll always attract people with higher and higher frequencies. It's never going to be easy, though, no matter what level you're at. If you think you want to attract your greatest, most romantic relationship, know that the grander the relationship, the more potential friction, disagreements, and chaos you're going to have. If you're going to have the peaks, you've got to handle the troughs. To think otherwise is an illusion. Again, don't wish for an easier life; wish to truly *live* life.

You think your life will be easier in a committed romantic relationship? Think again. You're going to have greater chaos being in a living laboratory called a home, with another research subject called a mate. The same is true in all relationships. That's why being in a relationship, whether it's with yourself, money, your business, or romance is the greatest tool for self-examination and expansion. It's a lot easier to be the Buddha when you're sitting in your living room doing nothing.

Your Been There, Done That List

When seeking your mate, the first question to ask is: what do I keep getting that I no longer want? Chances are there's a common thread that runs through your relationships, likely more than one. Think back to your last relationship, and the one before that, and the one before that. Do you keep attracting the drinkers and the potheads? What about the rage- or workaholics? How might a repetitive character flaw be satisfying something for you? What inside you mirrors this character flaw, and what are these traits attempting to teach you? How can you learn, love, heal, and grow?

In the Welcome, I asked you to write down things you know you don't want so that you could invert them and figure out what you do want. Have you done that? Let's try another exercise for relationships. Write down your 'Been there, done that' list – identify all the qualities you keep finding in the mates you've been attracting. Think of it as a 'What have I had that I no longer want?' list. Bill made his list and realised he always got the liar who's forever partying, not interested in settling down with any one partner. Nancy attracted the angry and wounded every time, and all her girlfriends were super-dramatic, blowing in the wind or crying every day. She used to joke that she was running some ad in her auric field: NEEDY INSECURE WOMAN SEEKS ABUSIVE GUY: ONLY DAMAGED EGOS NEED APPLY. The joke was on her.

Most people are so busy focusing on what they don't want that that's all they can draw to them – more lack. If you want marriage, but you don't want to answer to anyone, what are you really focusing on? Did your parents divorce? What do you really believe about the institution of marriage? How does your previous choice of partners reflect this?

What is the story common to your past relationships? What is that story satisfying in you? What are the benefits? Maybe being with a needy partner has helped you feel wanted and worthwhile. Perhaps an abusive partner has made you feel righteous, earning you the attention of people eager to offer you pity. Or maybe dating the diamond in the rough – that person with great potential – has allowed you to be the saviour. When you can pinpoint what's motivating you, it'll help you to understand why you're with the one you're with. That's where meditation and therapy can be invaluable, as we'll discuss shortly. Right now, just know this: when you change, your results change.

Relationship Intention Wish List

Once you've made a list of the qualities you keep attracting that you *don't* want, it's time to make a list of what you *do* want so you can attract that partner into your life. In most cases, if not all, it'll be the exact opposite of your don't-want list. In making my romantic relationship intention wish list last year, it became clear to me that I'm very male. Like many men, at least the ones who'll admit to it, I want a woman with a beautiful smile, a great athletic body, youthful, glowing skin, and so on. But more than anything, I'm attracted to spirituality, independence, and self-sufficiency from a woman who doesn't have to prove anything. She has her own life but loves to meld with mine. She's health-conscious and active, nurturing and affectionate, communicative, smart, fascinated with simplicity, and content with just being. What's on your list?

Make your list 🛈 ; make it specific and present time, and then let it go. I'm a big believer in using intention triggers and attention grabbers with regard to attracting your ideal mate. Intention cards and vision boards are a good start, so by all means take those actions. Then recognise that you don't have to get a relationship; you already have it.

Remember, the act of 'wanting' the perfect relationship keeps it away and affirms the not having. When you recognise that what you want already exists, it accelerates the process of its coming to you. I want you to become aware of that fact.

Nothing Is Ever Missing from Your Life

'I want to attract my dream mate,' Barbara told me during one of my workshops.

'He's already in your life,' I said.

'You're funny,' she said, punching me playfully on the arm.

'I'm not joking,' I answered.

'How can you say that?' she asked, rolling her eyes.

As I'd done for many before her, I had Barbara sit down and write down all the perfect qualities she wanted in her dream mate: loving, communicative, spiritual, good sense of humour, handsome, honest, hardworking, cuddly, healthy, fit. There must have been fifty things on her list. 'If you can find him in my life right now,' she said, 'you're a miracle worker.'

'I intend to, and it's the universe that's miraculous,' I said with a smile. 'Now go back down your list and write the initials of two or three people in your life right now who have each one of those qualities.' (This is your cue to do the same with your list.) 👁 She paused for a second and then played along, placing initials beside each characteristic. It took some thought but she eventually found them all. Her sister and her assistant always make her laugh. Her best male friend and her karate instructor are both handsome and fit. Her son and younger brother cuddle next to her while watching home movies, and so on.

'But James, I want all those things in one person.'

'You're not going to get it in one person,' I explained, 'if you're not grateful for having these qualities in the relationships you already have. In fact, your focus upon what's not there is sending out the very message that's keeping it away. You must acknowledge that you do have these things in your relationships, just in a myriad of people instead of in one person.' Barbara seemed confused.

'Look, Barb,' I continued, 'if this is a vibrational universe, and it is, and you're putting your attention on lack – he's not there, he's not there, he's not there – how can you attract anything but more lack? The offer wave you're sending out is being echoed right on cue. Your wish is my command.'

'All right,' she said. 'But what am I supposed to do?'

'Begin by recognising that nothing's ever missing; it's already in your life. Be grateful for what you have and lock your attention on all your goodness and gifts. Then, if you want to attract that into one person, you can. But you can't skip the gratitude step. Faking it won't work either.'

When you start to become truly grateful for the relationships you already have, the universe sends you more.

Barbara got married a year later to a man who fulfilled the totality of her list.

Please know that everything you ever want or can want you already have – it's just in a different form than you currently choose. Begin to notice and place your attention upon where it currently exists. Practise a feeling of gratitude and appreciation versus scarcity and depreciation and you'll quickly be able to transmute your results into a different form.

Acknowledge a Dualistic Universe

In my desire to attract my perfect mate, I sometimes forget that it's something I both want and do not want. I think Walt Whitman nailed it when he wrote, 'Do I contradict myself? Very well, then, I contradict myself. I am large, I contain multitudes.' How do I live with my contradictions? For me, it comes down to embracing my ambivalence.

Sometimes I dislike being alone and want a deeper and more lasting partner rather than a multitude of dates. Like the squirrel in the park, I run towards the nut but lose my courage and dash back. Hopefully inching closer to my heart's calling but feeling danger and uncertainty as I draw close, I lose my nerve. I long to commune and connect, but then I long to be alone. Sometimes the feeling of being perpetually single isn't always as sexy as it seems. It can be a roller coaster. Sometimes I'm excited to be free; I can do what I want when I want. I feel light and supple. I have lots of female companionship when desired. But then an hour later I'm sad and confused. How can one person want to be both so independent and yet so connected? Welcome to my world.

In this dualistic universe, being alone can be both freeing and exciting, and limiting and dull. But so can being in a romantic relationship. It's all about how you choose to experience it. We have to be realistic either way, and handle the sometimes-hourly variations whatever our relationship status.

No matter what, it's important not to lose yourself in relationships. The breakup of my relationship in 2000 contributed to my business collapse. Not only was I personally invested in my partner, but all of my financial organisation needs were being fulfilled by her too. I wasn't self-reliant in my partnership skills. The lesson here is not to pour all of the details of your life or business into one person. I learned that the hard way.

Become the Person You'd Like to Fall in Love With

You want to know the quickest route to having sound relationships? Become the person you want to attract. If it's romantic love you want, be romantic. Want someone with a great body? Get to the gym. Desire a compassionate partner? Be compassionate. Someone with a great sense of humour? Lighten up. Do you want friends who are loyal and true? Be loyal and true.

Relationships Either Grow or Die

Who we spend our time with has a huge effect on our lives, so it's important to be careful who you connect with. Feelings are contagious, and people will either raise or lower your vibration. When people grow apart, it's often because one person has raised their vibrational energy right up and the other one hasn't.

You see this a lot when one partner goes through a big transformation in her career or decides to heal his life and get out of an addiction while his or her partner stays in the same old mind-set. It's not that the person who's growing doesn't love their partner anymore, it's that on the simplest level their energies no longer match.

Most relationships (romantic and otherwise) aren't meant for life (as evidenced by the divorce rate), but they're all meant for growth. A relationship that grows together stays together. The law of spirit is fuller expression and expansion. So if you want to keep your partnership growing and changing, you must practise appreciation and gratitude in action. Think about it. When something appreciates it gains more value – real estate, jewellery, as well as your bank account. When you appreciate a relationship, it grows in value as well. Consequently, when you don't continually appreciate a relationship, it must move towards depreciation and death. Are you beginning to understand how all these things tie together?

Family Values

Many of us prize our relationships with family as much as our romantic partnerships. Yet when people come up to me at my live events, I frequently hear comments like this: 'When I get to this point in my career, I'll spend more time with my kids.' Or 'When I get to this income level, I'll start taking vacations with my wife.' Or 'When I achieve this reward, I'll wind down so I can really be there for the family.' Then these people describe some action or behaviour that they're going to put into practice *after* they achieve or acquire their magic bullet. When I hear these types of comments, regardless of the context or the promise being made, I typically think, *No, you won't.*

How can I be so sure?

Because if you haven't developed the habit now, you won't act on it later. Life doesn't miraculously change until you change.

'*Before enlightenment, chop wood and carry water. After enlightenment, chop wood and carry water.*'

This Zen proverb tells us that success, happiness, and even Harmonic Wealth are not a destination but a journey. You and I both know that no award, no income, no new toy, no promotion, not even the perfect mate will ever make us truly happy or fulfilled. Life will not miraculously change when your next goal is attained. You'll still have to chop wood and carry water. In other words, the activities of life will always be similar, but *you'll* be different.

The difference comes in the attitude with which you do these things. When you achieve true happiness and fulfilment, you'll learn that the journey is the adventure, the excitement, and the fun of life. You won't wait until you've achieved wealth to have quality time with your family. Do it now.

Long-Term, High-Quality Relationships

In 1900 there were 1.5 billion people on Earth. In 2000 there were 6 billion. Do you think we're being forced to learn how to get along?

If you want to revolutionise your relationship with others, you must find time to do what you value most. I'm not here to tell you what your values should be – I'm not qualified to do that – but what I can assure you is that if you want to change your life, you're going to have to change your values.

Many of the companies I work with today comprise virtual offices, meaning they have no central location. These home-based businesses are booming. Like all things in life, this is both good and bad. Remember the Law of Polarity?

While virtual offices give us our own space and allow us the luxury of avoiding traffic, it's easy to become isolated. Moreover, in a world where there is so much to learn, so much to do, and so many ways to grow, relationships seem to be becoming more and more difficult. I guess that's why, in this high-tech society, high touch is highly valued.

The quality of your life can be measured by the quality of your relationships. Keep in mind that what you're ultimately playing is a long-term game, building high-quality relationships with yourself, with others, and with the world around you.

So, let me ask you to consider. What are the small things you can begin to do right now for your loved ones, your children, your spouse, your significant other, your mate, your clients, your prospects, the people in your organisation, and ultimately yourself?

How can you provide more value to the world? Small things that consistently make a major difference, can provide tremendous value and very often cost you so little. Stop reading now and brainstorm ways in your notebook. Seriously – do it. Not for me, but for you.

Checks and Balances

Harmonic Wealth grows from two basic understandings. First, to the extent you focus on one or two areas of life to the neglect of others, you feel poorly overall. As much as you can focus on all five areas, albeit unequally at times, you experience true wealth and fulfilment. But remember what I said about balance being bogus. You're never going to be in perfect balance, complete stasis, until you're six feet under. Secondly, giving energy and attention to each pillar causes all the areas to flourish. None of them operates in a vacuum. They are all – we are all – connected. Everything affects everything, and all things are in relationship with all things.

How can you apply this to your own life? By constantly conducting checks and balances, recognising where surpluses and deficits exist, and shifting your energy when needed. If, for example, you want to focus primarily on business growth for a while, that may require sacrifices in your relationships. So make agreements with yourself (and anyone else affected) about how long you'll allow this temporary situation. Talk to your friends and family. Tell them you'll be absent a lot during the next two months, but after that you plan to spend some serious quality time together.

The structure of our society is such that we spend more time at work than we do with friends and family. Like it or not, unless you're highly unusual, that's just the way it is. We typically spend at least eight hours of our day at work so that only leaves a few hours to spend with our children, our family, our loved ones, and even ourselves. Because we have less time, it must be higher-quality time. If we're not careful, we work a long day, come home, and turn on the TV. We never talk. We never connect. We never get to know each other. We don't exercise our body or our spirit. Eventually the friends drift away. The kids are gone. The husband and wife don't remember each other. We become stressed because our time is less invested in the relationship we have with ourselves, our friends, and our family. We must have higher-quality time in these areas to be productive and fulfilled in the long term. We have to invest higher-quality energy and spirit for our most central relationships.

How many people do you know who get pulled into their job? Their job becomes their entire life, and they rationalise (ration lies) about why they're doing that. How many people do you know who work their entire life away and tell the good story about how they're doing it for their kids or their family when the truth is, spending time with their family would be far more exciting, joyful, and fulfilling for both? Harmony is the key to life. It's the key to true wealth and long-term success. If you don't have harmony, at some point, you're going to break.

One of my good friends called me recently. He told me about how, at one point in his life, he was totally consumed by his job, spending countless hours at work, investing most of his energy at the office. In the process, he became disengaged from other areas of his life, one of which was his family. At the time, he didn't realise that he had let the importance of his family slip until his father died unexpectedly. Or rather, unexpectedly to him! He'd been so busy with work that he didn't notice the signs of his father's declining health. It was a wake-up call. He had allowed key areas of his life to get skewed, out of harmony. Little by little he had lessened his appreciation for, and therefore the value of, his family – unintentionally and without noticing.

I remember reading about a top executive, one of the few women who'd risen to run a leading publishing house. When an interviewer asked her how she'd done it, she replied, 'Easy. I just gave up friends.' She was joking – or was she?

Outgrowing Your Peer Group

As you expand and grow, so will your relationships. When you choose to become great, people around you will do their utmost to keep you stuck and the same. Not because they're bad – they're not – but because they value security and dislike uncertainty. If your objective is to vibrate at higher and higher levels to attract higher and higher results in your life, you'll find it very difficult (if not impossible) to do so if everything around you is reinforcing the contrary. Remember the importance of triggers and grabbers.

If you look at the people you're hanging out with and they're not going in the same direction you are, they're not going to be doing the things you're doing or thinking as you're thinking. They'll hold you back, plain and simple. If you want to grow, your peer group must change.

Are you spending time with people who support you and are helping you move towards your intentions? Or are you investing your time with people who are holding you back? If your goal is to improve your relationships, are you in the kinds of places where you can build these types of relationships? Are you investing time with the people you want to connect with at a deeper level, the kind of people with whom you would want to be in a relationship?

This is a lesson I had to learn more than a decade ago. I had outgrown my friends, the crowd I spent my time with. I tried to 'ration lies' in my mind all the reasons I didn't have to change or why I should continue to hang out with them. After all, they were my friends. But in my heart I knew I was at a crossroads. While they were good people, their energy was toxic, and being with them was holding me back.

Sometimes the hardest thing to do is to let go of habits and people as you continue along your path. Until I left my old lifestyle, friends, activities, nothing new and better would come into my life. Like updating your home environment (which we'll talk about in the physical pillar), I learned that you must update your friends. If you desire new and bigger things to come, you must create a space for them to appear. I decided that I'd no longer spend high-quality time with people I didn't want to be around. It wasn't easy, but I have never regretted it. I started spending more time with people who aspired to qualities, traits, and accomplishments similar to mine in any of the five pillars. It wasn't long before I had new friends, friends who supported who I was becoming and where I was headed. I invested my social time more wisely, and it paid off. While many of my then current social group didn't understand my decision, it's without a doubt one of the most empowering things I've ever done.

Just accept the fact that when you choose to pursue your greatness, you'll represent the courage in many cases that your peer group doesn't possess. You can still love your old friends, but I recommend you don't spend high-quality time with people who aren't of the same mind-set. Surround yourself with big thinkers – people whose character and accomplishments you aspire to create in your own life, people who share a harmonic vibration with your thoughts and purpose.

Your relationships and partnerships are more important than your heredity. The people you spend your time with will be more significant than your upbringing. You may have heard before that you'll be the same person years from today as you are today with a few exceptions: the books you read, the decisions you make, and the people you continuously spend your time with.

Don't share your dreams with others unless you can guarantee that they'll support you. You know, certain people are constantly bitching, moaning, and complaining about everything. You know these people. You ask them how they're feeling, and once they start answering, you wish you hadn't asked? I call these people energy vampires. You know, they suck the lifeblood – energy – right out of you. They flit around with their fangs hanging out, complaining about what's not working, what's not perfect, what's not there. You go into a meeting with them, and you come out feeling drained, zapped. You might have one in your family. Life is precious and goes really quickly, so I have three words that are like garlic to an energy vampire. Get over it.

Look to your closest friends to see what you're attracting. Are they physically fit? Are they abundant? Do they have plenty of money or are they constantly harping about how broke they are? Are they happily married? Or if single, are they living a happy and fulfilling single life? You're five times more likely to be physically fit if the people in your life are. Think about it – the people you surround yourself with either help you up your game or pull your game down. They either help you want to succeed or not. Who are you hanging out with?

Masterful Support

Whether it's with two people or ten, the power of partnerships creates energy and innovation that cannot be accomplished on our own. The Bible tells us that where two or three are gathered in agreement, nothing is impossible. Many indigenous societies have a ritual where several people gather together and after opening ceremonies, speak with each other while passing around a pipe or talking stick. They believe that if they continue listening respectfully to each person, the gods will literally come down among them and give them ideas no single individual has had previously. For this reason, these rituals are held as sacred.

We're living in an era of collaboration, and a mastermind group is a wonderful way to create a more formal support network to accelerate your goals. This is where you join other like-minded people and meet on a regular basis, once a week or once a month, for the purpose of helping each other reach your dreams and the next level of achievement. You may begin by having one member express his or her intention to the group. The group then helps by brainstorming ideas on how it can be done as well as ideas on what that particular member will need to do to reach their desired outcome. The member can then ask the group for their help in acquiring and achieving these things. Your group can support you with ideas and/or contacts who can help you, or by holding you accountable to meet your deadlines.

The more you help others in your group, the more you will receive in return. The more you give, the more you get. A mastermind group also serves as a support mechanism to keep you on course when your results don't seem to come fast enough. I've been in a mastermind group where I'm the only member from my industry. We viewed our diversity as strength. It's exciting, and I strongly encourage you to get into a relationship of this type.

The bottom line is this: you cannot do it alone and these kinds of relationships and partnerships will dramatically improve your results. When you think about people in your industry you admire, people you'd like to spend time with, who you could mastermind with, who could be a mentor to you, do you get excited?

Keep in mind: you're constantly attracting everything you need to accomplish your intention. As long as you keep that offer wave flowing, your future-pull will echo in return. When you expect the right people to enter your life, they will.

Find a Mentor

All great achievers in life have had a coach or a mentor. Sometimes you can build a mastermind with one other person. The people I want to invest time with or have mentor me are the people who are ten or twenty steps ahead of me – where I have to hustle to feel like I can stay up with them. Regardless of what you may think, there are people who would love nothing more than to help you stay focused, on track, and use the skills you're learning. Remember, the truly successful in life are great givers. Expect them to come into your life. Just make sure you give and pass on your coaching energy to someone else wanting to move forward as well. To quote Gandhi once again, 'You must be the change you wish to see in the world.'

It starts with you and me. We are the ones the world has been waiting for.

Mental

What are you? Where are you? Who are you? However you choose to answer these questions, it's your marvellous mind that provides the response. The powers of your mind are virtually beyond measure. Yet, so much of the way we live conspires to keep our minds small.

There was a time years ago when your body was a fraction of its current size, yet your mind power was enormous. Remember? Back then, your unfettered curiosity propelled you constantly forward. You hadn't heard the labels others would apply to keep you small – 'not so bright', 'lazy', 'not talented', 'no staying power' – and you hadn't yet learned to apply those constricting labels yourself. You wanted to learn everything, know everything, be everything. It's taken a lifetime to douse the fire of limitless possibility.

But what if that sense of limitation is nothing more than an illusion? What if it's all just a bad joke that you bought into and believed to be real? What if you could learn to look beyond the illusion to the truths of your life. You are intelligent. You are capable. You are creative.

You can look beyond the smoke and mirrors.

You are absolutely unlimited.

What you may not yet be is disciplined or confident. That changes right now, right here. You must prepare your mind for the task of living your precious life to the fullest, because when your vision on the inside becomes more compelling and powerful than what you observe on the outside, the universe is at your command.

14

Your Marvellous Mind

A man is but the product of his thoughts. What he thinks, he becomes.

– GANDHI

Emotional Capacity

Our greatest cognitive challenge is one of direction. Do you know where you place your attention? Is the Radio Times your day planner? Do you flop down in front of the box 'just to relax', and then find it's three hours later and time for bed? Do you walk right past the local bookshop? When you read about other people's accomplishments, do you feel not just envy, but that familiar, nagging sense that, once again, you have let your own vague plans slip through your fingers? Amid the jumble of routines and responsibilities, have you made any concrete plans for achieving your goals?

Most people I meet have attention deficit disorder when it comes to what they truly choose for their lives, letting their minds wander into limiting and disempowering territory. They pine for a loving relationship but obsess about their last heartache. They want financial freedom but bitch every time they pay a bill. They want physical fitness but badger themselves for leaving the gym five years ago, so why even bother? Or like an excited puppy, their minds run from one fancy to another, leading to a whole lot of tail chasing. So, while attention deficit steals dreams, many have attention surplus when it comes to creating their misery.

They spend their intellectual and emotional lives barely meeting the minimum payments of their obligations to themselves. Bogged down in limiting and negative thoughts while the things they really wish to attend to are put off week after week, they give over their lives to routines and responsibilities while their hopes and dreams slip through their fingers. Remember, the only competition you'll ever have is the competition between your disciplined and your undisciplined mind. I want you to have attention surplus for what strengthens rather than weakens you.

There are two levels to the mental pillar of Harmonic Wealth, the intellectual and the emotional capacities. Your intellectual capacity is the ability to absorb and synthesise new information, generate creative ideas, and plan strategies to achieve them – to truly think, instead of deliberating and endlessly analyzing, which often masquerades as thinking. True thinking is instantaneous – all else is conditioned rumination. Your emotional capacity is your ability to live a life given colour, dimension, and intensity by your feelings, not becoming driven by them, to access, direct, and control these powerful vibrations, not be directed and controlled by them. Let's talk first about how to strengthen your intellect. Then we'll discuss how to discipline your belief system and master your emotions.

Your Unique Genius

Are you someone who has no power over your destiny, no control, or are you someone who sees all of life as a chance to embrace change, an opportunity to learn and grow? If you fall into the first category but want to be in the second that's not a problem. If you commit yourself to strengthening your intellectual pillar you can quickly grow and find the best way to use the opportunities that life presents you with. In the meantime, let me demonstrate how you're smarter than you know.

I briefly discussed the work of Howard Gardner, Harvard professor of psychology who concluded that our educational system fails us because it measures only certain types of intelligence. According to Gardner, there are actually eight different areas of intelligence, or competence, and he contends that almost everyone is a genius in one or two of the eight areas I describe below.

Linguistic Intelligence The ability to understand and master language and verbal expression. Are you good at speaking, expressing your feelings, thoughts, and ideas? Do colleagues look to you to say a few words at meetings? Do friends ask for your help with others because you always know just the right thing to say? Martin Luther King and John F. Kennedy are great examples of linguistic intelligence. Consider King's stirring I Have a Dream speech, how the power of his rhetoric invited a nation to share in his vision of unity. Or how JFK's famous inaugural address – 'Ask not what your country can do for you – ask what you can do for your country' – gave Americans a portrait of themselves as idealists and activists. It was their linguistic intelligence that caused them all to stop, listen, and learn.

Musical Intelligence The capacity to create and perceive musical patterns, musical expression, and composition. Do you walk out of a musical humming every new tune? Is playing a musical instrument easy for you? Mozart, who was composing before most children learn to colour, is an obvious example. Do you have the ability to hear all the complexities and intricacies of each instrument, building a magical tapestry, or can you empty a karaoke bar faster than a skunk?

Logical–Mathematical Intelligence The strong computational and reasoning skill most often displayed by mathematicians, chess players, and the billionaires who gave us Microsoft. This one is measured in our school system, with its emphasis on logic and deductive reasoning. Give me the word problem, and I'll give you the answer? But understand that it's only one of the eight available to us, and many are disadvantaged in this area. If you're an engineer or scientist, you most probably have high logical–mathematical intelligence.

Spatial Intelligence The ability to visualise complex problems and have an appreciation of large spaces and layout. Despite almost flunking out of school (seriously), Einstein fell into this category. He didn't speak until he was four years old; he didn't read until he was seven. His teachers described him as mentally slow, unsociable, and adrift forever in his foolish dreams. Einstein was expelled and refused admittance to Zurich Polytechnic School. Yet he had the ability to imagine himself on a beam of light, moving forward, while correlating that to time and ultimately coming up with his famous equation $E = mc^2$. That's spatial intelligence at its finest.

Bodily-Kinaesthetic Intelligence Excellent coordination in detailed physical tasks or in energetic large muscle tasks. A professional athlete would fall into this category, as would a dancer and a horse trainer. How many people have you known who are athletically inclined but don't do well in school?

Intrapersonal Intelligence Deep understanding of the self, of your own inner experience, your emotions, your motives, and your thoughts. People with this intelligence are really in touch with who they are. They're often highly skilled at communicating inner thoughts and feelings, but not always, because that crosses over into linguistic intelligence. Many of the philosophers and mystics, like Walt Whitman, Ralph Waldo Emerson, Buddha, or Jesus, shine in this category.

Interpersonal Intelligence The ability to easily understand others – their intentions and concerns. Do you get the difference? Intrapersonal is understanding the self; interpersonal is understanding others. People with this intelligence are highly empathic and deeply concerned about how any action is going to affect others. Many women have told me they only wish their husbands had some of this one!

Naturalistic Intelligence A person who has a deep appreciation and understanding of the environment and the ecology of all actions. In other words, someone who understands that every action has an equal and opposite reaction in the natural world.

The Hawaiians have a saying – *A ohe pau ko ike i kou halau* – meaning, 'Think not that all wisdom is in your school.' It's sad that our traditional school system causes many self-image problems because we're all expected as little kids to fit into the same mould, tested on the same limited criteria. While I'm a believer in continuing education, I also agree with Gardner that it totally misses the mark in a variety of areas. According to his research, we should be tested and taught in specialised ways that capitalise on our strengths.

Countless people in our world are incredibly high achievers who didn't do well in our traditional school system. I had a good friend who was in special education early in her life, which wreaked havoc on her self-esteem and self-image. Yet she was absolutely brilliant in bodily-kinaesthetic intelligence and grew up to become a master horse rider and trainer. Unfortunately, she had a lot of childhood pain to overcome that lasted well into her adult life. There was just no traditional measurement for her genius as a child.

Does Gardner's theory make you see others differently? I'd be willing to bet that if I were to ask you about the most significant people in your life, you could tell me fairly quickly where they fall within these categories, what their strengths are. Do you know where *you* fall? Maybe you are rubbish at maths, but in what other areas are you absolutely brilliant? Use this list to think through your natural strengths, your strongest areas, your innate capabilities, your areas of genius. ⓘ

What Makes Your Brain Light Up?

Now ask yourself: how can you use these intelligences to make your life richer? How can you improve upon them and make them stronger? If you want Harmonic Wealth, then you must use the areas in which you have the most skill, the most capability and natural strengths.

How can you utilise your genius at more optimum levels within your current profession? Do you need to change your work based on this new realisation of your skills? How can you improve upon your innate genius?

We might not be able to remember our PIN or what day we're supposed to visit the dentist, but we remember the stuff we love doing, don't we? My mother used to say, 'If only you could remember to do your homework as well as you remember passages from your favourite books, you'd get straight As.' We remember things with more emotional intensity when we're attached to the material – when we care.

Think about something that gets you excited. The reason why 'Follow your bliss' is good advice is because doing what you love makes your brain light up. It's this inspiration that creates the feeling vibration in your body that guarantees harmony and true wealth in all pillars of life. You and I both know that you learn most easily with your brain *and* heart engaged. If you're not sure where your genius lies, think about doing something you love, something that makes time fall away. Chances are, that path will lead you to where you need to focus your intellectual firepower. By the way, this may be nowhere near where the people around you think you ought to go.

'I'm going to become an estate agent and make a killing,' my friend Dave told me when he was having financial troubles.

'But you hate sales,' I said. 'You're an artist who sleeps in until noon; how would you ever handle the hours or the endless paperwork?' He laughed sheepishly, knowing I was right. But you've got to focus your magnificent mind on things that excite you – even if it's underwater basket weaving.

Here's a case in point. A friend of mine, Carol Allen, couldn't have chosen a more bizarre path or a more unlikely road to riches. After graduating from UC Berkeley, one of the most prestigious state universities in the USA, she made a failed attempt at becoming an actress and then picked, in her own words, 'one of the stupidest business models' she could find. She'd been taking astrology classes from an old woman in a house in Hollywood, and decided that she wanted to become a full-time astrologer. Okay. Not so bizarre for LA, but this wasn't even mainstream astrology but rather a form from India called Vedic astrology, based on ancient Sanskrit scripture. She wasn't Indian, didn't speak the language, and was entering a very difficult intellectual system mostly populated by men. Carol's school friends, who were now earning six figures, would say, 'What are you doing? You have a degree,' and she would answer, 'I don't know, but I get so happy anytime I'm in class, read an astrology book, or give a reading.' She was following her love.

The bad business model soon became apparent, however, because her clients only needed her services once a year, if that, and she averaged only

£60 for a two-hour session. It was draining work, too, with a limit to how much she could handle in a day since most people came to her in a crisis. Plus she continually had to network for new clients. But she paid attention to how good she felt, and her excitement remained constant despite the hard work and meagre yearly income.

After years of helping thousands of clients, Carol realised that 95 per cent of the people who came to her for readings were coming with one goal in common: to make sense of their romantic relationships. So Carol spent a few more years studying to become a relationship coach and writer, taking classes that again got her excited.

With time, the combination of her talents in astrology, relationship coaching, and writing skills led to her becoming a sought-after relationship coach, popular radio host, and speaker, with a weekly column read by millions of people and many television appearances. Recently she was paid handsomely to write a book called *Love Is in the Stars*. 'I never could have known how all the things I love doing could come together to form a career,' she said. 'I was just going towards what made my brain light up.'

You have to literally love what you choose to pursue. Think about when you first fell in love. Did you have to make yourself think about the object of your affection? No. You couldn't wait to e-mail, text message, phone, and most of all spend time with the object of your affection. You were inspired.

If you find yourself having to get motivated to do something, it's not something you truly love. Motivation is something that comes from externals, or at best must be generated. Inspiration, on the other hand, is something that comes from inside and requires no effort whatsoever. The prefix *in* from the Latin translates as 'to be'. Therefore when you are inspired you are 'being spirit', tuning into the ultimate creative source.

What inspires you? What makes your brain light up? Find it and feed it.

Feeding Your Marvellous Mind

As you begin to seek out ways to strengthen your natural intelligences, you'll need to find the specialised resources that will nourish the amazing machine you've got between your ears. But first, let's prepare you for receiving these new gifts by changing the care and feeding of your marvellous mind.

Your mind is the greatest gift you've been given by the creative source. It's what differentiates you from every other entity on this planet. What are you feeding it?

Statistics tell us that 85 per cent of North American households last year didn't buy one non-fiction book, not one. If that amazes you, here's something even more amazing: Ninety per cent of those who did buy a book didn't read it! Good intentions, maybe. Poor follow-through, definitely. Yet, during this same time period, North Americans spent £40 billion on movies, with televisions on in the average household six hours and forty-four minutes a day.

'But James,' you might tell me, 'that's not true in my house.' I ask you to be honest and add up the hours the TV is just on in the background or how often you use the remote 'just to see what's on'. Compare that to how much reading you do. I've never met one massively high achiever who has a large amount of time to sit in front of the plug-in drug. Are there good things on TV? Absolutely. I occasionally watch TV. But I'm selective about what I watch; I don't just switch it on. I'm careful about *when* I watch it. Not during dinner, when our opportunity to connect with loved ones and share ourselves is at its peak. Not as an avoidance tool, when feeling my feelings would be the healthier option. Most definitely *not* before bed, when the suffering and violence I see on the nightly news or in a one-hour drama or film will play in my unconscious all night.

I'm dismayed by how much soul-sucking programming is available morning, noon, and night. Even the most cleverly designed, so-called reality TV show is a distraction, even obstacle in the way of creating our own realities with our marvellous minds. Maybe we love seeing the messes on reality TV because our lives are boring or maybe it makes us feel better about our own messes. *Maybe my life's not so bad after all,* we think. If you're sitting on your bum watching a show about winning a million pounds, I guarantee you're never going to create it. When your life becomes enthusiastically inspired, the greatest, most exciting, and entertaining reality might just be the reality of your own life.

As I said in the financial pillar, show me your results, and in fifteen minutes or less, I can tell you how you're using your mind. No matter what you tell me, whatever you're putting into your mind on a consistent basis is driving your thoughts, feelings, emotions, and actions. If you're putting garbage or limiting energy into your mind, you're going to produce limiting energy and outcomes. It's showing up in your results, in your relationships, in your finances, in your health, in your fitness – everywhere.

If you look at socioeconomic studies for low-income households, you'll find maybe a copy of the *Sun* in their homes. Go to a medium-income household and you'll find a few books by the toilet, maybe a few more elsewhere, with a glossy gossip magazine in the sitting room. But what do you think you'll find in a high-income household? A library. As I've said, that's the most prized room in my home.

The question is: does the socioeconomic status bring the library, or does the library bring the status? I'll guarantee you it's the latter. *Poor* isn't just about money or education, but about a state of mind. All leaders are great readers. If you don't read, you might as well be illiterate. Mark Twain said, 'The man who does not read good books has no advantage over the man who cannot read them,' wise words from one of the wisest and most adored – not to mention richest – men of his day. If you can't afford the latest book in your field, there's always the nearest library.

You'll never grow by watching the news and reading tabloids. Is there a time and place for these things? Maybe. You may need to be informed on how developments affect your business and your world, but you don't have to be inundated. There's a big difference between scanning for relevant headlines and feasting on lurid stories of murder, mayhem, and gossip. Remember, there are only two things you can do with your brainpower as it relates to time: spend it or invest it. Time spent (or wasted) is gone forever. Invested time (in the form of learning) creates a lifetime annuity. Remember your worth-per-hour figure, and make sure you're constantly investing the great asset of time.

A South American Indian shaman I used to study with could point to the sky and create rain, literally – a practice that came in handy more than once or twice, as you might imagine. But this same man, whom I admired so much, couldn't turn on a computer or use a cash point if his life depended on it. He couldn't hail a cab or use a mobile either. Are these things important? You bet. They're vital skills in this era of integration.

15

What You Believe, You'll Achieve

According to your faith, be it unto you.

– MATTHEW 9:29

Information: Potential Power

You and I live in a changing world with changing needs. For this reason, we must do things in a new and different way. A recent IBM study predicts that by 2010, digital data worldwide will double every eleven hours! What that means is that if you received a PhD five or six years ago, you used to know a lot. Unless you aggressively pursue new knowledge, what you know quickly becomes obsolete.

You're either moving forward in life, or you're moving backwards – either growing or dying. There's no standing still.

Contrary to what we've heard so often, information is not power. It's potential power. Information – the big commodity/resource of our time – put into right action in alignment with universal principles is true power and wealth. So, if information is potential wealth, and information put into right and big action *is* wealth, the experts who have knowledge and use it wisely are the ones getting rich now. How can you become one of those people?

Think independently, for starters. Listen to and act on your original thoughts versus the endless reruns of social programming. While it's important to get continuous information and feedback from the outside world, information is nothing more than organised data. When you take the information and act upon it wisely – that's where your life begins to change. It's not what you know that changes your life – it's the action you take with what you know that separates the truly wealthy from the constant dreamers.

Beyond books that strengthen your native intelligence, how else are you feeding your mind? Do you go to lectures, seminars, or workshops? What's playing in your car: educational CDs or corrosive talk radio or something just to fill the space? Everything has its time and place, and again, it all has a direct effect on your personal and spiritual expansion. There is no real good or bad per se – everything you do and every decision you make is either adding value or taking value away. There is no neutrality. The decisions I've made in this part of my life have totally transformed my world because I've made a commitment to focus on and consistently surround myself with high-calibre energy and information.

Turn It Off to Turn On

I'm going to hammer home the issue of TV one last time because it's so very important. Four hours a day of television equals twenty-eight hours a week; assuming that you sleep eight hours a night, that's one fourth of your waking life. That habit adds up to 1,456 hours a year. That means you spend sixty days, or two entire months, out of every year plopped down in front of the visual drug. Reflecting back on our earlier financial model, at £400 per day that's £24,000 per year that you invest in this addiction! Come on, my friend. Anything that takes twelve years out of your life – remember, that's the lifetime average – without giving a hell of a lot back is something you need to drop. We're now in denial about our abuse and dependence upon this habit-forming substance.

I've already talked about how TV wastes your time and therefore your money. But that's not the only reason I want you *at least* to minimise the influence of this black hole on your life. Has anyone ever told you, 'Stop watching so much TV – it's rotting your brain'? Turns out they knew what they were talking about. Watching TV actually alters your brain waves, your most precious asset. The brain primarily generates four different levels of energy in the form of vibrations or frequencies at any given time: beta, alpha, theta, or delta. Beta frequencies, which you're experiencing right now, are normal waking consciousness. When you talk to another person – absorbing information, thinking of imaginative responses, asking engaging questions – you're using beta frequencies. As you begin to relax the mind, you produce more alpha waves, which are good for calming you down and helping you be open to changing limiting patterns, but the alpha state is also a vibration in which you're more easily influenced.

Researchers have shown that watching TV causes your brain waves to slow down from beta to alpha. For example, psychophysiologist Thomas Mulholland decided to measure the attention spans of children. He programmed an EEG machine, which measures brain waves, to turn off a TV whenever kids produced more alpha than beta waves. Then he challenged the kids to concentrate as hard as they could in order to keep the TV on. Much to his amazement, most of the kids couldn't keep that TV set going for more than half a minute. That's how little time it takes to lull our brains into that hypnotic (some would say almost comatose) state.

There's a physiological reason we crave this state. When our brains produce more alpha waves, we also produce more endorphins, those feel-good brain drugs that are the body's natural opiates. We become like rats trained to press a lever to get more opium; we watch more and more TV because it pulls us into a trance-like high. Plug-in drug is right.

So maybe you're thinking, *But I need to relax and de-stress after my hard day.* TV does a lot more than just relax you. There's evidence that it inhibits your ability to learn while you're watching, so if you're telling yourself that your TV habit's okay because you only watch educational shows, you may be just kidding yourself. Jacob Jacoby, a psychologist at Purdue University, has done a great deal of research on how well people comprehend what they see on TV. In one of his studies, involving 2,700 people, he discovered that 90 per cent misunderstood or failed to remember salient details even from simple commercials or a TV show they watched regularly. When quizzed about shows they'd seen just a few minutes earlier, viewers missed anywhere from 23 to 36 per cent of the questions.

No more excuses. Unplug now. Hopefully you won't get the cold sweats.

Your Total Belief System

What you believe you'll achieve is the driving factor of your results: your lack of abundance in terms of money, peace of mind, relationships, physical health, or anything else. This is the cumulative effect of your current total belief system, which is exactly what it sounds like – the totality of everything you believe, your habits, experiences, values, and assumptions. Most people try to change their results by dealing with the effects, throwing new solutions at the results, thinking they're going to change things. But if you want to change the results, you must deal with the cause. You have to change what you believe.

Have you ever sat in a cinema watching the images in front of you on the silver screen and found yourself lost in the realness of it all? Then you looked behind you at the projection room and saw the stream of light exiting the box, creating those lifelike images. It's a strange experience, isn't it? Maybe it hit you that you and all these people sitting around you were staring at the projected images, believing they're real. The screen is a lot like your life; think of the images on the screen as the outcomes of your life. If you wanted to change the image (your results), you'd have to change the film, wouldn't you?

Ever watched people yell at the actors up on the screen, 'No, don't go in there!' or throw popcorn at them? Pretty ridiculous, isn't it? They act as though what they're doing or saying has an effect on what they're seeing, but everybody knows that the screen is only showing what it's being given. You could take a hammer to the projector, too, but that wouldn't change the film.

Everything around you is being projected upon the screen of your life, and your mind is the projector. Change the film (your total belief system) and you change your results.

Stages of Belief

One of the reasons it's so hard to change what we believe is that we don't understand how those beliefs got into our heads in the first place. Why do we believe what we believe?

Well, for one thing, our unconscious programming and our overidentification with the culture around us keeps many of us from creating an independent sense of self, our unique identity. It's a rare individual who begins operating authentically by living a more closely examined life. If we want to change our total belief systems, we need to bring our unconscious beliefs into our consciousness, examine whether they're true or useful, heal them, change them, and release them if they're not.

My friend Elizabeth grew up as a strict Catholic in a small suburban town. She took First Communion, went to confession regularly, sang in the church choir, and danced at church socials. Listening to the music from *Godspell* was her idea of a walk on the wild side. One day in catechism, the priest told the class, 'No one but Christians will see the Kingdom of Heaven.' Elizabeth shifted uneasily in the pew – for the first time she began to doubt her religion. They'd just finished learning about world religions in school – she and her friend Robin had papiermâchéd a golden Buddha – and she found herself thinking, *But what about all those nice people in China and Japan and India?* As a teen, she dropped out of catechism, which displeased her very religious mother greatly. In her twenties, she stopped going to church, angered by the pope's position on women's issues. She shed the belief that premarital sex was a sin and began to enjoy her sexuality. In her thirties, she railed against all organised religions as bastions of groupthink, and enjoyed poking fun at Christian fundamentalist rigidity. But by her forties, she came back to embrace her own idea of God, doing volunteer work side by side with many Catholic friends whose devotion to a local charity moved her deeply. Only by questioning her religious upbringing was she able to create a total belief system, embrace what worked for her, and discard the rest.

As you know, when I grew up, left my small town, and moved away from home, I went through my own anguished search for God and truth. I questioned everything. What I'd been taught seemed so full of holes and didn't answer the probing questions I'd asked for as long as I could remember. I felt as if contact lenses had been fastened over my retinas, causing me to see things through a now grey filter that was totally irrelevant and incomplete. Nothing looked as it had, and I had no idea what to feel about anything. I chucked it all, and even felt at one point as if there was no God. This was what they call in esoteric traditions the Dark Night of The Soul, and it feels more lonely and confusing than words can express. As you may imagine, when I left my town and my church, my father and I fell out of sympathy with one another for a while, leaving us both deeply wounded. But guess what? I wasn't the only one going through a metamorphosis. As I grew, so too did my dad. The shift in his beliefs wasn't as dramatic as mine, and still isn't. But through a more holistic and less rigid space, we forged the deep friendship we now share, one rich in lengthy, open-hearted conversations about the very issues that often used to divide us.

It was Socrates who stated, 'The unexamined life is not worth living.' I went on my own quest and found my own answers, some of them different from what I'd been taught and some of them similar, but somehow strangely altered. Unless you have the courage to ask the questions, you'll never have your own answers but instead the often unsolicited 'gifts' from outside sources.

Knocked Unconscious

Your programming comes from deep-seated values, beliefs, and assumptions that are fixed or locked into your unconscious. Again, most of these are gifts (some of which you probably wish you could give back to Santa) you received at a very early age from your parents, grandparents, teachers, religious sources, and anyone else in authority, typically during the ages of three to eight. Sociologist Morris Massey conducted exhaustive research on personal values and found that most of our core level values lock in by the age of thirteen and rarely if ever change. What that means is that most of the people you interact with on a daily basis are thirteen-year-olds walking around in thirty-, forty-, or even eighty-year-old bodies. According to Massey, your values only change if you experience what he called a *significant emotional event*, or SEE – something that rocks your world and causes you to step back and reconstruct your viewpoint.

By and large, you are the by-product of other people's habitual ways of thinking, and those thoughts are the cause of many of your results. Amazing, isn't it? You may not even like those people! Most often your conscious mind isn't aware of everything your unconscious mind is putting out, yet your programming, your unconscious film, or total belief system, continues to operate as though everything you think or believe is literally true. It's not.

Thankfully, because you've chosen your own beliefs to start with – even if you did so unconsciously – you can now learn how to choose new ones consciously for new results.

Here's the secret about your mind. While the thoughts and beliefs you hold in your conscious mind are vital to attracting what you want, the programming and beliefs you hold in your unconscious mind hold even more weight. As I said at the start of the book, they're stronger than your willpower. Willpower, no matter how strong, is on and off, while your unconscious programming runs 24/7. In order to have harmony in this pillar, you need to understand the elements you're dealing with.

You operate from four parts of your being: Higher Conscious Mind (HCM), Conscious Mind (CM), Unconscious Mind (UCM), and Body. In corresponding order these are the spiritual, intellectual, emotional, and physical parts of you.

When I refer to the *Higher Conscious Mind*, I'm talking about the all-knowing intelligence of your soul. It has been called by many names throughout many great traditions: Holy Guardian Angel, the Higher

Self, or even God. The Higher Conscious Mind is the part of you tapped into cosmic or divine intelligence, the part of you that is never separate, no matter how you may feel to the contrary, from your source.

Your *Conscious Mind* is the part of you that's reading this right now. It's the rational, reasoning part of you, where your unique personality resides. This is the part of you that talks and thinks, reasons and rations. It's also the part of you who watches TV when you should be reading. (I just had to sneak that in.)

Your *Unconscious Mind* is what really drives all of your actions, and it's where your habits lie. When you're learning something conscious, like driving, it's difficult initially, but at some point the actions drop into your unconscious mind and become habit. The unconscious mind just takes care of it from then on, with very little effort.

As you can appreciate from the work of developmental psychologists, your unconscious is where the totality of your programming, your total belief system, resides. Your unconscious mind created the story of you for many years before you were developmentally capable of bringing conscious thought to the process. It houses a major portion of the film that runs through the projector and onto the screen of your world. Your unconscious mind is the emotional, receptive part of your mind. Nothing is ever forgotten here: your unconscious stores it all beneath your conscious awareness, although you can learn to access it through meditation, visualisation, relaxation techniques, rapt observation of reoccurring results, and the like.

High achievers learn to use their unconscious minds properly by planting the empowering seeds of their vision, intentions, and pictures into their unconscious, which is what we're doing in this book. Whatever seeds you plant in the garden of your unconscious mind will spring forth, bringing actions that attract the same kind of result. There's no way you can get diamonds by planting potatoes, right?

The *Body*, of course, is where all action and subsequent results reside. We'll get into that in the next pillar. Interestingly enough, the unconscious mind runs the body.

Your goal is to reprogramme your total belief system so that your conscious and unconscious work in tandem to move you forward. There are many ways to do this. Find a good teacher (or therapist) who is trained in this type of work, constantly observe your results in the physical world (they're mirroring back to you your unconscious beliefs by the minute), and continuously train your mental focus to lock onto new beliefs and realities.

What Do You Really Believe?

Beliefs can do one of two things: they either move you forward or they hold you back. The problem is that we're often held back by beliefs we don't even know we have! In conducting seminars around the world, I ask people what their beliefs are and very few people can tell me.

As I mentioned, we either choose or create our beliefs, consciously or unconsciously, from an early age. As time goes on, a shift occurs, and our beliefs begin to create us. Does that make sense?

Beliefs convey the way you've decided the world works. They are convictions, or an acceptance, that certain things are true or real. They can be anything you want, and remain true for you as long as you no longer question them. When you believe something, this belief largely determines what you will and will not do and how you can achieve your values in life. The craziest thing is that once you've accepted a belief about something, you do everything in your power to make sure it remains true, *even if it doesn't serve you.*

William James, the father of modern psychology, said, 'Believe that life is worth living, and your belief will help create the fact.' He claimed that one of the greatest discoveries of our time is that a man can change the quality of his life by changing the quality of his thoughts.

Beliefs can change, though, can't they? I knew a Jewish man who was sure he 'had' to marry a nice Jewish girl, but then he met and fell in love with a somewhat naughty Catholic girl and that was it. He fell hard, married her, and they've been happy for twenty years. He surprised himself by how easily he'd put something aside on his must-have list and changed his beliefs.

Group beliefs change too. If you reflect on history, you'll find that the most profound shifts in humanity haven't been the result of government actions or even wars, but from a fundamental shift in our collective thoughts. (You could call the total belief system of the planet our global beliefs.) Remember how we talked earlier about how anything new tends to create fear? Let's not forget that the masses once believed the Earth was flat, sea monsters lived in the sea, fairies flew, and dragons roared.

Attitudes shift as well, but not always for the better. In today's world, for example, most young men are taught to avoid emotion and intuition and are being reared on violent video games and movies which dull their senses and increase aggression. The popularity of horror films, for instance, is at an all-time high. We 'adults' have become complicit in saying to our children that it's okay to watch people being shot and mutilated, their limbs maimed and severed in the name of entertainment.

By the same token, many young women are being conditioned to believe that their value and self-worth are directly correlated to their desirability. Movie and video game images are rife with buxom beauties that make even Barbie look plain. Is it any wonder, then, that our current economic model has us believing that it's okay for less than 5 per cent of the world's population to be consuming over 25 per cent of its resources, while causing more than 30 per cent of its pollution?

Yes – more validation that we're in a collective trance.

Please understand that I say all this without judgment, as strange as that may sound. I consider none of this bad, for it's all part of the process of changing our individual and global beliefs. The current issue of global warming, for instance, is now making it very apparent to larger and larger groups of people that sustainability and world harmony must be considered. We could argue that it should have been considered all along, and maybe that's true. However, recognition is the first law of learning and transformation. You'll never change your beliefs and behaviour until you recognise the need to do so. Human beings, individually and collectively, rarely change unless and until they experience enough pain or discontent with the current model and its results.

All transformations begin with a transformation of consciousness. Critical point.

Even when recognising that a transformation must occur, changing your beliefs can be scary stuff. Resistance is a reflex. The paradox is that we have a need for certainty in our lives but also a need for variety. Ongoing certainty creates boredom; variety and change are essential to growth. I can promise you, though, at least from my experience, that no matter how much you grow, there's still a tendency to stay in your comfort zone. I know; I've learned this the hard way. (Sometimes I wonder, *Isn't there an easier way?*)

Living Your True Beliefs Brings Peace of Mind

In the spring of 2000, I was on a boat off the Baja Peninsula. A cold wave crashed down over the bow of the small boat, dousing me with crystal clear water from the Sea of Cortez. I stood with my back to the Mexican mainland, bracing myself for the next hit. Every inch of my body dripped seawater, the salt wreaking havoc on my bloodshot eyes.

The piercing wind penetrated my insides. Tony, my mate, sat with his head between his knees, his wide-brimmed fishing hat producing its own miniature Niagara Falls. A key element in defining our signature sports fishermen attire, our hats were meant to provide a bit of good juju, to call in the spirit of heroic fishermen from local legend, or at least that's what the guy on the dock had said when we forked over our four hundred pesos.

Good juju, my arse. We'd been sloshing around in the boat all day, water up around our ankles for hours. Not one bloody nibble. So, this was deep-sea sports fishing. It had sounded so much more macho and exciting, even romantic, when I signed on. Every fibre of my being wanted to call it a day. My stomach, queasy from the incessant rocking, begged me to return to solid ground. But I hung in there. According to

Ernest Hemingway, real red-blooded men loved deep-sea fishing. I'd convinced myself that I craved the challenge of man versus nature, of taming a wild beast and making it submit to my will. After all, testosterone *was* in my nature, wasn't it?

Just then, my reel spun. I heard for the first time what would become an unforgettable clicking whirr, the noise signalling that my bait was rapidly travelling to the depths of the ocean.

'Marlin! Marlin!' yelled Domingo, our guide. 'James! Marlin!'

'Man, that's a hell of a powerful fish,' I yelled over to Tony. Marlins are at the top of the food chain in these waters. Tony jumped to his feet, looked at my reel and then over the edge.

'Shit, James! She's over a thousand pounds; only the females get that large,' he said. I slipped and nearly fell over my severely bent rod, fumbling to get my waist belt on.

'Bring her in, James! Bring her in!' Tony shouted. I removed the rod from its secure holding place and the war began.

The next hour and a half was the longest continual pain and panic of my life. No elaborate fighting chair to strap into in here. I stood spread-eagled with a foot in each corner of the small boat ('Damn – we had to go economy class!'), the fish and I married, bound together through struggle. I've had less stress in an entire year. I spent the entire time on my feet, my arms pulling with full strength every moment. A fire raged in my shoulders and lower back; the muscles in my legs were killing me. Screw Hemingway! I hated fishing! I hated Tony for talking me into this. I hated the Sea of Cortez. Most of all, I hated that damn fish!

Domingo and Tony continued shouting words of encouragement. 'You got her, James. Hang tough, man.'

Time after time, I reeled in my opponent with three hard-earned spins, thinking I was making headway. Yet every time she took it all back and then some. Five spins for her in only half the time it took me to earn three. The powerful beast shot straight up in the air, spinning and kicking, her brilliant blue, silver, and green tail glistened in the sun before diving back into the ocean's depths. This was never going to end. But I couldn't give up now. My shoulders, lower back, and thighs felt like they had ice picks shoved into them. But I wasn't a quitter. *Be a warrior, James. Warrior.* The word gave me resolve.

Our dance raged on. Eventually, the marlin's magnificent leaps became less mighty and then disappeared altogether. Her days were over. I was the victor.

Reeling her in took several minutes. At five times my weight, she was the largest fish I'd ever seen. The men around me were out of their minds; they slapped and patted my aching back, snapped photos, estimated her measurements from every angle, but I was somewhere else: gone, disconnected, in another world. Another boat joined us. Congratulations abounded. My prize was admired by all.

In surreal slow motion, I focused on the task at hand, taking the final turns of my reel, trying not to look at the marlin lying on her side just below the waterline. I wondered if this noble beast had completed her business in this life. Was she a mother in this aquarium of the world? Would she be missed?

I attempted to bat these thoughts away immediately. *Don't go there, James. You've achieved your goal. You've won the prize. It's meant to be.* Why, then, couldn't I really look at her? Was it my place to play God in this way for the sake of sport?

In this suspended moment, I forced myself to face my soon-to-be mounted prize. I stared into her big, confused eye. I could feel her exhaustion, her fear, her sense of betrayal. Could the others not see this? The cheers from the men around me were muffled, far-off background chants for an undeserved hero. Blaring in the foreground was the sound of my heart, playing an empty song. This was not my goal. This is not what I wanted. This is not who I am. I had signed up and waged war for something that was never mine to take on.

Domingo began to raise the gaffing hook, the final action to end the marlin's life. A shot of certainty flooded my system. I grabbed his arm, perhaps too forcefully. 'No,' I said.

I moved my hand swiftly to the base of the hook she had so innocently swallowed and yanked it from her powerful jaw. She was free. She
and I made eye contact one last time, only for a millisecond, but it was all
I needed to sense her forgiveness as she swam away. My heart pounding,
I watched to make sure she was moving unencumbered: poetry in
motion. Inside, I thanked her for a powerful life lesson.

The men stood in disbelief, their mouths hanging open. One piercing
look at Tony and he backed off. 'Cool, man,' he said. 'I get it.' I took a
deep breath and hid my smile from the others, determined to save my joy
and awakening until I was alone.

The next morning, I was drawn back to the dock. As I sat nearby on
the beach meditating in the morning sun, two dolphins leaped into
view, not sixty feet away, jumping, diving, splashing, slapping their tails on
the surface of the water. I wondered if this was God's way of reminding
me of the importance of counting the cost before any journey? I grabbed
my journal and wrote, 'Make sure that your destination is in alignment
with your true heart's desire.'

I glanced up at the dolphins and continued my writing: 'Other
people's values will bring you other people's results. But your values
bring fulfilment and joy.'

I'd been chasing someone else's beliefs and values, not my own. Where
else in life was I doing this? I needed to uncover and question my own
definition of what victory meant. I was eternally grateful.

You can't have a harmonic relationship with your self or others – true
Harmonic Wealth – if your total belief system has been hijacked by
others. The lesson the marlin gave me is that it doesn't matter how much
time or energy you've spent on a path; it's more than okay – honourable
and imperative, actually – to get to the destination and realise that you've
been living someone else's version of truth based upon their experiences
and belief systems.

It's okay if you look up one day and realise that you're living a lie, even
if you've committed great time, money, and attention to the path you're
on, even if you're breaking records, about to win a huge prize, or if

everyone is cheering you on. Whether it's a job, relationship, group affiliation, or religion that you've outgrown, it's okay if you've got caught up
in ways of thinking that aren't your own. Truth happens. Recognition is
the first law of transformation and growth. Be glad you're figuring it out
now rather than ten years from now.

I don't care what you were taught to think was right in your life. If it's
not right for you, it's not right. Always remember, it's more noble to
imperfectly pursue your own vision than to perfectly pursue the vision
of another.

Your Internal Thermostat: Changing Your Habitual Programming

Remember that your unconscious mind can't tell fact from fiction. The
upside is that when you give a command to your unconscious mind by
imagining how you'll feel when you have your desired outcome, the
mind thinks you've already created it and calls for an encore performance
in the real world. Positive thoughts, words, emotions, actions, and results
follow, repeating the cycle that continues to instill the positive habit.

But the downside, as you know, is that your unconscious can perpet-
uate a world of hurt, attracting more of the same, because you haven't
challenged those beliefs.

Dr Maxwell Maltz, a cosmetic surgeon–turned–self-help author, wrote
Psycho-Cybernetics, a classic in the field about such mental mechanisms.
Although he dedicated the first part of his professional life to improving
people's outward appearances, he ultimately decided that it was more
transformative to change our beliefs. He talked about the importance of
emotional surgery and the need to dehypnotise yourself from false
beliefs. He compared the unconscious mind to a thermostat that equalises
the temperature to a set point whenever it gets too hot or cold.

Let's dissect the analogy. In your home, if you set your thermostat to
68 degrees, and the temperature goes up to 75, what happens? A measurement device or cybernetic mechanism measures the change in
temperature, triggers a generator, which switches on the air conditioner,

and brings the temperature back to 68 degrees. If the temperature falls below the set point, the cybernetic mechanism detects the difference in temperature and uses the same process to switch on the heating.

Your programming is your unconscious and your Total Belief System is the cybernetic mechanism.

Maltz theorises that we all have our internal psychological thermostat set to what we're comfortable with – our comfort zone – even if our results leave us anything but comfortable. I had a client named Susie, for instance, who lived with her family in a small house where she, her husband, and two kids were cramped and constantly fighting for space. They couldn't wait to afford a home where they wouldn't be bumping into each other.

When they were finally able to save enough to move to a much nicer and larger home, she later admitted that the first few days after their move were painful. You've heard of buyer's remorse, and in many cases it's just a simple matter of the discomfort of becoming bigger – of expanding. 'It made no rational sense because I couldn't wait to leave that place,' Susie said, 'but all I wanted to do was run back to our old house and curl up in the fetal position in our old bedroom.'

Another couple I knew, Phil and Penny, couldn't get beyond the $80,000 mark. For years while Penny was a stay-at-home mum, Phil made $80,000. But as soon as Penny started working, pulling in $40,000 herself, Phil's income fell to around $40,000. Then, when she made $55,000, his income fell to just over $25,000. Their inability to get beyond $80,000 felt mysterious to them because their thermostat setting was outside their conscious awareness. They had no idea that buried deep within their unconscious was the mutual belief that they were $80,000-a-year earners – whether from one income or two. As Penny's income grew, the cybernetic mechanism (thermostat) measured the deviation from that set belief, finding that things had become too hot, and automatically brought the couple 'comfort' at the amount they were used to.

You'll see this with people who get a bonus at work of, say, £5,000, but then have car troubles totalling that same amount. You'll often hear them say things like, 'Easy come, easy go,' or, 'Can you believe the irony – it was for the exact amount?' Yes, unfortunately, I can.

Before I met Phil and Penny, they'd tried getting more organised, forcing themselves to make elaborate lists, schedules, and time management plans. But they always slid back to their unproductive habits of watching daytime TV and overeating, taking long naps when they should have been working. The root of the challenge wasn't in the actions they were taking but in their cybernetic programming. This programming drives all action. You see, if I have a cybernetic mechanism that says I can't earn more than a certain amount of money, I'll hold myself back from taking the actions of someone who earns twice that. It's unconscious.

One of the greatest needs in human existence is to remain consistent with how we've defined ourselves – even if that definition limits us! Do you follow me? Phil and Penny had decided who they were and the limits they would have to live with. But once they realised that their thermostat was locked in position, they worked hard to change their programming, doing all the things we've talked about so far and more to bring about growth: intention and goal work, vision work, avoiding things that weakened them, taking their critical action steps, managing their use of time more effectively, self-honesty, and so on.

Within less than a year, they were able to change their thermostat. The last time I talked to them, they had a combined yearly income of $185,000 – far more than they'd ever seen in any twelve-month period. As they get more and more comfortable earning greater and greater amounts (and believe they're worth it), the thermostat in their minds will only keep adjusting, their actions will follow, and their combined income will continually rise.

Ditching Self-Limiting Beliefs

Is your mind racing trying to find all the ways your cybernetic mechanism has thwarted you? Did your results stay the same despite a job change or promotion? Have you lost twenty pounds only to gain it back almost immediately? Have you married for a second time, with the same emotional issues you thought you'd left behind?

In order to change your internal thermostat and discover the beliefs you truly want to live by, it's crucial that you uncover and let go of any limiting beliefs that are holding you hostage. Phil, for example, had a false belief from his blue-collar childhood that all rich people were lazy, dishonest, and spoiled. Would you be inspired to step out of your comfort zone to take the daily actions required for expansion if your reward at the end of the day was that you'd become a lazy and spoiled liar?

I'm going to ask you to ask yourself some crucial questions. The goal is to get very comfortable being uncomfortable. Your comfort zone either holds you back or expands with power and opportunity. View that opportunity as an adventure in growth.

Consider these questions:

1. Who has influenced my thinking about myself, others, life, and success?

2. What beliefs, attitudes, and habits of thought have they passed down to me?

3. What societal attitudes, religious beliefs, or teachings are part of my mind-set?

4. Are these thoughts, attitudes, beliefs, and teachings enhancing my success or limiting it?

Now ask yourself, *Do I ever have thoughts like these?*

1. *I haven't been in business long enough to be successful.*

2. *I've never earned £50,000 a year before. Who am I to think I can do it now?*

3. *My parents never saved for retirement. I can't either.*

4. *I don't deserve to be happy in love.*

5. *Fat runs in my family. We're just built that way.*

6. *I've never had a good memory. I can't even remember people's names.*

7. *Some people are just born lucky.*

8. *I've already had more than I deserve in this life. It's greedy to want more.*

9. *People in positions of power aren't trustworthy.*

10. *The world is a dangerous place.*

Take out your notebook and write down a list of twenty beliefs you have about life. ●

Do it quickly without thought, and don't judge what you come up with. Write down as many as you can, both negative and positive beliefs.

What would your best friends or children say are your top beliefs? If you don't know, ask them. Then go back to your list. Just get ideas down, even if they appear to conflict. Then look at your list and see what needs some thought. Could you prove that belief in a court of law? If not, consider rethinking it. For each belief, try to pinpoint where that particular belief came from. Conflicts will show you where you need to grow. Ask yourself, *Is this a belief I want to keep, or something that needs updating? Is it useful or counterproductive to think this way?*

It's not unusual to discover that you hold conflicting beliefs. Perhaps you tell yourself, *I believe women should stay home and take care of their children, but I also believe women should earn their own money.* Where did those two contradictory beliefs come from? Start with your parents. You know what they believed, don't you? Parents often hold opposing views, which confuses the heck out of their kids. Maybe your dad believed that children should be seen and not heard, and your mum believed that kids should always express their opinions. Or maybe your father believed that inner peace was impossible, so why even try, whereas your mum felt that an unexamined life wasn't worth living.

For example, as you know, I spent a large part of my life making a lot of money and then invariably losing it. I couldn't figure out why until I did this exercise and realised that my mother held a belief that you should always save for a rainy day, while Dad believed you should spend it while you have it because it may never rain. Until I recognised and harmonised them, these unconscious and conflicting beliefs, which I had embraced equally as my own, caused me to be in a continual financial push-pull.

Making this list helps you appreciate that for the most part, you've just unconsciously accepted other people's beliefs without question – even when they're contradictory. From that point on, they've driven your behaviour and often limited you – until now. We're going to change some of your thought patterns by doing positive and powerful repro-gramming. Your reprogramming will be driven by your own passion and placed in your unconscious mind by your own choosing, a choice to create a new and powerful life of Harmonic Wealth.

Harmonic Wealth is not a start-and-stop programme, but one that builds upon itself. Once you really commit to it, if you haven't already, you'll see that you start creating some serious momentum. It'll get easier and easier as you stick with it. It's like riding a bike: the first few feet are the hardest until you get going. Once you reach a respectable speed, the principle of momentum kicks in and it's easier and easier to keep going. Each day synergistically builds on every other, dovetailing into the next, creating new behavioural patterns and ways of thinking and acting that bring harmony and wealth. Practise these lessons you're learning and apply them each day as an ongoing way of life – forever.

16

Thoughts into Action

Thought is action in rehearsal.

– SIGMUND FREUD

Thought Precedes Action

If you don't clean up your thoughts, you'll never change your actions. To under-stand why, try to have a thought without an image. Think about your neighbour without visualising him or her. Think about your car without seeing it in your garage or drive. Think about wanting to feel healthier without at least a fleeting image of what that would look like. Can you do it? It's not possible.

To take this further, images, depending on the meaning you attach to them, that come to your mind always bring with them corresponding emotions. The union of these thoughts and emotions creates a feeling in your body. Guess what thoughts, feelings, and emotions bring? Corresponding actions. In turn, actions have corresponding results, don't they? Do you see how easy and logical this is? It's not rocket science, but it is mind science – James Ray style. No matter what, all the results in your life have followed one fail-safe, logical sequence:

1. Thought (You had an idea.)

2. Emotion (You created an energetic response and label to what you thought: energy in motion.)

3. Feeling (The marriage of your thoughts and emotions created a visceral vibration in your body.)

4. Action (You did something about your thoughts, emotions, and feelings.)

5. Result (Voila: 'Your wish is my command.')

This is why the brain is referred to as a computer. Unless your computer gets a virus or your hard drive crashes, 1-2-3-4 always leads to 5.

So, if you want different results, you must interrupt your habitual way of thinking and create new habitual thought. You must think your way to new results. However, the key distinction that's almost always left unsaid is that while thought starts the chain of events, if you don't have the whole process, thinking alone gets you nowhere. You must go 3 for 3.

Groove with Your Thoughts

Scientist and prolific inventor Elmer Gates, whose ideas for generating creative thought were profiled in Napoleon Hill's *Think and Grow Rich,* hypothesised that thoughts produce a slight molecular change in the substance of the brain. Therefore, repetition of thoughts causes a repetition of the same molecular action, until an actual channel or groove is formed in the brain. Neuroscientists today believe that thinking the same thought pattern over and over reinforces that neural pathway, allowing other neuron connections to wither. Neurons that fire together wire together. The good news is that we can create new grooves, new neural pathways, by the reverse process of thought that created them.

Imagine for a moment a very well-worn path through the woods. The trees are densely overgrown to the right and left of that path. As you enter the woods and consider travelling through it, which path are you going to take? It's easiest to take the path of least resistance, isn't it?

However, if you choose to go on a new path, to blaze a new trail, then you'll have to hack your way, you'll have to step over things, knock things down, and it will be a rough journey the first time. The second time you go back along that path, it will be a little less difficult, but it would still probably be much easier to walk on the old path, would you agree?

Just suppose that we travel that new path every day, multiple times a day, for several months. What would happen? That path would get easier and easier to follow. Pretty soon it'd be the normal piece-of-cake way to travel.

So, let's get ready with the machete to cut that new trail. Expect the going to be really rough for the first three weeks, okay? Every time you catch yourself walking down that grooved road of limited thinking, stop, reboot, and then pick up that machete again.

I'm often asked, 'What about a person under medical care – with bio-chemical imbalances and such?' I'm not a doctor, yet I have many healthcare professionals who are graduates of my programmes, and what I have learned is that you're more than your biology.

I have numerous examples of individuals I've worked with, who were taking multiple medications and dropped them in short order, becoming totally healthy and whole. I never recommended or suggested that they stop their medication; what I do is continually remind them of how amazing and unlimited they are.

When I met Angela, she'd been diagnosed as bipolar. On twelve different types of medications, she had two failed suicide attempts behind her, and on both occasions she'd been committed to an institution. Angela couldn't even move or get up in the morning without her pills. When she came through my Harmonic Wealth Weekend, I reminded her of who she *really* was. I never recommended (nor will I) that she come off her drugs; I only continually reinforced her unlimited capability and taught her how to utilise her mind. Within one year she was off all medication. Recently she got promotion in her job with a handsome rise, and she's now highly functioning.

If you find yourself in a dire situation, work with a skilled healthcare professional while continuing to remember with greater certainty who you are. With time and perseverance, you'll access your infinite capability.

Reframing Your Thoughts

We are surrounded by limitation and negativity. We're surrounded by people who think small and limited. We are surrounded by potentially perceived problems. This is why it's so easy to act like a passive victim, someone to whom things merely happen with no control. Your negative thought patterns reinforce this sense of passivity.

To reverse this mind-set, start today – right this moment – by actively reframing your thoughts. Today and every day from this day forward, use the Law of Polarity – the law that states that everything in existence has its opposite and cannot exist otherwise. If there's an up there has to be a down, if there's a right there has to be a left, hot must exist in polarity to cold, and if something appears to be really truly bad, there must be something absolutely amazing as well. Use this law to your advantage. Understand that every single thing that comes into your life is actually facilitating what you want. When somebody suddenly cuts you up in traffic, you might consider asking yourself, *What's really great about this?*

Realistically, you'll want to say, *Nothing!* But if you're persistent enough and committed enough, you'll find something. Maybe you were sleepy and that jolt of adrenaline really woke you up. Or it made you stop and count your blessings, which made you feel good. Perhaps it allowed you to test your level of emotional control. Or maybe you just felt grateful that you didn't get hit!

If your old programming kicks in – *Why do I always get stuck driving behind arseholes? Great, now I'm going to be late. Why am I such a wimp?* – ask yourself, *If I really wanted to find something good, what could I find?* This may seem silly or crazy in the moment, but I guarantee it'll change your life. One thing I can always find about a perceived negative situation is: I learned something, which helps me grow and improve. If you understand that you're attracting and creating everything in your life, then you also have to accept that every single thing that comes into your life is coming in for a reason and is moving you towards your goal. Find that reason by reframing your thinking.

Beautiful New Beliefs

Go back to that list of twenty beliefs you made. Which ones don't help you? Which ones are holding you back? Once you've uncovered any negative underlying belief, choose a new belief to take its place.

As we did earlier with your anti-intention, you'll be choosing the opposite of your old belief. 'I don't have enough education' becomes 'I have a PhD in life experience.' 'I'm fat' becomes 'I'm strong, healthy, and vivacious.' 'I'm too old' becomes 'I have a wealth of wisdom to share with others.' 'I'm too young' becomes 'I'm fresh, hip, and creative.' 'I don't have enough time' becomes 'I am the master of each moment and how I utilise it.' These are the new beliefs you must reinforce with your new habits.

I want you to write down your new beliefs now, followed by the habits/actions you'll produce to keep them in place. ⓘ Then you must keep your attention upon all positive results no matter what. Constantly ask yourself the question, *Where do I see evidence of my new beliefs and intentions in my life?* It doesn't matter how small or insignificant the evidence may seem; all references are good references.

When you grow and expand by reprogramming your total belief system, you're creating a clear mental picture that you constantly step into, running the new film that helps you redefine what you can receive. You're resetting your cybernetic mechanism from 68 degrees to 70, 80, and then a smoking hot 110. Again, change your thoughts to change your actions. Your external world is a reflection of your inner world. Remember who you are.

Aladdin's Lamp

You've probably heard me talk about Aladdin's lamp – the best illustration I've found for explaining the interplay between the Conscious Mind, Unconscious Mind, and Higher Conscious Mind. Remember the story? A young boy stumbles upon a lamp, picks it up, dusts it off, and out pops a genie. The genie looks at him and says, 'Your wish is my command.'

You've probably heard about those three wishes, right? As a kid, weren't you always trying to get around that? 'My third wish is that I get more wishes!'

If you trace the story back to its roots in the eighteenth century, you'll see that the original version carried no limitation to the wishes. Forgive me, but I feel a metaphor coming on.

Your Conscious Mind is your Aladdin, your Unconscious Mind is the lamp, and your Higher Conscious Mind – your Higher Self is the genie – with no end to the gifts it can (and will) give you.

The reason you might experience something you didn't consciously wish for is because of your programming, which sends out a consistent offer wave, a path of energy or vibration that calls forth and pulls similar vibrations into your life. According to this unconscious energy broadcast (your lamp, or the pathway to the genie), your Higher Conscious Mind is saying without judgment, 'Your wish is my command.'

Until you change your programming, the offer waves you put out into the universe may be contrary to what you consciously want. That's the downside of the unconscious. By nature of its being unconscious, you're not aware of what it's broadcasting and asking for until it shows. I often have clients tell me that they don't understand why something bad is happening to them, and yet their closest friends and family members aren't surprised at all by their results and outcomes. You see, while the person is trying to change the screen, the friends can see that the wrong film has been spooled onto their projector. Another way to explain it is that their unconscious is full of minimised programs.

Allow me to illustrate.

Imagine that you're sitting at your computer screen working on a Word document. You get tired of looking at it, so you go to the upper right-hand corner and click the little minus sign, immediately minimising your file into a small icon at the base of the screen. Ah – relief. Now you don't have to look at it any longer. You feel like it's gone, but it's still there, isn't it, taking up RAM space as if it were still in full view.

Do you follow the metaphor? Your Unconscious Mind houses all of your unresolved emotional issues: limiting beliefs, decisions, and emotions that, while out of your awareness, still send out offer waves and attract echo waves that are harmonious with these issues.

This is why a large percentage of women who have abusive fathers grow up and marry abusive men or why a large percentage of people who grow up on social security become benefit recipients. The reason why 90 per cent of people who lose weight gain it back in two years isn't because they love the taste of food more than the next person. It's because of their programming, which isn't always conscious. Have you ever asked an overweight person why he or she ballooned back up after losing a lot of weight? 'Why are you eating the whole pie?' 'I don't know,' they might have said. They're right; they honestly don't know because their unconscious needs are out of their awareness, like the computer program that's been minimised but continues running in the background.

Some people think that ignorance is bliss. No. Ignorance is just plain ignorance.

I'll be beating the drum to get you to avoid anything that weakens you, to surround yourself with things that strengthen you, and to continue to take the actions you're already taking – setting your intentions, completing your six critical action items each day, visualising, and so on. These are the positive behaviours that will help you swap your film, delete those minimised programs, and change your life.

Accentuate the Positive

Are you wishing positively but commanding negatively? Through the use of Aladdin (your Conscious Mind), you can reprogramme your Unconscious Mind on a consistent, repetitive, and committed basis. The projector can only project exactly what's on the film – no more, no less. That film is created based upon the things you think about on a consistent basis. Do you think more about your worries or about your blessings?

When imagining what you want, know that the mind cannot process a negative, so if you say to yourself, *I don't want to be broke,* what are you going to immediately think about? I had a client who was constantly worried about being homeless. She would say to herself, *Stop thinking about carrying everything you own in black plastic bags,* and then that's all she could see. She was freaking herself out so much that she got insomnia.

Take out your notebook and write down your top intention today. We've been here before, but just as a reminder: maybe it's that you want to hire a cleaner to help you once a week. Maybe you need to find that workout companion to help make you more accountable for your fitness goals, or you want to muster up the courage to register for the evening classes that will lead you to your new career. Whatever it is, get a clear mental picture of your result in your mind. Write it down on your intention card. Visualise it and feel it at least twice a day – morning and night – during the time when your Unconscious Mind is the most receptive and open for programming. Then make sure and act upon it – big, bold, immediate, and consistent! When you visualise, look through your own eyes; make it a big, bright, colourful, exciting, full-of-noise film in which you're the star.

Remember you must go 3 for 3: your thoughts, feelings, and actions must all be firing in alignment. Thinking and visualising about it alone won't cut it, yet thoughts are the starting point. Thoughts give direction to your feeling and actions.

Thoughts are a directional system like the steering wheel of a car. Remember when you were a little kid and your parent allowed you to sit in your family car? You had a great time making noises with your mouth and turning that steering wheel back and forth. But you went nowhere. To make it real, you would have had to turn on the engine.

That's what you're doing now. Your engine is the motoring device we'll call your feelings. But although they bring you further along, you're still not really getting anywhere. You still have to place the car in gear and get the car moving. Once the tyres start rolling, you've got action. This is going 3 for 3.

So, thoughts are the starting point and they're vital – setting you and keeping you on the right course, just like the steering wheel. But in and of themselves they're insufficient. Go 3 for 3 in high gear!

17

Energy in Motion . . . Emotion!

There can be no transforming of darkness into light and of apathy
into movement without emotion.

– CARL JUNG

The Emotional Mind

To achieve true Harmonic Wealth, you not only have to take control of your thoughts and beliefs, but your emotions as well. Harnessing and directing your emotions versus being harnessed and directed by them is key. We all know people controlled by their emotions and they're like a wild boar on steroids: up and down, up and down. Emotions are part of the human experience. Is there a time to get angry? Sometimes. That's part of the human experience. But there's a time and a place and it's probably not at the supermarket checkout.

As we've discussed, if you're going to be able to be an incredible creator in this world, you have to get into action. As long as you're living in a physical body, this is the game. Most of the word *emotion* consists of the word *motion*. Emotion is nothing more than energy in motion. So, if you want to be highly motivated and moving forward, then you have to access this emotional component of your mind masterfully.

I once did a radio interview for men and the host asked me, 'What's one of the biggest problems with men not getting what they want?' I said, 'Suppressing their emotions.' It's not their fault, but it is their responsibility.

Everything is your responsibility. I was blessed because my father always told me, 'Real men can cry.' That's unusual. Maybe you were taught to have a 'stiff upper lip'. If you fell over onto your head, you were told, 'Don't be a sissy.' Women also have been programmed to suppress their nature, particularly in business.

It's challenging to find the line between directing, controlling, and suppressing our emotions. Until we are courageous enough to express, feel, own, and appreciate our emotions, they can and will block our energy. Anything suppressed will be expressed. The author Gregg Braden quotes scientific evidence proving that negative emotions leave a six-hour residual of negative vibration in the body. My friends at the HeartMath institute have shown that negative emotions continually expressed literally tighten up your DNA, hampering your spiritual and physical capabilities. The negative, disempowering energies you're putting out pull in (attract) universal energies that are in harmony with that dark energy. In short, when you're playing the victim or pissed off with someone else, who are you really hurting? Like our dumbbell example, you're the one suffering.

Owning Your Emotions

Want to own your own power? Then first own your emotions. The first step is to appreciate that *your experience in life has nothing to do with external events*. Remember our estate agents? Nothing in life has any meaning besides the meaning *you* give it.

Sound radical? Think about it. How do we create meaning? In many cases we're taught what matters and what doesn't by our culture and by the people around us. The truth is that it's all subjective. Some of us are taught that long blond hair and diamond rings mean beauty; other cultures believe that short curly black hair, lip plates, and long earlobes are the real standards of attractiveness. Some of us are taught that a person's death means a sad situation that requires mourning; others grow up learning that it's a joyful reunion with a higher power.

Imagine you're in the sea and you're a poor swimmer. Behind you comes a huge wave. Now what do you think? Do you think, *What an exciting and fun wave?* No way! You're scared as hell. Now, imagine you're a professional surfer and that same wave comes up behind you. *Cool, hang-ten, what a gnarly wave, dude!* Did the wave change? Obviously, it was just the meaning you gave it. As Hamlet said, 'There is nothing either good or bad, but thinking makes it so.' If you want to get all twenty-first-century about it, picture quantum physicists today tussling over the Copenhagen Interpretation, the idea that there's no such thing as objective reality. These are some of the world's greatest scientific minds stating there's nothing outside you that doesn't come from inside you! As within, so without.

Earlier in this chapter, I urged you to challenge your beliefs, so you could understand that they're only as real as you allow them to be. The same is true of your emotions. You may seem to be at the mercy of your emotions, but that's only because you allow them to dictate meaning to you. Have you ever had a friend say something rude to you, but you think it's funny because he said it? Yet if a stranger said that very same thing to you, they'd be fighting words. No one can make you angry; you make yourself angry. Harmonic Wealth means controlling and choosing your emotions, or acting versus merely reacting. Please remember, there's a difference between choosing your emotions and suppressing them – that's not what we're discussing here.

If nothing in life has any meaning besides the meaning you give it, then your experience in life has nothing to do with external events but everything to do with your internal experiences and how you attach meaning to an event. It's all about how we interpret things. This is a deeper level of accountability. Just because you're accountable when something you're doing seems to turn out badly or wrong, it doesn't mean that *you* are bad or wrong, does it? You are not what you do – you are so much more than that.

What it does mean is that you're now responsible for finding what is necessary to move forward. When you place blame, you get stuck, your intellectual and emotional wheels spinning like tyres in the mud.

Emotional Honesty

What I'm talking about is emotional honesty, or mastery. The key to emotional mastery is self-honesty. That might feel like a foreign concept right now, and if so, start with the little things. Do you eat what you want for breakfast or do you tolerate the cardboard-tasting cereal your wife buys because it's easy for her and makes her happy? Have you been putting off taking time for yourself because you were taught not to be selfish? When would be a better time to take time for you – when you're laid up on forced bed rest? Don't wait for fate to take its course. If you find yourself lying to neighbours when they ask how you are, impart a little honesty: 'I'm having a bit of a challenging day today, thanks. But I'm getting through it.' People may or may not appreciate your candour. If nothing else, you'll make them think.

There's a big difference between putting on a smile during difficult times and transcending the difficult times. It's like the difference between filling up your car with petrol or smacking a smiley face over your petrol gauge and continuing to drive on an empty tank.

Later Days in Uglier Ways

I was having breakfast with some friends recently after a particularly challenging situation in which my entire home was flooded by a leak in the bathroom. On the same day, while waiting for the plumber (who of course was late), I decided to run out quickly and get some lunch. I made maybe half a mile before I realised I had a flat tyre. One of those days . . . I stopped and asked myself, *Okay, how does this help me?* The only answer I came up with at the time was that it allowed me to notice how much I'd grown in recent years. There were several years of my life where I was really what you might call highly strung. If these challenges had happened back then, I would have gone ballistic – DNA so tight it could've ground carrots – and then ended up feeling regretful in retrospect. Obviously neither of these emotions would bring value into my life.

My friends couldn't believe I hadn't been angry. One of them asked, 'But James, don't you believe that you should vent your emotions? Isn't it unhealthy to keep them bottled up?' There's a big difference between transcendence and suppression. For example, take a pair of dirty gym socks and underwear, stuff them into a locker, and go away. Coming back one year later, do you think they'll have cleaned themselves? Hardly – they'll be rank.

As you know, anything that's suppressed will be expressed in later days in uglier ways. Suppression shortens your life span and stores toxic energy in your body. One of the quickest ways to lower your body's vibrational field is reacting negatively. That's what happens when you vent ugly emotions – lose it when someone grabs your parking space, become jealous of a colleague's promotion, and the like. The higher vibrations brought about by states like love, gratitude, appreciation, joy, inspiration, and enthusiasm guarantee a longer and healthier life.

So, don't clamp down your emotions or vent them with a roar. Take a deep breath and then transcend them by asking, 'How does this help me?' 'What does this teach me?' 'How will I grow from this?' or 'How will I use this experience to my benefit in the future?' Quantum physics tells us that every electron, which has a negative charge, must have a matching positron, carrying a positive charge. In layman's terms, that means if something seems really, really terrible there has to be something incredible there as well. It has to be there – it's a scientific law.

I recall my dad telling a story about Glenn Turner, the owner of a company back in the 1960s called Koscot. One day Glenn came home to find his wife sitting on the floor in tears, 'They came and repossessed all our furniture,' she cried, looking up through tear-stained eyes. 'That's great!' her husband replied. 'Now we don't have any more payments!'

Recently, when Michael J. Fox was interviewed about his feelings concerning the role Parkinson's disease has played in his life, he replied, 'It's a gift. I've learned so much, experienced so much, and been able to give so much that I never could have before.' I haven't a clue as to whether these men understand physics or the Law of Polarity, but at least in these circumstances they exhibited mastery.

In my experience, releasing limiting unconscious emotions is paramount to more powerfully and productively handling life's situations in the moment.

The Internal Game

Understanding that you have the ability to control your emotions gives you tremendous power to change the quality of your experiences, the quality of your results, and the quality of your life. If you feel angry at any time or get upset, I want you to stop and ask yourself one crucial question: 'What does my emotional reaction say about me?' In other words, what do I have to believe to be experiencing this emotion right now in this situation? Remember, you don't control others. You only define yourself and your own experience.

You create your own meaning. People tell me time and time again that learning and using this one new question has totally changed the quality of their lives.

Good Vibrations

Many think that emotion and feeling are the same things, but while they're closely related, they're not the same. Feelings are visceral – you feel something in your body. While emotions are the labels you place upon your internal experience (and which ultimately put your body into motion), feelings are the vibratory rate created by the *union* of your thoughts and emotions.

As we've discussed, your feelings affect your results because you first have a thought about something, and then you create an emotion around that thought. Feelings (vibrations) then come into your body and merge your thoughts and emotions.

In a vibratory universe, the feeling energy literally emanates from your body in waves of vibration, calling forth from the corresponding vibrations in the universe. Feelings of doubt and insecurity are a biofeed-back mechanism of work to be done.

Mastering your feelings and emotions will consistently allow you to create the vibration of what you intend. Since the Law of Attraction never ceases to work, I know you know the importance of mastering your feelings to your overall success.

You truly choose your direction and make a decision to pay the price to make it happen. Most individuals are unwilling to pay the price for the prize, and you must be unbending in your resolve.

Let this next section on optimism inspire you. It did me.

Happy or Crappy? Only You Decide

Have you lost your sense of wonder?

Psychologist Martin Seligman, godfather of the positive psychology movement, has conducted exhaustive research on optimists versus pessimists. What he found was that optimism is something that can be learned. He discovered that optimists consistently talk about what things are rather than what they aren't, what's there instead of what's not there. Pessimistic people talk about what things aren't. Now, we're not born pessimists. Children are optimists. Stand outside Disneyland on any given weekend and talk to the families as they exit. Kids come out with candy floss in their hair. Ask them, 'What did you think of Disneyland?' They'll gush, 'It was great. Mickey and Goofy were fantastic!' Now talk to the parents following them. 'What did you think of Disneyland?' Here's what they say: 'Queues are too long. Food's overpriced. That mouse gets on my nerves.'

So, is Disneyland the happiest place on Earth or the crappiest place on Earth? It's both — it all depends upon the observer.

How does this happen? How do we go from being born optimists to inveterate pessimists? Somewhere along the way, something or someone changes that, but what Seligman has found is that we can learn — or relearn — how to be optimistic. According to his research, optimists out-perform pessimists ten to one and, as we'll cover next in the physical pillar, your diet, and exercise, has a lot to do with how you feel and therefore how you view your life.

Reprogramming your thinking ('What's good about this situation?') and asking the question 'What does my emotional reaction say about me?' can help you retrain your mind to see the sunny side of life.

Your Very Own Crystal Ball: Your Intuition

Reprogramming your thoughts and mastering your emotions are essential to manifesting a life of Harmonic Wealth, but let's face it: there will still be times when you're not sure you're thinking straight or when you get caught in the undertow of your emotions. How, then, can you know you're moving in the right direction? There's one foolproof source to consult: your intuition.

Your intuition, or 'inner tuition', is the angel on your shoulder. Studying the ancient tradition of Huna in the Hawaiian Islands, I learned about the Na'au (pronounced Na-ow), housed in my gut. The intellect only understands the tangible, but the Na'au perceives the intangible.

According to the ancients, your Na'au never ever lies. Your head will mess you up every single time because you will analyze (anal lies) yourself right out of the opportunity that beckons at your door. Have you ever analyzed yourself right out of a great new job or love interest? What if this, what if that? We all have.

The kind of meditation techniques we'll cover in the last pillar help – not the kind where you contemplate your navel, but the kind where you sleep without sleeping. The whole point is to get to know yourself.

When you start to pay attention to that inner voice, it'll start to sharpen. Your intuition will become spot-on in its clarity. You'll learn to tell the difference between fear and a challenge that will help you grow, or something to truly stay away from. A good opportunity will feel expansive, exciting, like your brain is lighting up.

Start by paying attention to that tiny, faint voice inside you. Many of my students ask me, 'How do you develop this?' All I can tell you is to pay attention, listen, and act.

I started this practice many years ago with little things. Like when I was driving home from the gym, if I got an impulse to go a different way, I did. Did I avert an accident? Who knows? But I would follow those intuitions and things would turn out brilliantly a lot of the time – I might meet a new person, see a flyer for an interesting seminar, notice a book in a shop window. I came to see it as my Higher Self, the genie speaking to me. When I followed that urge and it turned out less than brilliant, I came to see that I was having an emotional response that I thought was my intuition. I continuously documented the fine differences and distinctions in my journal – are you keeping yours? I truly hope so. With practice, I started being able to chronicle and understand my physiological responses, my inner pictures and visions – those feeling vibrations in my core. Soon I could distinguish between the two. Now I understand why some people call intuition 'second sight'; it's the difference between seeing with the eyes and seeing through the eyes. Seeing with the eyes is a physiological act. But when you see through your eyes, you develop the kind of inner vision that can create the outer reality you desire.

It takes some time to develop your intuition, but once you get it, you get it. I've been really successful in property for the last few years, for instance, and I've never studied it. I just walk into a place and check my gut. When it's right I know it, and when it's not, I know that too, and I know it very quickly, regardless of what the numbers say.

It's hard to describe a feeling, and everyone is different, but feelings are vibrations, so you can experience them in your body. I've heard it described as a pull, a still small voice, or visual reinforcement. Get to know the signs of your own inner knowing.

When you get really tuned in and you're following your intuition, you begin to listen and when it says go, you go, even if it's illogical to do so – most often it is. You see, logic is part of your conscious mind and intellect. Intuition is your Higher Self – your future-pull – challenging you to become what you're destined to become.

Following your intuition is taking emotion (energy in motion), and moving the body into action. Emotions move the body to act, which is critical because again, the universe loves speed. As one of the ancient teachings of the mystery schools states, whatsoever you resolve to do, do it quickly. Leave not until tomorrow what can be done today.

What must you do today? Clarify your intention and direction and move boldly. Fortune favours what? Ah, *the bold*!

PILLAR IV

Physical

Your results in the physical world are an exact mirror of your efforts and attention. You can hide your mental and emotional issues, at least for a while. You can spend to the limit on your credit cards and act like a big shot when you're broke, you can even fake a good game of spirituality – saying all the right things at the right time and meditating or going to church. But when your habits are poor, the damage is most obvious in the physical pillar. The minute your body walks in the room, people can tell a lot about your habits as well as what you think about yourself.

The physical pillar encompasses anything and everything tangible – the physical world as well as the physical body. We'll start by focusing on your physical surroundings and then we'll delve into the physical body, because without good health and fulfilment, all of the riches in the world can never be enjoyed. This pillar will inspire you to take care of yourself. Pay attention, treat yourself with love, and move forward. You have a lot to learn and a lot to give. What better area of life in which to be patient and thoughtful than with your precious human body?

18

The Universe Loves Order

Quality is not an act, it is a habit.

– ARISTOTLE

Put Your House in Order

Have you ever noticed that tribal people in Africa, India, and Mongolia often wear beautiful textiles or jewellery? It seems that even in poverty we're drawn by instinct to make some aspect of our lives rich. Whether through music, stories, ritual, ceremony, or physical embellishment, we long to express outwardly the wealth we feel on the inside. In shamanic traditions, indigenous tribes surround themselves with objects that represent wealth in their culture to constantly remind them of what they choose or intend to create. Husks of corn hang from the ceiling, and animal skins, ceremonial costumes, and visual images adorn the insides of their dwellings to help them focus on all that's good and abundant in their world.

Growth brings wealth.

As you expand, your ability to receive more expands in kind. The number one way to speed the inevitable process of growth is by raising your vibration. The best way to do this is by constantly immersing yourself in things that give you strength and power and conversely by avoiding anything that weakens you. Willpower comes and goes but environment is 24/7. That's why it's vital to surround yourself with triggers that grab your attention and keep it focused in the right direction.

Let's begin by looking at your environment. Ask yourself, 'What am I surrounding myself with?' ⓘ

A client once complained to me that his wife was always trying to 'keep up with the Joneses'.

'Every time we're about to have guests,' he said, 'she runs around the house trying to see what "they" see. Like a detective, she suddenly finds everything that's wrong with our house – stains on the carpet, holes in the sofa, dead plants in the garden. She becomes shallow and materialistic and wants it all fixed right away, and then we fight.'

'Be grateful that your wife does this,' I answered.

'What?' he said, eyes bulging. My response wasn't what he was expecting from a spiritual teacher. He didn't yet comprehend that a beautiful, organised, fully functioning environment sets the stage for growth, for attracting what you choose into your life. While just impressing others may not be the best motive, the process of improving your surroundings is wise.

Beautifying your environment may take time, but you can and should commit yourself to an organised environment immediately. I'm a big advocate of being organised. The universe loves order. A chaotic external world is a reflection of a chaotic inner world. Thinking back to how much money you're worth on an hourly basis, do you really have time to waste living in chaos? Despite the fact that the majority of Americans say they would be more satisfied if they were neater, the National Association of Professional Organizers reports that Americans spend fifty-five minutes a day looking for things they own but can't find. That's almost two weeks a year. Based on our previous example that costs you at least £8000. It seems impossible, doesn't it? Well, even if they're out by half, that's still a whole week.

How can you expect the universe to deliver your goals to you if you're otherwise occupied searching for your car keys and overdue gas bill? Prepare your space to receive all the good you want and deserve. Make the space for your goals, intentions, and higher purpose to find you.

If you still think the spiritual world and the physical world are separate, would *now* be a good time to widen your focus?

Recognition Is the First Law of Transformation

Remember, it's all energy. Everything, from the clothes you wear, to the decor in your home, to the state of your car is vibrating energy that constantly affects you, pulls you forwards or backwards. So, get outside yourself and look with fresh eyes at what you've created. No judgment – just a powerful experience.

It's easy to get into a rut on our way to expansion, which is why I'm such a proponent of travel. Have you ever had the experience of staying in a fine hotel or visiting the beautiful home of a friend, only to come home and realise the limitations of your own life? Maybe all your getaway did was inspire you to rent a steam cleaner and plant new flowers in the garden, but taking that action changed you internally, didn't it? It kicked you into gear and inspired you to ferret out other areas where you could clean up, organise, beautify, and grow. Afterward, every time you looked at the clean carpet or saw the butterflies flying through the garden, you smiled inside, knowing you created that beauty.

But what if visiting a home that's nicer than yours makes you depressed instead of inspired? Getting depressed indicates that you don't believe you can have that nicer home, which in turn means that you're having trouble believing in yourself. By doing the work, reading this book, you're starting to change that. So, understand that recognition is the first law of transformation, and that you can change. When you recognise your need to grow – and you are recognising it, aren't you? – you're already beginning to vibrate at a higher frequency. Stay with it, keep increasing your vibration, and results will follow. What if you're jealous? That tells you right away that you're ready to take action. When you truly realise that there's an unlimited supply, you'll never be jealous again. Until that time, use what you have.

I can't urge you enough: update your surroundings. Repair anything broken. Replace anything missing. Get rid of anything soiled or stained.

Make your environment a constant reminder of where you're going versus where you are or where you've been. Have a dinner party, take a trip and return with fresh sight – whatever helps you run around your home with the perspective of a first-time visitor. Look with new eyes. What do you see? Is it a constant reminder and reinforcement of your true values and desires or of things you've outgrown long ago?

Do you have old posters stuck on your walls? Do springs poke you in the arse every time you sit down on your sofa? Even the biggest big-screen TV won't make you feel abundant if you're watching it on a cheap beanbag chair.

Be honest with yourself. Do your surroundings support and reinforce the lifestyle you consciously choose? If the answer is no, then chances are you're having a difficult time staying in the correct vibratory rate to create and attract true wealth.

Quality Before Quantity – Always

You may say to me, 'James, how can I get nice furniture, clothing, and surroundings if I don't have the money to do it?' Well, first of all, make a commitment that if you have to choose between ten cheap outfits and one of a higher quality, choose the one. Ten cut-price paintings that are space fillers or one that moves your spirit and makes you feel wealthy? Again, choose the one.

I made a decision early in my life that if I was going to buy something, I was going to buy the best. Obviously the best is relative to where you currently are, but that's not an excuse for holding yourself back either.

If you think you still can't afford something, maybe it's that you're not thinking creatively enough – or maybe you don't want to make the effort. Could your ego or laziness be getting in the way? Can't get the table you want? Take a beautiful piece of fabric or even a shawl and use it as a tablecloth. Get creative. There's always a way to upgrade. The goal here is to put more beauty and inspiration around you, to think always in abundance, and to remind yourself that you live amid endless creative resources.

The monetary value of an item doesn't matter as much as the feeling of abundance it generates. When I go to a good shop and get one of something instead of ten of something less expensive, I feel good. But if you truly feel great getting some rich woman's cast-offs at the Salvation Army, by all means do it. Remember, the goal is to do what strengthens you.

I decided that if I had to be patient to get something of high value instead of something of lower value right away, I would develop patience. This strategy has served me well and I encourage you to become patient, even with regard to shopping for discounted treasures. Being an impatient 'now' person is a big deterrent to creating financial wealth. Decide to become a patient 'later' person now if you haven't already.

Find What Works for You

I've just told you to do some things now and some things later. Confused? Fix and clean up your surroundings as soon as you can so that everything in your world vibrates with the highest frequency possible, so that *you* can vibrate with the highest frequency possible. Then have patience with regard to new things. I'm about to show you how to realise your physical goals in quick time, so that as long as you remain vigilant and committed to beautifying your environment, your changes will be swift enough.

For example, you may want to consider the 'now', 'later', and 'much later' approach. When you're weighing a purchase, ask yourself how's it going to make you feel right now? Then ask how's it going to make you feel for the life of the object? If you buy an expensive car that makes you feel excited at the time but in just a couple of months you start worrying about the payments, that's not a good move. If, on the other hand, you buy an expensive piece of clothing that makes you feel fantastic whenever you wear it for years and years, in many different social situations, that is a good move! So, look at your financial goals and ask yourself, *Will buying that thing now help me or hurt me?* Will it help my goals by, say, helping me look more presentable for meetings and making me feel more successful, or will it hurt me because I really should have spent that £500 on, say, new equipment that would help me move forward? People tend to buy for emotional reasons (thank you, Madison Avenue!) and then justify purchases for intellectual reasons. Get clear on how your spending serves your long-term goals.

Oh, and by the way, one of the things I learned early on is that every single pound I invest in my own capabilities and growth very conservatively brings me *thousands* of pounds in return.

19

Nourishing Your Temple

To keep the body in good health is a duty . . . otherwise we shall not
be able to keep our mind strong and clear.

– BUDDHA

Taking Stock

We covered many of the tangible aspects of life in the financial pillar. As
we discussed, it's not really the money you want anyway, but what you
think the money will bring, right? So, after a quick exercise, we're going
to invest the majority of our time discussing your physical body – the
vehicle that, when in harmony, allows you to enjoy all those worldly gifts.
We'll talk about the usual basics – what to eat, how to exercise – but also
a lot of things that you probably don't think of as physical fitness: intuit-
ing your body's wisdom, reframing your language, using the power of
your breath, sexual healing, and much more.

If you've done the work recommended in the previous pillars, you're
already becoming very aware of and skilled in what you must do to
create physical results in your world. It's just a matter of practising what
you already know and going 3 for 3.

If you haven't done so already (and even if you have), make a specific
and measurable list of what you want in the physical realm, excluding
your physical body, because we're going to do that at the end of this
pillar. I'm talking about the home of your dreams, the sports car, starting

the foundation that helps children, buying your mother a house, a second honeymoon in the Caribbean, the lush corner office in the building where you work, a new kitchen or bathroom or walk-in wardrobe. Whatever you're dreaming of, get it down.

Now, if you could only have one of these things, which would it be? I know you want all of them, but here's what I've found: if you pick the one you absolutely MUST have before you leave this lifetime, then many of your lesser goals will be realised in the process.

Love for Your Body

Let's shatter any delusions you may have that it's somehow not spiritual to want a beautiful, healthy, and fit body. Your body is the vehicle through which Cosmic Consciousness has chosen to materialise, grow, and evolve, so limiting your physical strength, health, or beauty doesn't serve you in any way. Hiding behind a body you don't like is a cop-out. Sure, plenty of spiritual people think that taking great care of your physical form isn't a worthy spiritual pursuit, but that's part of a tired old argument that equates spirituality with poverty and the nonphysical world. You and I both know that's nonsense.

That said, there's a difference between having love *for* your body and being in love *with* your body. Did you get that? We live in a society by and large in love with the physical form, and many of us even sacrifice our health to look and feel good in the moment. We worship fitness, an external thing, often to the detriment of true health, an internal thing. Where's the logic in that? Please remember this axiom: health comes first and fitness follows. Yes, you should have love *for* your body because it's the only vehicle you have to ride in from now to the end of this lifetime. So, take care of it. But understand that it's not who you are. I learned this powerful lesson in the most difficult way.

A Million Little Pieces

I was the kid with the big Coke bottle glasses and buck teeth who everyone made fun of. Do you remember the jokes? 'Four eyes', 'Bugs

Bunny', 'so skinny you have to jump around in the shower to get wet' –
I heard them all and they weren't very funny – at least not to me. To
make matters worse, I failed at every sport. I just curled up inside myself
to avoid the pain.

Since I knew I'd never get the girls being a nerd (or at least feeling like
a nerd), I somehow made it to the gym and realised rather quickly that I
had muscles in those weak arms after all! I became a workoutaholic. The
bigger my body got, the more addicted I became to lifting heavier and
heavier weights, having no idea that a good thing taken to its extreme
could become a bad thing. All I knew was that becoming a competitive
bodybuilder seemed like the answer to all of my problems.

But getting attention from girls for the first time in my life didn't
diminish my feelings of being a loser, an imposter. If anything, it made me
more nervous (flirtation from a gorgeous trainer one day sent my cybernetic mechanism into panic mode). My body had become big and
strong, and yet in my mind, I was still that weakling who sat alone in the
cafeteria, terrified of his own shadow.

So I got a new motorbike, believing that having monster horsepower
at my command and all the physical freedom that comes with that would
finally do the trick and morph me into a bona fide stud. The last thing I
remember about my first ride was a set of headlights coming towards me.
Then I woke up in A and E. That sense of power was gone, replaced by
searing pain.

After six weeks in the intensive care unit, with a smashed left forearm,
two herniated discs, and two fractured knees, I had lost every one of
those hard-earned sixty pounds gained at the gym. It was as if all those
countless hours of focus and commitment had never happened. I felt
cursed, doomed to remain small and insignificant.

My doctors told me I'd never be able to lift any real kind of weight
again, so I fell into the deepest depression imaginable. If you didn't think
I know what it's like to lose yourself on the sofa, believing that television
is not only the real world but also your best friend, now you see where
some of my perspective comes from.

Yet, one morning I realised that the accident hadn't taken away *me*, not the real me. I still had the same values, dreams, and goals. I still had the same heart. Just because I was back to my normal weight didn't mean that my parents and brother loved me any less. In fact, unless I looked in the mirror, I was the same person I had always been. So, maybe it was time to learn to love that guy? I couldn't see why not.

Realising that I was not my body got me excited. I would never again allow the external world to define my success or failure. I would find my inner wealth and harmony and build from there. What a gift!

I turned off the TV, continued my reading with renewed enthusiasm, and changed my thoughts. As my thoughts changed, so did my life. I went back to the gym, not just to prove the doctors wrong (which I did), but to give myself the best possible chance of supporting all those hopes and dreams.

When the Universe Knocks on Your Door

You were born into greatness but conditioned into mediocrity. Sometimes it takes a sign from the universe to wake you up from the bad habits that keep you from treating your body like the worthy vessel it is.

Does it start with tiny warnings? Yes. The esoteric traditions maintain that there are seven levels of warning. Ignore the smallest whisper of a warning, and you'll get a louder one, then an even louder one. My teacher in Hawaii said to me years ago, 'James, for everything in life, you must pay attention. To the degree you don't pay attention, you pay with pain.' He got that one right – I have the scars on my body to prove it.

Let's say, for instance, that you're completely ignoring your physical pillar. At the seventh level, you'll get a sign – the very first one. This sign will most likely be really discreet, perhaps a dream. Or for some strange reason the waistband on your trousers seems to have shrunk just a little bit. 'Hmmm, the dry cleaners must have done something different.' If you pay attention, take responsibility, and address it, it stops. If you don't, then it comes into the sixth circle, and it's a little more intense. Then the fifth, fourth, third, second, and boom! Heart attack! Cancer! At any level, if you pay attention and address the issue, it stops. The universe says, 'Okay, he got it,' and it stops.

Jan fled a cheating husband who stole her money. Heartbroken, she ran right into an affair with a married man. This wasn't in keeping with her beliefs and values – that much was obvious because hadn't the same thing just happened to her? – but Jan justified the affair by telling herself, 'You can't help who you fall in love with' and, 'He's not happy in his marriage.'

Then, according to Jan, 'The creepiest stuff started happening.' First she had a slight accident in a parking lot at the supermarket. A week later she skidded on black ice in her cul-de-sac and hit a telegraph pole. Alarming, but what came three weeks later scared her senseless. As she was driving on the motorway, the car ahead of her hit its brakes and she went slamming into him at 40 mph. Whiplash, a near-demolished car, and a lawsuit forced her to look at what wasn't working in her life, and the most obvious offence was her relationship with the married man. She felt as if the universe had been warning her to slow down and stop the reckless behaviour driving her, but she hadn't listened.

How many times do we let things go without noticing? We make a change when it's too late or after something has happened that gives us an abrupt wake-up call. Many people begin to take care of their health only after they have a heart attack. Many people decide to take care of their marriage only after one party threatens divorce. It doesn't have to be that way. Truly wealthy and successful people look at all key areas of their life and keep them in harmony.

Let me ask you: are you going to wait until the universe gives you a wake-up call? Or are you going to take charge of your physical pillar right now?

Taking Charge of Your Precious Body

I've studied many spiritual traditions, and every one of them will tell you that you must master the body. How can you ever expect to channel and direct universal energies if you can't even control your appetite? You can't and you won't. How do you think you can ever direct and utilise universal energies if you can't control your sex drive? You can't and you won't. It's all part of the body. Physical mastery is the most basic to an integrated and harmonious life, and if you can't master the basics you'll never truly graduate to the advanced degrees.

Oh, sure, you might neglect it for a time and have a great romantic relationship, make a lot of money, or have a mystical experience. However, you and I both know that eventually neglecting the physical pillar is going to bite you in the arse. You're a spiritual being having a physical experience, sure; but if you're one of those folks who wants to eat pudding all day, miss the gym, and just meditate while skipping the whole physical pillar thing, arguing that everything's temporary and you're going to lose this body anyhow, do you need this pillar!

Various religious traditions call the human form the precious human body or the temple. I doubt you'd want to travel through the most beautiful temples in the world with a greasy cheeseburger in one hand and a milkshake in the other. Yet, what are you putting into your temple? Do you treat it so that it'll easily and elegantly carry you through a long and fulfilling life? Or do you stuff it with junk to satisfy your short-term desires? In order for you to treat yourself as the priceless artefact that you are, you've got to see yourself as such.

So I ask you, do you know how valuable you are?

Have you been conditioned to believe that you're lazy or unattractive or, as one client put it, 'a waste of space'? How unfortunate, but as I've said before, that was the past and you can change that now. Perhaps you're at the other extreme: you think you're terrific, proud as can be about how you've turned out, and yet you still don't treat your body with the respect you know it deserves.

Please understand that I'm not speaking of the physical attractiveness that Hollywood has conditioned us into worshipping. We can't all have the abs of Matthew McConaughey or be put together like Giselle Bundchen. However, you can be healthy, strong, and fit with what the Creator has given you to work with.

I want you to step outside yourself for a minute and think about a racehorse named Northern Dancer, who in 1964 won the Kentucky Derby. This magnificent animal later went on to become the most successful thoroughbred sire of the last 300 years, and one of his yearlings, a colt later named Snaafi Dancer, was bought at auction for $10,200,000. Assuming you were the one bidding against Sheikh Maktoum of Dubai that day for the colt and you, rather than he, had gone home with him, what would you have fed your thoroughbred for his first meal? Would it have been lush organic grasses, vitamins, and fresh, clear water? Or maybe a big bag of chips, chocolate, and a super-sized cola?

The question is ridiculous, right? No one in his or her right mind would feed any animal, much less a champion, a diet of junk food. But let's assume for a second that you did. Would it be any wonder if the horse ceased making its usual fast times around the track? Of course not.

But you're not worth $10 million, right? Actually, you're even more valuable. In fact, you're worth even more than your weight in gold. In 2003, *Wired* magazine gathered price estimates from US hospitals and insurance companies on the worth of the human body. Turns out you're worth somewhere around $45 million! Your bone marrow, for instance, is priced around $23 million, and your DNA at around $9.7 million. Your lungs? they're worth $116,400 apiece, with your kidneys coming in at a whopping $91,400. While you'd never sell your vital parts for cash (nor is that legal), isn't it empowering to know that you're literally worth a fortune? You're already a multimillionaire – literally! How are you tending to your fortune? The way you're valuing or devaluing yourself is sending a powerful message to your unconscious (as well as your Higher Self and the universe at large) as to how much you appreciate the gifts you've been given.

Remember, things that are appreciated increase in value. When you're grateful for what you've got, your offer wave is stating, 'Thank you for this. Send me more. Your wish is my command.'

What I want you to embrace is that you're an absolute treasure, a highly valuable entity. (For instance, 150 pounds of gold is only worth around $1,600,000.) You carry at least $45 million around with you at all times. Think about it – isn't it time to start looking at your worth with a clearer perspective?

You Really Are What You Eat

Research has proven that your diet plays a large part not only in your physical well-being and performance but also in your spiritual evolution. You're not going to grow to your full spiritual capacity with poor nutrition and an out-of-shape body. If you think you're going to scale the mountain of evolved consciousness carrying twenty pounds of excess baggage, think again. You need to monitor what you're putting into your body as vigilantly as you monitor the thoughts you're letting romp through your brain. It's that important.

In the following pages I'm going to give you some of my favourite tips on bringing your physical pillar into harmony, because if you've ever seen me racing around the globe, you know I need a lot of energy to do what I do, and so far, so good. I'm not a nutritionist, and certainly everything I do may not work for everyone. But no matter where I teach, people ask me detailed questions about my health habits and philosophies, and I'm happy to share the practices I've come to believe in and depend on.

You can find a diet philosophy that recommends just about anything, and then turn right around and find something that contradicts it. You may have noticed that there are books that tell you to live on pineapples and grapefruit. Some recommend eating only raw, uncooked foods. Macrobiotic, on the other hand, says that raw food is often too hard to digest. Some vegan books love grains, while others warn you to steer clear. Of course I have my own approach, one I've embraced from a lifetime of trial and error – travelling the world, stressing my body, and being frustrated by all of the varying rules, determined to find answers that work!

I'll start with my general philosophy on goals for wellness, and then give you specific advice on diet, exercise, and bodywork. Then I'll help you pull it all together as part of setting your goals for Harmonic Wealth.

Take what feels right to you, but don't take my word for anything. Test it for yourself – and be sure to check with your doctor and your gut before making any drastic changes.

Obesity Steals Vitality

According to the Centers for Disease Control and Prevention, 64 per cent of American adults aged twenty years are either obese or over-weight and the UK is not far behind. Obesity (defined as being more than 20 per cent above the ideal weight) puts your health at risk for things like type 2 diabetes, heart disease, high blood pressure, strokes, and arthritis. But obesity doesn't just make you a sitting duck for disease; it also contributes to wrinkles and sagging skin. From tests done at St Thomas' Hospital in London, Dr Tim Spector found that a person's body mass heightens oxidative stress and causes accelerated aging at the molecular level.

Unless you have a lot of muscle, which requires another calculation, you can plug in a combination of your height and weight to test yourself to see if you're obese with the body mass index (BMI). A 30-point score (or higher) shows that you're in physical danger, and a score of 25 to 29 shows that you're overweight and need to take action. The National Heart, Lung, and Blood Institute has a simple page online (http://www.nhlbisupport.com/bmi/), and once you enter your height and weight, you get an immediate BMI score to tell you where you stand.

However, if your body has a large portion of muscle, you'll weigh more than the norm and these one-size-fits-all measurements fall flat. One thing that's important to remember when you start working out (and a big issue for many of my female clients especially) is that weight training will often make a person gain weight because muscle weighs more than fat. However, as your body composition changes, you'll be healthier and more fit (and look smaller and leaner, by the way), even when tipping the scales.

So many women have complained to me that the men in their lives tend to lose weight faster than they do. While there are exceptions, of course, this is often the case because of one critical point: a large percentage of women do exercises and aerobics but don't lift weights on a regular basis. Muscle burns calories! If you're not building muscle, you're not going to burn as many calories. That's why everyone needs to incorporate not only aerobic training, but also muscle-building anaerobic training into their lives. If your goal is better fitness, you're going to get there a lot faster by building more muscle, burning more calories, and losing more weight. Make sense?

The most accurate measurement for calculating body fat is an underwater process called hydrostatic weighing, but it's more commonly found in California than anywhere else. A less accurate calculator, but still something I'd recommend if you can't do the hydrostatic approach is called a body composition test, given at most gyms and by many doctors. At least it'll give you a gauge that will move you forward with your health and fitness programme. Using that same measurement calculator each time will allow you to see if you're improving or sliding back.

No Free Lunch

You're smart, so by now you know that there's no easy fix to being out of shape, overweight, and unhealthy. You know you have to get moving and take in fewer calories than you burn off. You're not going to be able to live on fast food (which is fast, but not really food) and look and feel your best. It's just not going to happen.

'But I'm so busy, James. When my schedule slows down I'm going to take better care of myself.' I know. We all are. That excuse is wearing thin, but you're not. Remember that you are who you are now, and your habits are your habits. You can't be other than you are. Doing comes from being. And isn't the opposite true? Being comes from doing. I know people – myself included – who often have better health habits when they're busy, eating less, and eating more simply. A handful of nuts here, apple slices there, water bottle everywhere. In fact, it's often when we have all the time in the world that we lounge around eating snacks, cook up huge gluttonous meals, or spend too much time having lunch with our friends. Busyness can be a blessing, keeping you otherwise occupied and focusing on something other than the ice cream you're craving. Here's a key: never let yourself get too hungry. You'll tend to overeat when you're totally empty and your stomach's growling versus when you're not.

All it takes is a little forethought to bring healthy snacks with you so that you're not famished sitting on the motorway next to the golden arches exit. I travel over two hundred days per year and I always carry a backpack filled with snacks (usually protein bars and raw almonds) and a water bottle – no exceptions. You can do it too and you'll be happier and healthier when you do.

Stop waiting for some far-off wake-up call to motivate you to change your habits. Find a way to take care of yourself and your family right now, regardless of your circumstances. Remember, you're a long-term thinker and planner.

Pay Attention to What's Keeping You Healthy

We all have our areas of addiction. I knew a grossly overweight woman who would eat huge tubs of ice cream every time she felt depressed. She'd feel horrible about herself the second she'd finished, but at the time she was eating, she was fully engaged in the fleeting buzz of her pleasing activity. Only afterwards did she experience the displeasing results of her self-perpetuating cycle. But she never took any steps to break that cycle.

If you're committed to losing weight, you've got to give your time and attention to health and vitality. Consider this: who are you spending your time with? Who are your lunch partners? Who are your dinner companions? What are their habits when it comes to feeding their precious bodies? You may be wondering if that really makes much of a difference. Who you surround yourself with is more important than your genes. Obesity or thinness is contagious. An American study recently discovered that if your friend is heavy, there's a 57 per cent probability that you'll be heavy. If your sibling is heavy, 40 per cent of the time you will be too.

So, if you hang out with people who are fat, chances are you'll be fat too. Think about it: when you go out with your friends and they don't order pudding, do you? If your nearest and dearest are heavy, perhaps you're less critical of the spare tyre around your own middle. The old saying, 'Birds of a feather . . .' – it's the Law of Attraction.

I'm not suggesting that you totally jettison your rotund friends, just that you don't go out to dinner with them frequently, not if you really choose to be healthy and vital. People who typically go out for a burger and a beer are rarely going to choose an eatery specialising in healthy salads. Are you spending time with people who inspire you to take better care of yourself, moving you closer to your goals? Or are you hanging out and investing your time in people whose limiting or negative beliefs and habits drag you down? If they're not supporting you in your goals and dreams, where are they taking you? What about everyone's most popular dinner companion, the TV set? In between the trashy programming, it's broadcasting commercials urging you to stuff your body with more trash.

How do you move your temple through the world? Have you ever thought about the fact that it only takes a few minutes of your time – an investment in yourself – to walk a couple of flights up instead of taking the lift? Just yesterday I was dashing through the airport to a flight, and I jumped on the people mover belt. These things are great when you're moving fast, as you can fly. That is, if other people work with you. I was shocked (and then again I wasn't) as I had to continue saying, 'Excuse me, excuse me,' to a large number of people who were actually just standing there, letting the belt do all the work. *Whatever you do, don't walk. You might get cramp!* Even if I have all the time in the world, this doesn't make sense to me. Besides, it's fun to figure out those last few steps at the end and make sure you hit solid ground at the right speed.

I encourage you to choose the things that strengthen you – the activities that keep you focused and continuously on track to living in Harmonic Wealth.

We're back to attention equals love. If you want to be healthy and strong, you have to pay attention to the habits that keep you lean. Truth be known, some people are in love with being out of shape because they're attending to it all the time. 'Oh, my job keeps me so busy, I just don't have time to eat right.' 'With the kids and my charity work, who's got time for the gym?' 'Who'd want to go out with a fatty like me?' All excuses, good stories to stay comfortably small and safe. Remember, energy flows where attention goes. Every single time you look in the mirror and say something derogatory about your body, you're in love with that out-of-shape self. You love it because you're attending to it all the time.

I was on *The Oprah Winfrey Show* once when a lady asked me, 'How do I use the Law of Attraction to lose weight?'

I said, 'Well, what do you love about your body?'

She sighed. 'Nothing.'

'Right. Okay, back up here a second. What do you love about your body?'

I just kept digging and finally she said, 'Okay, I've got pretty good legs.'

'Great, great, what else do you love?'

'Well, I've got pretty good feet.'

'That's awesome. Do you know how many people have gnarly feet?' Instantly this woman began to shift her attention to what was good and lovable about her body, what she was grateful for.

A shift in consciousness will make all the difference. I worked the same way with a woman in her mid-forties who was ten stone overweight. Think about it – that's the equivalent of carrying around a small adult on your back all day long! She lost more than five stone in a year. The critical shift was as much in her thinking as in the changes she made in her diet. Now, I'm not suggesting she didn't take action. She did, and plenty of it. But the action stemmed from her learning to love and appreciate her current body. As she placed her attention on what was beautiful, she stopped telling herself she didn't have time to work out and she started going to the gym at least three or four times a week. As she placed her attention upon what she loved about herself, she stopped saying she was too busy to cook healthy meals and actually started eating the way the diet books she'd been reading for years recommended. Success breeds success. As she shifted mentally, emotionally, and physically, her image in the mirror began to morph and reflect what she thought and felt. She stopped blaming her over-forty metabolism. No more excuses. A lot more action. Her body and her life were changed – forever!

Remember 3 for 3. Start by asking: *What do I love about my body? What do I appreciate about my body?* As you love and appreciate and are grateful for who you are and what you are, then you begin to take different care of yourself. Suddenly you'll start thinking, *I love my legs, maybe I should go work them out a little bit.*

Energy flows where attention goes. The fastest way to lose weight is to be consistently grateful for the health you have.

Cybernetic Self-Sabotage: Why It's Hard to Change Eating Habits

In the last pillar we talked about Maxwell Maltz's work regarding the cybernetic mechanism, the internal thermostat that regulates how much change you'll make at any one time. Otherwise known as your conditioning or programming, this same mechanism kicks in when you decide to make even positive changes in your diet. Until you're aware of it, it can really sabotage your best intentions to change.

At some time or another, you've probably tried cutting back on sweet things. People around you were eating dessert and you said no. You went to a birthday party and declined the cake. How good did that feel? Then the next night you sat down and devoured an entire packet of chocolate biscuits in ten minutes, wolfed them down like a starving person.

What happened? In the simplest of terms, your cybernetic mechanism measured the deviations between where you were and your goal, and noticed that the temperature had risen to seventy-five degrees. So it kicked your generators on and pumped cool air into the room until the temperature came back to sixty-eight degrees (or sixty-eight biscuits). Then your cybernetic mechanism went, 'Ahh. That's where I'm supposed to be – sitting on the sofa with plenty of sugar. That's my comfort zone. Besides, we all know I'm a fatty anyway.'

Now, please understand that you probably didn't consciously think this. However, in your Unconscious Mind – which is totally out of your awareness – your conditioning or programming is always running and will continue to run until changed.

Eat for Energy Efficiency

Have you ever gone out for a big lunch, then slipped into a food coma at your desk an hour later? What's happening here?

It takes a tremendous amount of energy to digest your food. When you fill your stomach with foods that are harder to digest, such as meat, more of your body's resources are called in to aid the digestive process. If you eat a lot of the white devils – white bread, pasta, rice, and potatoes – you get a quick spike of energy, then a huge plummet. The result: food coma!

Fruit and vegetables take a lot less energy to digest than meat. As you'll see below, I'm not suggesting that we all become vegetarians. Been there, done that – didn't work. What I am suggesting is that you take a look at putting only high-performance fuel into your body.

Any extra energy going towards digestion is energy you're giving away. We don't get energy, we give it. It doesn't make sense to run your system a lot to get a little. As a kid, I watched a cartoon that showed a toothpick factory where they took a big tree and shaved it down to a single toothpick. Now I'm sure it was a high-quality toothpick, but not worth the energy invested for what they received in return. You want to make energy-efficient choices in what you eat.

Carbonated drinks are a perfect example of an energy-inefficient substance. Brief sugar jolt, huge food coma payback. Plus the acidity will kill enzymes in your body and literally kill you – I'm not kidding! A recent study in the *American Journal of Clinical Nutrition* reported that a can a day can add up to fifteen pounds a year. Even more than that, a recent survey published on CNN found that individuals who have only one fizzy drink a day have a greater likelihood of heart attack. Replacing your favourite soft drink with a bottle of water can save you 120 calories a day, or 15 pounds a year, and it might just save your life.

Back to the Stone Age

If you want to trim down, eat mostly meat and vegetables. I'm a big advocate of what researchers call the Paleolithic diet. But the key is lean meat and a LOT of high-water-content vegetables (the vegetables help digest the meat easier and in less time). Personally, I choose not to eat red meat, even though I like it. I eat primarily fish and some chicken.

It's a fact that the amount of grain we feed our beef cattle, if redeployed, would solve world hunger. Also bovine belching and flatulence are major contributors to global warming and ozone depletion. It just seems like an easy sacrifice to make for me. You see, this is another great example of how all the pillars work together. The choices that you make nutritionally can affect your relationship and harmony with the world at large.

Here's the really cool thing about this way of eating: you'll *never* have to count calories. Just cut out those white devils – pasta, pizza, bread, rice, and potatoes – and you'll lose weight and have tons of energy. You can't eat enough vegetables to get fat even if you tried. But again, don't just do it for appearances; do it for your health and vitality. As for me, I'm going green inside and outside, my friend – as within, so without.

I eat good levels of protein every day. When I was bodybuilding, I ate too much and it just packed on the fat. Your body can only digest 24 to 32 grams every three to four hours. Any more and you're into excess. In case you're wondering, I never count how many grams I take in either – forget that. Just have a lean piece of fish or chicken with each meal (make sure and pull the skin off the chicken before cooking – this is where the majority of fat resides), and you'll get plenty of protein.

I eat a lot of dark greens. I love sushi: I could eat sushi four times a week and not be tired of it. Asian cultures eat lots of rice and they have low rates of heart disease and cancer. I think it's because the health benefits of the fish and seaweed offset the rice. I've done a lot of research on the Paleolithic diet and think it makes a lot of sense. Our ancestors didn't eat potatoes, rice, or bread. Hundreds of thousands of years ago human body chemistry evolved to match an environment that changed extremely slowly. That environment had no grains or sugar, and certainly no abundance. But today, in only a few generations, we've made enormous changes in that environment and our bodies haven't been able to keep up with them. The book *Health Secrets of the Stone Age,* by Philip J. Goscienski, MD (a pediatric infectious diseases specialist with a forty-five-year career in clinical and academic medicine), links our modern dietary excesses to the rise in diseases that were rare until early in the last century, including chronic diseases and the twin epidemics of obesity and diabetes.

We can tell from fossil evidence that Stone Age men were strong. They showed no evidence of osteoporosis. Present-day hunter-gatherers, who live the same lifestyle and who follow the same subsistence pattern, typically enter the sixth or seventh decade of life without obesity, hypertension, coronary artery disease, and diabetes.

Interestingly, according to a report on ABC News, Americans have recently become the shortest (not to mention the fattest) population in the industrialised world. We used to be the tallest nation in the world, starting in colonial times when our president, George Washington, measured 6'2". Currently, in the Netherlands Dutch men average 6'. In America 5'10". Why aren't we as tall as we used to be? It's how we live. Aside from healthcare deficiencies here in America in our early lives, researchers suspect that our fast-food diets are mostly to blame. Overeating and growth hormones in our junk food cause kids to grow quickly and stop growing at younger ages. 'Height says a lot about a country's well-being,' the report said.

Eating a Stone Age diet with plenty of lean meat and vegetables can help you avoid many of the illnesses of modern times. Leafy dark green vegetables, for example, help to beat osteoporosis.

Many of my clients have been surprised that as a spiritual man I still eat meat. I understand their confusion. I was a strict vegan for five years, and I really bought into the idea that it was spiritual. But I got fat and weak because I was eating pasta, rice, and bread all the time. I had a thirty-seven-inch waist (now it's thirty-three). When you're doing high-energy work, pulling energy into your body for the advancement of consciousness, you've got to have some meat. One of the reasons new agers are sometimes so airy-fairy is that they can't stay grounded. When I study in the jungles and do rituals, the shamans take me off all meat because they want me to soar. But one shaman in particular, one schooled in the West as well as the jungles, helped me understand that if you want to operate in the third dimension and have an intelligible conversation, you've got to stay grounded.

Integration is about being *in* the world but not *of* the world. When I wouldn't eat anything with a face, I wasn't grounded. My muscles started to atrophy. I was told that I would get brittle bones. My teacher at the time told me I needed protein, and I started buying organic chicken and fish so I could strengthen my body with the least environmental impact.

You may be a vegetarian, and if your reasoning comes from a humane place where you just can't justify the killing of animals, I respect that. I've been there and I understand it – totally. I just have a question you might not have thought of: if we stop killing animals for food, do they stop killing each other for food? As hard as it is to wrap our minds around killing anything, perhaps being part of the food chain is part of the bigger plan. I'll ask you at least to consider that animals are going to die no matter what – just like we are. That's why shopping organic is all that much more important, to ensure that the animals are treated with greater care.

Eat Less, Live Longer

Want to live longer and have more energy? Don't eat so much food! I apply this principle in my own life, and there's a lot of research to support it.

There are more than 76,000 people in the USA at the hundred-year-old mark or older. Recently, Harvard researchers studied a number of centenarians to see if there was any correlation between their age and how they lived their lives. They were a varied bunch. Some of them ate bacon every single day, others smoked cigarettes until they were a hundred, some exercised, some didn't. The one common denominator? They all ate light, minimal meals. In other words, they were nearly undernourished.

This doesn't mean that you need to follow the Buddha and sit under the Bodhi tree until you can count the vertebrae in your spine from the front of your body. The Gandhi fasting diet will never catch on in the West – I'm sure of it. I'm not talking about starving and we're not discussing making a fashion statement either. We're talking about making sure your body uses everything you give it. Living at a tolerable level of hunger before you eat means that you're eating to refuel, not for entertainment, out of habit, or for emotional fulfilment. Some research suggests that if you take in 30 per cent fewer calories every day, you'll extend your life by 30 per cent. So, if you want to eat more food, then here's the secret: stay around longer and eat all that food over time. Eat less to eat more. As my good friend Dr John Demartini says, 'You'll add life to your years and years to your life.'

Acid Eats Your Body

Current statistics tell us that 38 per cent of Americans get cancer. Most doctors agree that cancer thrives in an oxygen-deprived environment. Cells with a higher, more alkaline pH are higher in oxygen. So, my priority is keeping my system slightly alkaline at all times, with a pH ranging from 7.35 to 7.45. I usually clock in around 7.4.

The following are some great alkaline-forming foods (not to be considered all-inclusive):

apples, apricots, bananas, berries, melon, cherries, dates, figs, grapes, grapefruit, oranges, peaches, pears, strawberries, tangerines, watermelon, wheat grass, most edible grasses and their juices, sprouts, grains and beans, fresh cucumbers, spinach, celery, watercress, garlic, cayenne pepper, endive, green beans, cabbage, lettuce, red cabbage, fresh peas, horseradish, parsley, coriander, lime, fresh lemon, tomato, green pepper, avocado, aubergine, rhubarb stalks, lima beans, fresh soya beans, baking soda, sea salt, seaweed, asparagus, Brazil nuts, artichokes, raw sweet potato, almonds, hazelnuts, pumpkin seeds, sunflower seeds, flax seeds, sesame seeds

The following are some acid-forming foods (again, not to be considered all-inclusive):

Pork, veal, beef, sausages, bacon, turkey, chicken, sea fish, eggs, white bread, white rice, white biscuits, shrimp, lobster, crab, pastries, cakes, pasta, macaroni and cheese, sugar, corn syrup, artificial sweeteners, popped corn, spirits, wine, beer, coffee, sweetened fruit juice, milk, ketchup, mayonnaise, prepared mustard, most microwaved foods, most canned foods, all fried foods, ice cream, pudding, jam, jelly, all sweets, packaged snack foods, peanuts, cashews, walnuts, chocolate, cola, and all soft drinks

I recommend using pH test papers (used with urine or saliva) several times per day. These are relatively easy to find at most health food stores and pharmacies. Food and drink aren't the only factors. Regular exercise, meditation, and stress reduction also have a positive effect upon the body's pH levels.

A Piping Hot Mug of Battery Acid

What you drink can affect your pH as much as what you eat, and when it comes to lowering your pH and spiking acid, coffee is a major offender.

I used to drink a pot of coffee every day, so I don't judge anyone. I was a wreck when I came off the stuff: acne on my face, foul breath, headaches, and a shaking body. Some logic would say, 'This is bad; I'd better go back to the stuff,' but I understood that I was detoxing. We don't tend to value detoxification in our society. When your nose is running, your intelligent body has something it's trying to purge. But what do we do? We take medicine to keep it in. I say, 'Better out than in.' If your body has mucus, toxins, and poisons and wants to get rid of them, and you take something to suppress that, you're basically saying, 'I want to keep that crap inside me.' When I was detoxing from coffee, my body intuitively knew it didn't want or need that caffeine and acidity.

Alcohol

The latest research in health and longevity are loudly touting the benefits of resveratrol, a compound found largely in the skin of red grapes. While still uncertain, many scientists believe this to be the substance found in red wine that's known to decrease heart disease and cancer. Whether resveratrol is indeed the amazing answer to the French paradox – why some argue that the French suffer a lower incidence of coronary heart disease despite having a diet rich in saturated fats – or not remains to be proved, but we do know that red wine in moderation (emphasis on moderation – and not white wine, which is pure sugar) has definite health benefits. My anti-aging doctor believes strongly in the resveratrol research and recommended that I drink more red wine. I like a good Pinot Noir with a nice dinner, but I'm such a lightweight, I'm gone after two glasses. So, I take a resveratrol supplement instead.

Clean, Clear Water

Your body is comprised of 70 per cent water, so after oxygen, water is the most important nutrient. A dehydrated cell is a dead or unhealthy cell. A friend who lives in Las Vegas tells me the number one cause for admittance into A and E there is dehydration. Under a microscope, the difference between a healthy hydrated cell and an unhealthy dehydrated cell is best illustrated by the difference between a grape and a raisin. Bottom line, if you have raisin cells you can bet you're going to have a raisin face sooner than later!

My experience and research suggests that you should drink a minimum of 1.5 litres of pure water per 100 pounds of body weight per day. Obviously, your climate, ingestion of diuretics such as caffeine and alcohol, and other factors will affect this.

I'm talking about pure water, not the polluted water you find in fizzy drinks, coffees, and teas. Herbal teas are preferable (green tea especially), but they're diuretics and leach water from your body.

Most people tell me it's too hard to drink enough water. This is most often due to two things: force of habit and drinking too many polluted liquids. People also tell me that when they start drinking more water, they have to go to the bathroom too often. From my experience this is temporary and once your body gets accustomed to being hydrated, it'll settle down.

I drink one gallon of water every day at least. I have it delivered to my home. I just had a water filtering system placed in my office, which is much more eco friendly, and I plan on doing so in my home soon. I've heard that tap water is good in some places, like in some deserts, but I sure wouldn't recommend you drink it in most cities. I personally never drink it anywhere – ever. The trouble with buying water in shops is that you have no idea how long that stuff has been sitting on the shelf, and some plastic can break down and get into the water and pollute it. Also, some brands of bottled water are nothing more than filtered tap water. Add that to plastic fragments and you're probably doing yourself no favours.

I buy oxygenated water drops and put them into my water. I also mix aloe into my water for my internal organs and chlorophyll to keep my system alkalised.

You Are What You Eat – Really!

Again, we both know I'm not a nutritionist, but I know what works for me and what seems to work for those individuals I work with. Here's how I put all the principles I've just discussed to work in my diet.

As I've mentioned, I stay healthy and vibrant by eating a good mix of protein and carbohydrate – lean meats and vegetables – and minimising my fat intake. I'm a big advocate of vegetable carbohydrates, but I stay away from starchy carbs because they can have a dramatic effect on your insulin levels, cause your body to hold fat, and mess with your energy levels. I think of most starchy carbs as dead food. (Think there's much life left in that serving of boiled pasta?) It you're going to eat starch, go for healthful organic oatmeal and brown rice instead. Generally, I prefer vegetables because they're higher in water content, have more roughage, and make your system more alkaline. I use organic ingredients whenever possible because they don't contain pesticides and buying them helps support more responsible farming.

Pack your diet on a regular basis with plenty of salad and green vegetables and you'll not only live longer but you'll be stronger and healthier in the process. A good rule of thumb is the 80:20 rule: 80 per cent alkalising vegetables and 20 per cent healthy acid-forming foods like lean meats.

It's healthy to have frequent smaller meals throughout the day. When your eating is inconsistent, it tends to cramp your intestines and cause stomach problems. I eat small meals every three hours. Breakfast, snack, then lunch, then snack, then dinner, so I'm eating around five times a day. Really, 99 times out of 100, I don't feel full. I eat to the point of satisfaction because a long time ago I decided to eat to live versus live to eat.

I start every day with a glass of water with lemon juice. Even though lemons are acidic, the way the body processes them leaves an alkaline residue.

I follow that with my veggie drink, which I make in the blender. I prefer a blender to a juicer for a couple of reasons. First, a blender leaves all the roughage of the vegetable or fruit, and second, it's a hell of a lot easier to clean. I remember when I used to juice, it seemed like all I ever did was scrub the thing.

My life-extension doctor gave me an awesome recipe for a blended drink that not only helps the system become more alkaline, but also removes excess estrogen that can cause disease from the body. I use all organic ingredients:

1 handful Chinese leaves – just tear off a few

1 small baby pak choi or 1 large leaf and stem from large pak choi

1 carrot

Blueberries or raspberries for the antioxidants (fresh or frozen – I buy them frozen and put in half the bag)

About 3/4 pint water

Blend with added supplements if desired.

I blend this up and drink it before the gym. It took a while to get used to it, but now I really enjoy the taste. When I'm on the road and can't make my concoction, I take my supplements – green capsules – first thing.

I like porridge in the morning after my veggie drink. It's a complex carbohydrate that has healthy oils for your brain. The carbs spike insulin, so I mix in protein powder to help offset the insulin spike and a little non-fat organic milk to keep it from getting too thick. Oh, and blueberries to add flavour and antioxidants.

For my first snack I have ⅓ cup of nuts and ⅓ cup of raisins or dried cranberries (carbs and proteins). I eat a lot of nuts.

When I use salt, which isn't often, I make sure it's sea salt. Normal table salt is devoid of minerals, but sea salt contains over fifty trace minerals.

I eat salad all the time. Greens are a great energy source and I go for dark green lettuce and vegetables because they have the greatest nutrition. Spinach or mixed greens are great, while other than the high water content, iceberg is a waste of time (but still better than a burger and fries). Since restaurant servings of lettuce are often too small, I'll ask if it's a meal portion when ordering. My philosophy is that if you're paying for your meal, you might as well get what you want. I'm not a pain about it. If I don't get what I want I'll say, 'Would you be so kind as to find a way to get me more lettuce?' or 'What would have to happen to get me a bigger portion here?' It's that simple.

Seaweed is my thrice-weekly staple, lovingly wrapped around sushi. The oceans of this world are filled with underwater plants that have absorbed vital minerals that can be harvested for our consumption. They're renewable, don't threaten endangered fish populations, and are some of the most nutrient-dense foods available anywhere. Your local health food store will carry flakes, sheets, or capsules, so it's easy to find a way to eat seaweed that suits your taste buds. I also request wild-caught fish whenever I go out, which is healthier than farmed. I advise going online and checking for mercury rates in your area, which can be dangerously high. Some fish have higher densities of mercury than others.

I stay away from refined sugar – it isn't energy-efficient, and the crash that comes after the initial rush is dramatic. If you miss chocolate, try eating raw cacao nibs. These beanlike 'nuts' are one of the most powerful sources of magnesium found anywhere on the planet. Studies show that a large percentage of us don't consume the daily recommended amounts of magnesium, resulting in many common health problems like migraines, attention deficit disorder, fibromyalgia, asthma, and allergies. Raw cacao beans are a mood elevator without the crash you get from sugar in the chocolate you're used to eating, since they contain tryptophan, an amino acid that helps produce soothing serotonin in your brain. This form of chocolate won't be as sweet as your taste buds have become accustomed to with chocolate (they can be downright bitter when eaten alone), but when used in trail mix with raisins or thrown into a smoothie, you'll appreciate the effects.

If you haven't tried raw, organic honey yet, you might like it if you have a craving for sweet things. My friends' teenage son stuck his finger in a jug of it recently and freaked. 'That's like candy!' he exclaimed. The real deal – straight from the bees without being cooked – contains important enzymes, phytonutrients, and a high level of antioxidants, which can restore muscle glycogen following exercise and help lower cholesterol. Some studies link it to a reduced risk for certain cancers. The best raw honey is the organic kind collected from bees drawn to local wildflowers – without the chemicals added to nonorganic honey. So, if you're craving something sweet, resist the temptation to reach for sugar and grab some raw honey instead. (One note of caution, however: don't feed raw honey to babies because the spores in it can cause illness to children with immature immune systems.)

Your best bet is to slowly condition yourself away from sweets of any kind. This, along with plenty of green vegetables and proteins, will keep your energy high and cause the ups and downs to disappear. Even natural sweets mess with your insulin levels and give you some energetic roller coaster moments. I never use sugar or artificial sweeteners – or even honey, for that matter – because I don't need them anymore. If I can do this, so can you. I was the guy who used to put five sweeteners in his coffee!

Daily Supplements

Perhaps nobody takes more supplements than I do. Many try to tell me, 'My grandfather never took supplements and he lived to be 100.' Well, you're not eating the same food Grandpa ate.

I highly recommend a really good multivitamin and plenty of essential fatty acids because your body needs this good fat for healthy skin, good joints, and plenty of energy. Contrary to popular belief, this kind of healthy fat will not make you fat. In fact, if you *don't* take in enough fat, your body will hang onto the fat you have because it needs it. Research has also found that essential fatty acids aid tremendously in brain function; they dramatically increase alpha brain waves – the brain vibrations created in a relaxed creative state. I take up to 15 grams per day of essential fatty acids (which is a lot) and my body is not fat. Also, my dermatologist constantly compliments me on my skin.

When looking for a good multivitamin, make sure you get one that your doctor recommends or that comes from a legitimate health food store. Many of the chain health food stores carry supplements that are packed with fillers and synthetic garbage. If you start working with hormone-related supplements like DHEA, pregnenalone, melatonin, and the like, I strongly recommend you do so under the guidance of a well-educated doctor in this field – emphasis on well-educated. Most doctors have very little knowledge of this area unless they've chosen to specialise. This goes back to the quick-fix mentality of our culture. Most of us would rather take a quick-fix medication and put a plaster on an open wound than deal with the cause and eliminate the wound.

Prayer: Laying Down the Vibes

The way I prepare to eat my food is as important as what I eat. I believe very strongly in pausing for a moment of gratitude and performing a type of blessing to send good energy into my food. Every time I sit in front of a meal, I rub my palms together several times, as I was taught to do in the mystical traditions before performing any kind of energetic work, because it ignites the palm chakras. I immediately feel an increase in energy before placing my hands over my food.

If I'm sitting with other people and don't want to make a scene (which can be comical with sushi, with all the different plates delivered in intervals), I hold my hands briefly over the food and just breathe. I go to that calm space I go to in meditation, shift my brain-wave patterns, and send that energy through my body into the food. I can keep my eyes open and continue talking with clients while my hands are over my food and a lot of times they don't even notice. If they do ask what I'm doing, I just say I'm taking a moment to be grateful for this food.

At my home, however, I'll hold my palms over my meal for a longer interval, really open my heart, and send out thoughts of gratitude not only for the meal before me but also for everything in my life. It's not the traditional type of prayer or grace I grew up with – 'Dear God, bless this food to the good of my body . . .' – but I know I'm helping to ensure that no matter what I'm eating, it's getting a jolt of good vibrations.

If you want a powerful visual for how our cells respond to our thoughts, I refer you to the work of Dr Masaru Emoto from Japan. His photographs, highlighted in the movie *What the Bleep Do We Know?* and in a series of books starting with *The Hidden Messages in Water*, are proof that thoughts and feelings affect physical reality.

Using a powerful microscope in a very cold room, along with high-speed photography, Dr Emoto developed a way to photograph newly formed crystals of frozen water samples. Then he asked subjects to direct specific, concentrated thoughts towards them, for example, *I love you* or *I hate you*. Sometimes he played beautiful music in the presence of the water, at other times harsh, discordant music. His cameras recorded that clear springwater, when exposed to loving words, shows brilliant, complex, and colourful snowflake patterns. In contrast, polluted water, or water that's been exposed to negative thoughts, forms incomplete, asymmetrical patterns with dull colours.

The implications are vast, since our bodies, some of the food we eat, and the entire planet are all over 70 per cent water. Those of us trained in shamanic and mystical traditions are elated to see his technology make sense of our often misunderstood practices. The implications of this research create a new awareness of how we can positively affect the Earth and our personal health. If saying 'I love you' and projecting that intention to a water bottle can produce beautiful snowflake patterns, why wouldn't putting your hands and positive thoughts over a plate of lettuce do equally beneficial things inside your own body?

The Futility of Fanaticism

So, the basics of my personal rules: eat lean meats and lots of vegetables, stay away from simple carbohydrates, always eat organic whenever possible, only drink pure water, avoid sugar, and snack on nuts – pretty simple. But let me make a disclaimer here: if you become a fanatic about your diet, you become a prisoner. If you walk around thinking and saying, 'If I don't eat organic, I get a headache,' or 'Every time I eat oils, I get acne,' or 'Butter goes straight to my thighs,' your Unconscious Mind says, 'Okay, your wish is my command,' and then works to give you the headache, the zits, or the cellulite. You've just programmed yourself to believe these 'facts' and therefore put yourself in bondage.

Give yourself a rest. You're human!

Given the choice, yes, I always buy organic. But I'm on the road two hundred days a year, so how often do you think I get the pleasure of ingesting pesticides with my salads? So, if I believed my body was in danger every time I ate away from home, I'd never get out of bed.

Do the best you can and let the rest go. You'll be far easier to be with and you'll be much more at peace. If I'm invited to dinner at a friend's house and all they're serving are big plates of pasta covered in butter, I eat it and enjoy it because my relationship with my friends is more important than my relationship with food. It's not what you do once or twice that makes a huge impact – it's your consistent habits that determine the results in your life. I encourage you to have flexibility so that if you do something different, it doesn't change your core habits.

That's another reason I like blessing my food. Knowing that I can change the energy of my food helps me to feel less fanatical about what I eat, less imprisoned by beliefs around food. People ask me all the time how I can eat airline food. I don't have a belief that I have to overcome airline food. I do what I always do: hold my hands over the food and let the rest go. I eat the lettuce, the vegetables, and the cardboard meat, and leave the roll and slice of cheesecake for the guy in seat 3B with the add-on belt extension.

There's room for some fanaticism depending on who you are and where you are in your life. If you're twenty pounds or more overweight, I'd say, 'Never eat pizza or bread or a piece of cake, *ever*, until you're back in shape.' That sounds harsh, I know, but when you get to the place where your health and vitality are where you want them to be, then you can pick and choose. But being a little fanatical at first can get you there fast; big results come from bold action.

20

Exercise: Moving Towards Life

A healthy body is a guest-chamber for the soul;
a sick body is a prison.
– FRANCÌS BACON

Move as If Your Life Depended on It – It Does

Exercise makes you feel better and have more energy. It's a major component of a life of health and fulfilment.

Our bodies are filled with toxins from the air we breathe and from the pesticides on the food we eat. Our good health depends on moving them out of our system. That's one of the things exercise does: gets the blood and lymphatic systems pumping. Doctors of longevity tell us that all that increased blood flow is good for the brain and also lifts our mood. Consider this: dozens of studies have been conducted with people who suffer from depression, and the results show that a walk around the block is one of the best treatments going. It seems that depressed people feel better when they're taken outside to smell the air, feel the sunshine, get moving, and oxygenate their system.

Years ago, when I first started personal coaching in Atlanta, I was hired by Richard, a guy in his late forties who wanted me to help him get his life back. Richard was a manic-depressive who was on numerous medications from the psychiatrist he'd been seeing for years. He also had a daily routine that would make anyone depressed. Basically, Richard would take his pills, sit on the sofa in front of the plug-in drug, and feel sorry for himself all day long. He hadn't worked in years.

The first thing I did was tell him that he had to take a walk around his neighbourhood with a pad and pen every day at 12.37 p.m. He was to write his observations in great detail. This was to be done on time, all the time, and if he ever missed, I would fire him as a client. I then told him he was to bring me a detailed report on his reflections each week. The timing and the execution of this exercise were imperative and had to be carried out impeccably – all would be revealed shortly. I delivered this assignment with much pomp and circumstance, emphasising its importance to our overall project together. Little did he know that I just pulled the time, the pad, and the pen exercise right out of thin air because I wanted him to get out of the house. I wanted to help him feel as if he had an important task to accomplish; I wanted him to have movement *and* meaning.

I was simultaneously working with him on how he held memories, how he thought and felt in various areas of his life. It seems that he had set up a self-fulfilling downward spiral psychologists call secondary gain. In other words, deep inside he believed that his situation brought him the emotional attention he desired from his wife and others. It also gave him excuses for not doing many things he disliked. I assisted him in finding new and more empowering ways to get the same attention, as well as being able to do more of what he loved. As he began to shift his attention, his world model followed suit. Remember, quantum physics tells us that we hold our current world together with our attention – energy flows where attention goes. Within less than three weeks he was off all medications and preparing to go back to work. His wife called me, crying, filled with gratitude, stating that she finally had her husband back again.

High-energy performance comes from motion. So, how much do you move? Many of us have jobs that keep us sitting at our desks for most of the day. If you're one of those people, get up and move around every hour or so, even if it's just to get a glass of water. Again, take the stairs. It is probably not as comfortable initially, but the more you do, the more comfortable it will become.

Commit to getting out and getting fresh air and sunshine, particularly if you're in a building that has poor and/or limited ventilation. You'll feel better and you'll be more productive when you return to your desk. After suffering from daily bouts of midday depression, my friend's mother started walking to a park in her lunch hour to sit by a rose bush to read and eat her lunch. That made all the difference to her mood and her day.

Your Personal Best

To achieve a truly harmonic physical pillar, you need to integrate structured exercise into your life. Think of this structure as a scaffolding with three elements: building stronger muscles, a stronger heart, and a more flexible body.

Exercise takes motivation and most people make the mistake of thinking they have to be motivated to start exercising. But that's faulty logic. Do the thing and you'll get the energy to do the thing. Start exercising and you'll get motivated, not the other way around. Haven't you ever felt exhausted or even a little sluggish and the minute you started running around, you felt renewed? Movement increases serotonin in your brain and will make you feel better. So get your bum up off the sofa!

Building Stronger Muscles

Man or woman, the same is true for all of us: we need muscle. We've been given muscle for a reason and if we don't use it, we'll lose it. We're only made up of a few things – water, fat, muscle, and bone. If we don't use a muscle in seventy-two hours, we get about a 40 per cent atrophy of muscle tones. That's not a pretty picture because if we lose our muscle, then we're more water and fat.

As we grow older, our bones lose density. Applying any kind of stress to our muscles, which is what we do when we lift weights, for example, builds up bone density. Muscle mass also decreases as we age; exercise can help reclaim it.

Have you ever wondered why elderly people fall so often? It's usually because they don't have strong thigh muscles. If you work your thighs every day, just by sitting down and getting up over and over, you'll be far less likely to fall because your legs will stay strong. Think about it; if you can easily get in and out of a chair well into your later years, you can help prevent the falls and broken hips that are the number one reason people go into nursing homes today.

Choose a rigorous weight-bearing exercise you enjoy and stick with it. Whether it's weightlifting or heavy work of some type makes no difference – hiking and dancing are great as well – as long as you place stress upon your muscles on a frequent basis and then follow with the needed rest and recuperation.

To build muscle, you need progressive resistance, meaning that you gradually stress your muscles more and more. I apply this principle when I lift weights, increasing the number of repetitions and weights little by little. The idea is to work very intensely in short bursts. When I see people chatting away on their mobiles while they're doing curls, I think, *They're doing nothing. It's a waste of time. They might as well be having a cup of coffee.*

Helping Your Heart

I believe we all need around thirty minutes of aerobic exercise at least five days a week. At the minimum, with rare exceptions, I do aerobics and yoga every single day – even on the days I don't lift weights. Often people ask me, 'Do you think you should work out every single day?'

I answer, 'Do you eat every day?'

Exercise is either aerobic or anaerobic. Anaerobic exercise is brief, intense exercise where your heart rate is at 80 per cent of maximum capability or above and you're taking in large amounts of oxygen. It's working the heart, but it's not burning fat. Weightlifting, sprinting, and intense interval training are anaerobic. Aerobic exercise works the heart below 80 per cent of its maximum capacity for a longer time; examples are running or walking on the treadmill, using the cross-trainer, swimming, or cycling. While anaerobic exercise builds muscle tissue, aerobic exercise helps strengthen the heart and burns fat. You need to incorporate both kinds of exercise into your fitness routine for maximum health. A good example of the different results of aerobic versus anaerobic exercise is a distance runner versus a sprinter. The distance runner runs for long distances at a slower pace while the sprinter goes full-on for a short distance. The distance runner's legs look like pieces of lean meat, while the sprinter's legs look like oak trees. Get the difference?

To get heart benefits, the key is to go slow and steady, so you can go for thirty minutes, boosting your heart rate but not burning out. Aim to keep your heart rate at about 60 per cent of capacity, which burns fat. Fat is a slow-burning fuel, so keep your pace on slow burn. Most gyms now have equipment with built-in devices to check your heart rate. If yours doesn't, the next best thing is to buy a good heart rate monitor. If you're exercising aerobically, you'll be able to carry on a conversation without huffing, puffing, and gasping for air.

Flexible Body, Flexible Mind

An inflexible body is a reflection of an inflexible mind.

On a physical level, it's crucial to stay mobile and fluid. Ask yourself this: when you wake up in the morning and you feel stiff, maybe in your back or neck or knees, do you feel young or old?

Rigidity and rigor mortis are closely linked.

For years I lifted weights religiously but neglected to stretch. At the time I was locked into the mass mentality that venerates physical appearance. Everyone could see the benefits of my lifting; no one could tell whether I was flexible or not, so I didn't pay any attention to that. Unfortunately, after years of heavy lifting and no stretching, I was musclebound and tight. My father was constantly telling me to stand up straight, to which I would angrily reply, 'I am!' The truth was that I was standing up as straight as I could but my chest and shoulder muscles were so tight that they were permanently contracted. After my first exposure to Rolfing (which totally changed my posture), I adopted the daily practice of yoga.

Many in the West believe that yoga means putting your big toe in your ear, but increasing flexibility is just one aspect of yoga. The word *yoga* translated from the Sanskrit means 'yoke' or 'union', and this body of knowledge is a comprehensive spiritual practice. Increasing flexibility, inversion, torsion, strength, and the ability to breathe deeply are yogic preparation for meditation. While meditation and spiritual practice are vital keys to growth as well as longevity, at this juncture I'm actually only speaking of hatha yoga, which is the bodily practice of the yogic path.

Regardless of whether you attend a yoga class or not, it's a good idea to learn enough of the postures to stretch your shoulders and chest, hips, lower back, hamstrings, and thighs on a daily basis. Think about it – what's the first thing a dog or cat does after getting up from a nap? Stretch! (But of course we're smarter than they are, aren't we?)

Your Exercise Routine

So here's the game plan. Lift weights to rev up your metabolism into a fat-burning machine and tone your body. Tone your most important muscle – your heart – with aerobic exercise. Do some stretching to keep everything flexible and supple.

Join a gym? Get a personal trainer? Work out with a friend? It doesn't matter which route you go, as long as you *go*! Please don't tell me you can't afford gym membership. You can't afford not to have one. Are you going to tell me your schedule's too tight to get yourself to a gym? Fine – you've got a million tapes and DVDs you can use at home to work out. Don't have room for a set of dumbbells? Fine, grab some water jugs or cans from the cupboard.

Are you getting me by now? I won't buy your excuses. Every excuse you throw at me is just a story to keep yourself stuck. But let's not talk about stories and excuses. Let's get inspired. Let's talk about results! A friend showed me the Body-for-Life website. Every year they sponsor a contest for people who want to follow their programme of diet and exercise for twelve weeks. In 2000, the winner for the inspirational category was Jared Horomona, a man whose cerebral palsy has made it impossible for him to stand unaided. At the end of the challenge, Jared looked like one of the Spartan warriors in the movie *300*. He's since run two New York City marathons on crutches. My friend Sean Stephenson was born with a rare bone disease and was predicted to die in infancy. The disease caused his bones to be very brittle, breaking over two hundred times and confining him to a wheelchair. Sean is a professional speaker, and whenever we're in the same town, I invariably see him in the hotel gym working up a healthy lather. When you go 3 for 3, anything is possible.

It's a good idea to work with a trainer to customise a weightlifting routine that works for you. All those fancy machines at the gym can look pretty intimidating, and it helps to have someone take you through how to use them. A trainer can also be really helpful in showing you proper technique and safety tips, not to mention motivating you to stick with it. As you progress with your workouts, it's great to have a buddy to go to the gym with, someone who can cheer you on to help you reach your fitness goals.

An initial consultation with a trainer can also help you zero in on an aerobic exercise that fits your fitness level, interest, and skills. Just be sure you pick an exercise that lets you monitor your heart rate and stay in your own aerobic zone. If you want to go to a class, then just know you have to work out for results; you're not there to compete or compare with others. You won't always be able to be a good little student and follow instructions if they're not taking you towards your goal.

There's nothing better than a great yoga instructor to make sure you're positioning your body correctly. I love a well-led class even though it's rare these days that I make one due to my travel schedule. However, there are tons of top-notch yoga tapes and DVDs out there, not to mention ones for just stretching. You can master a few strategic moves and do them every morning on your own.

My Exercise Plan

People are always asking me what my own fitness routine is. I'm going to share it here, not because I want you to rush out and duplicate it, but so you can get a sense of how to combine weightlifting, aerobics, and stretching into a busy day. The key is to find the exercise you like, and switch it up when you crave a change of pace.

When I'm in my hometown, I typically work out with weights three days in a row and then take a day off (other than my aerobic exercise, which is daily because I believe you should move your body every day somehow or some way). I lift for twenty to thirty minutes, which is a huge breakthrough for me – for the guy who used to lift for two hours twice a day. But I also recognise that the whole acid/alkaline issue is very important, and extensive lifting builds too much acid in the body.

Here's what my four-day cycles look like:

Day 1. Chest and back. I believe you should always work from the largest muscle group to the smallest, so I start with a movement for my back. I then immediately do something for my chest, with no rest or pause in between because my back is resting but my chest is fresh. Then right away I do something for my abs, and finally I take a break for a minute or so. This type of training in the bodybuilding world is called supersetting. Once I'm done with all nine sets (three different exercises for three sets each per body part), I'll do thirty minutes of aerobic exercise.

Day 2: Shoulders, arms, and abs in this same fashion. Again, I follow with thirty minutes of aerobics.

Day 3: Legs and abs followed by thirty minutes of aerobics.

Day 4: I take the day off. Often I'll still do thirty minutes of aerobic exercise. It depends on how I feel. If I feel like I need to rest, I do. But even if I take the day off from the gym I still do my yoga movements in the morning.

I see a lot of people just going through the motions in the gym and really getting nowhere. Weightlifting is often called progressive resistance training for a reason. If you're not progressively taxing your muscles, they adapt and you (and they alike) get little if any benefit. To get ongoing benefit, you must consistently increase your workout intensity. There are only two ways to increase your intensity: 1) consistently increase the weight you're lifting (very difficult to do indefinitely) or 2) decrease the time.

In a busy schedule, I've found that the decreased time approach gives me the benefit of consistently making it harder for my muscles to perform and therefore increases the ongoing intensity. By mixing up my exercises after hitting twelve reps on any one movement, I never allow my body to get fully comfortable so it must constantly adapt. It's really important to emphasise here that moving quickly through a movement that is easy to get your designated repetitions in is a waste of time. Go to the pub instead. Have a bag of crisps while you're at it.

The key here is that the last two repetitions must be very difficult to complete, and by moving in supersets with very little rest, your muscles never fully recover between sets. Hence, constant intensity for a brief time (like a sprinter) builds strong bodies and minds as well. Your mind will often tell you to stop this nonsense when your muscles are burning and you still haven't totally caught your breath. But you'll have the satisfaction of being strong.

I like the cross-trainer for aerobics because it's nice and smooth and easy on the joints with little jarring. I'm not big-boned. Remember I was 6'1" and under eleven stone. I now weigh fourteen stone, so for me to run or do something jolting can hurt because I've truly got toothpick ankles. When I weighed seventeen stone, guys would come up to me in the gym and say, 'How are those ankles holding you up?' I'd hit the roof. It really pissed me off because there wasn't anything I could do. There's not one exercise in existence that builds bigger ankles! I've had to work through a lot of emotions to let go of my many hang-ups.

I've paid attention to my wake-up calls as well, so like I said earlier, I now stretch every day – like a cat.

I don't lift weights on the road and that's another huge breakthrough for me because I used to be manic about it, racing to rent a car wherever I was and find a good place to work out. But I wasn't giving my body time to recover, which is absolutely necessary when you lift weights.

The way you know you're overtrained is when you're tired and listless.

You're not giving your body enough recuperation time. There's probably nutritional issues there as well, that you're not fuelling your body properly for high performance.

While I'm travelling, I'll just do a little yoga and meditation in my room to help collect myself for the day and thirty minutes of aerobics in the hotel gym, and that's it.

Pushing Too Far

I've learned the hard way that there's wisdom in listening to your body and taking time to rest when you need it. A couple of years ago I was out on the road nonstop, getting very little sleep – two hours here and there – just pushing my mind and body to the limit. I've always had this idea that I was invincible and nothing could stop me. Boy, was I in for a big wake-up call.

I was working out in Vegas when my right elbow started hurting during a triceps exercise. I basically used the walk-it-off philosophy and kept pushing. For weeks it kept hurting each time I was in the gym, but since I was invincible, I figured it was temporary and would work itself out.

Early one morning in my San Diego gym with about three hours sleep I was pushing my triceps to the limit with overhead weighted extensions. With a heavily weighted barbell over my head there was a snap so loud that they could hear it across the gym. One of the trainers came running as I dropped the weight to the floor and almost passed out. My right lower arm was just dangling. I couldn't bend it or anything – the tendon was torn clear through. I'm right-handed, but I managed to make the forty-five-minute drive to A and E in heavy traffic and excruciating pain. I sat there in the waiting room and no one would see me. My elbow was as big as a grapefruit.

At first I started down the self-pity road. *Why are they ignoring me? Can't they see I'm screwed up and in intense pain?* Suddenly I got a grip on myself and realised it was time to practise what I know. I started meditating and visualising my elbow healthy and normal. I went back in my mind to the gym and replayed the whole scenario, completing the set, totally healthy and whole, setting the weight down. I did that several times in this meditative state. A nurse came in and said, 'Oh my God, what are you doing?' My elbow was suddenly a third less swollen, and she was shocked.

'But if you heard a loud snap, it's not going to heal for a long time,' she said. I was thinking to myself, *That's not me, that's not me, that's not me. Thanks for sharing that but that's not me.*

I ended up having to have surgery and running around with a cast and an immobiliser on my arm – not fun, especially since I had to wear it while delivering a Harmonic Wealth Weekend. I had been told that I wouldn't be back to full strength again for at least a year. *That's not me, that's not me, that's not me. I'm healthy and whole – strong and vibrant – and I'm going to heal in record time.* When they took the cast off after surgery, my arm looked like a stick. I went through physical therapy and it was absolutely brutal.

I had another Harmonic Wealth Weekend a month after that and while telling the story, I got so inspired that I dropped down and did four press-ups on stage. The doctors couldn't believe it. *This is me, this is me, this is me.*

Never underestimate what you're capable of accomplishing – you're totally unlimited. Put into practice what you're learning here, and you'll amaze yourself and the world.

Once again, despite a dire prognosis, I recovered completely. But I paid a dear price for the lesson. I truly believe that if I'd just listened to my body and eased up, I could have avoided the whole painful situation. That's why I'm not fanatical about working out anymore. If I wake up and realise that I gave my workout a little too much the day before, I make sure I give my body the rest it needs.

21

Body Language: The Power of Your Words and Emotions

Language is the blood of the soul into which
thoughts run and out of which they grow.
– OLIVER WENDELL HOLMES

Words as Weapons

When we talk about the physical pillar, it's easy to equate physical with tangible. We pick up the food we feed our body with. We feel our muscles burning, toning as we run or lift. Yet, as we nourish and rebuild the temple of our bodies, we must be aware that we construct it upon an invisible, intangible foundation of thoughts and words: the way we live our lives, the sustaining air we draw in, the way we interact with the temples of others, the energy of the emotions in which we bathe.

Many people have a physical weakness, or two or three – maybe a weak neck, a problem back, or a sensitive stomach. We're quick to point out this frailty to ourselves and others, thereby sending it a fairly constant stream of negative energy.

Everything in this universe can be broken down into love or fear, or love or the lack of love, including your body. Your overall health has so much to do with: are you loving yourself and your life? Are you living in joy? Are you feeling empowered?

It's easy to get lazy in your thinking and your speech, but what you need to understand is that your language can be dangerous – a physical prophecy.

Maybe you're fond of self-deprecating jokes – you put yourself down so no one else can do it for you: 'God, my arse is so big I have to buy it its own bus ticket.' Or you float out a put-down, perhaps hoping a friend will offer a soothing correction: 'I look fat in these jeans, don't I?' Understand that every mean, negative thing you say about yourself, you believe about yourself – and your body will obey your beliefs.

My friend Brenda started working out with a trainer a year ago. For the first three months of training she spent more time coming up with jokes than focusing on her workout. Her trainer would say, 'Okay, now we're going to . . .' and she'd complete his sentence with, 'go get some doughnuts?!' It was all a big joke until she realised that she was, in effect, telling herself that she didn't take the sessions seriously because she didn't believe in herself seriously. That was a big wake-up call for her. 'No more jokes,' she announced. After that one decision, she said, 'I entered into a new phase of training, and a new phase of me.'

I pride myself on my laser-like focus at the gym when I work out, but that doesn't mean I don't have bad days where I'm tired or lazy or feeling bad about myself. I usually start my day with my workout so these toxic thoughts tend to try to creep in early in the morning – usually when I've had too little sleep. In these weak moments I use all kinds of declarations inside my head such as, *I'm getting younger, stronger, and more attractive every day* or *I am eternal youth and vitality and can do everything and anything*. When doing a particular exercise that seems impossible, the bench press, for instance, I'll declare, *I'm god of the bench press! God can do anything*. When those last few repetitions of an exercise just seem near impossible, I'll say to myself, *Last reps, best reps*.

I realise that some of these things may seem a bit silly, and I've never shared them before, but if they work (which they do) who cares? I only care about results.

The next time you hear yourself saying, *You're a pain in the neck* or *That kills me* or *This is a pain in the arse* or *You break my heart* or *I could just die* or *That's a killer,* ask yourself if that's what you really want to put out into the universe.

Your wish is my command. In the meantime, *I'm becoming stronger, more vital, and youthful every day.*

Oxygen: Breathing Exercise

Oxygen is the most important nutrient in the body. You can go weeks without food, days without water, but only minutes without oxygen. Most people oxygenate their system poorly, which is why breathing practices are so vital for the physical pillar.

All traditions have their breathing practices because breath is life. In the ancient traditions of China, for example, some of the breathing exercises were considered so sacred that if they were shared outside the king and his court, it was punishable by death. While studying the Huna spiritual tradition of Hawaii, I learned that the indigenous people of the islands recognised the importance of breath. The ancients started every day with deep diaphragmatic breathing. Do you know the reason they call the white man *haole* (pronounced how–lees)? Not because of our pale skin, but rather meaning 'people who don't breathe'. When settlers first came to the Hawaiian Islands, the Hawaiians asked, 'How could these people live without breathing?'

Most adults breathe high and in their chest. When breathing properly, deep from the diaphragm, your abdomen should extend; this isn't popular with a population that spends a lot of energy sucking it in. If you want to see a great example of how to breathe, watch a small baby. When a baby breathes, its stomach extends.

A great way to practise breathing properly is to lie on your back on the floor. In this position, you cannot help but breathe from the diaphragm. There are several different ways to breathe (depending upon the outcome you want to achieve), but in your normal daily activities healthy neutral breathing consisting of a 1:1 ratio of breathing in and out is good. So, for instance, if you breathe in for four counts you would likewise breathe out for four.

Make it part of your day to practise conscious, deep, diaphragmatic breathing and very shortly it will become a habit that you'll no longer have to think about. You may be surprised how much more energy you'll have. In fact, next time you're tired, instead of reaching for some caffeine, try some really deep breaths instead and you may find a total shift in your energy – very effective and much healthier.

Sexual Healing

I don't claim by any means to be an expert on sex – I've had it a few times and I expect to have it again (hopefully soon). While this topic is something I'll probably write a lot more about in the future, let me just say that if you're thinking it's not spiritual to be sexual, get over it. God made sex fun for a reason. My wish for you is that you're so healthy and you make so much money that maybe you'll have a lot more time and energy for sex!

We've been conditioned to believe the things that often cause trouble and internal conflict (money, sex, food, power) should be avoided, suppressed, or transcended to be spiritual. Yet, the most amazing teachers I've met in my life don't have less of these things – they have more! Yet, for some strange reason, they're not troubled and they suffer no internal conflicts. Hmmm – more on that topic in the next chapter.

How Your Emotions Affect Your Health

Some of the most fascinating research in the last two decades by Candace Pert and others has uncovered the profound physical effect our emotions have on our bodies. You can't achieve true harmony in the physical pillar until you free yourself from the thrall of negative emotions.

So many of us torture ourselves by seeing the world in black and white, by labelling every experience good or bad. I've learned experientially what my study of quantum physics had been telling me all along: when you get stuck in the duality of good and bad, you're really just stuck in the emotion of illusion and bound by gravity pulling you more rapidly to the grave. The more intensely you experience these negative emotions, the greater the toll it takes upon your youth and vitality.

Two of the most common time-bound states that people experience are the emotions of fear and guilt. Fear is nothing more than a future imagined state that you're going to experience more pain than pleasure. What most people do is use their imagination to project themselves into the future and fail, then bring that failure back into now and get worried and fearful about it. Not a clever idea, when you stop to think about it, is it?

Fear brings rapid age into your life and body. It sends a call to the universe to bring the things to you that you don't want. Not only does fear call in the wrinkles, it shortens your life span. Guilt, on the other hand, is also time-bound, but it's the opposite of fear. Guilt is an emotion of the past. When you're experiencing guilt, you're using your memory of past imagined actions to create more pain than pleasure.

You think your past is real? Think again. Remember, you have an infinite number of pasts and you're only recognising one of them.

When you transcend (end the trance) the duality of good and bad and embrace both sides of the equation, you'll find that you live in a perfect universe that is always supporting and teaching you. You'll stand in a state of wonderment, appreciation, and gratitude for the perfection of it all. When you're in this inspired state for a moment or a month, you're literally beyond third-dimensional space-time and therefore ageless.

There are so many things you can do to increase the value and vitality of your life while decreasing the effects of age. First and foremost on the list is to strengthen your physical pillar by doing some of the mental exercises I described in the mental pillar to free yourself from negative thoughts. It's equally important to feel inspired, as we've talked about here as well as in other pillars. When you tap into a higher purpose, contributing to and making a difference, studies show that you'll be more enthusiastic and live longer.

Put an End to Stress

Research into longevity proves that people with less stress in their lives and lower blood pressure, which are closely related, live longer and more fruitful lives. Edward Hallowell, author of *CrazyBusy: Overstretched,*

Overbooked, and About to Snap! was recently interviewed. He said that we're all being sucked into the 'grand seduction of multitasking', where we think we're getting a lot done at once, but in fact we're not. We're simply increasing the sense of stress and pressure in our lives, and it's harming our health.

Vanderbilt University recently conducted a study showing that drivers who multitask (putting on make-up, talking on the phone, texting) are five times as likely to get into an accident.

But as you know, the universe loves speed, so what does this mean? The answer lies in what we talked about back in Chapter Three: just because you're busy doesn't mean you're being efficient. This kind of chaos takes a toll on our minds and bodies. We're in chaos and therefore not present, so everything suffers – our relationships, our sanity, our spiritual peace and well-being, and our physical health. What do you do when you're rushing and stressed? Grab whatever you can to eat when your stomach's rumbling, miss out on sleep, and miss exercise, for starters.

So, achieving true health has to mean getting a handle on stress. It's one thing to read a good book while you're at the gym. It's another to feel your attention pulled in a thousand directions, fully present for none. Here mindfulness and paying attention can help. Be fully present in everything you do when you can. Return to meditation. Twenty minutes of deep meditation has been shown to lower stress. It's also the equivalent of two hours of sleep, which makes you look better, less old, and gives you more energy and focus.

Bodywork: The Power of Touch

I've seen healers at work around the world and I'm a big believer in alternative medicine and mind-body interactions. While those are lengthy topics in themselves, I'd like to cover a few of the alternative, preventative things I do to keep my body in harmony.

Acupuncture treatments, which I have at least once a month (especially pre and post a big event like my Harmonic Wealth Weekend), are one of my favourite forms of self-care. In this ancient Chinese system of healing, disease is seen as a loss of harmony between the yin and yang energies, which we'll talk more about in the next pillar. Tiny needles are used to open up energy meridians along the body, and although this doesn't sound like a fun activity, it's actually quite relaxing.

I'm an addict for massage, and rightfully so. When you're as physical onstage and off as I am, often teaching for sixteen hours at a time, massage can be a lifesaver (especially when combined with a good chiropractic adjustment). There are many different types of massage, and I prefer deep tissue massage, which I get at least once a week, sports massage, lymphatic massage, Rolfing, and Swedish massage, given by two beautiful Swedish women at once. (Just testing you on that last part, to see if you're paying attention.)

Unresolved emotional issues are stored at a cellular level and are shown to create adhesions in the muscles. They also reduce collagen and create rigidity. I have a home close to the sea in San Diego. During a gale the wind will blow off the ocean with a mighty force. A tree that is rigidly rooted is often torn right out of the ground while a tree that is flexible to bend and flow with the wind will withstand the storm. I think you get the point.

Again, an inflexible body is a reflection of an inflexible mind.

Because emotions are stored at a cellular level, many individuals have quite cathartic experiences during Rolfing sessions. You can also have a similar experience but to a lesser degree with deep tissue massage.

There've been many times during which I'm receiving very deep massage and a memory of someone or something I haven't thought of in years arises seemingly out of nowhere. Regular bodywork will not only affect your life vitality and longevity but it's very nurturing to the spirit as well. Studies have shown that people who are alone or feeling unloved need touch and pampering for their peace of mind.

We think our adult workaday lives cause us to need bodywork, but human touch is good for everyone, no matter his or her age or stress level. I knew a mother once who rubbed her baby's feet every day because she'd heard it would be good for his internal organs. The child loved it, and throughout his childhood the boy never had a real illness – never went to hospital, had a runny nose or an earache. So she continued until he was a teenager. The father finally said, 'No more. Now it's my turn.' The mother never knew if the foot rubs were part of the boy's overall health, but she never regretted that one small bonding, preventative health effort she took over the years.

Self-Care: Check-ups

We've already addressed how important it is to listen to the messages our bodies give us, and in addition it's worth going for check-ups with your doctor every six months or so. Check your eyes and teeth, and keep them in good shape with your optician and dentist. If you've got a cavity, I can help you deal with the pain psychologically, but go to the dentist to get to the root of the problem. There are plenty of modern services out there that can help us be in the best shape we can, so it's ludicrous not to make the most of them. Remember, when caring for yourself you're focusing on becoming the person you'd like to fall in love with.

Your Physical Goals

So, your opportunity on a daily basis is to practise healthy habits. You build a life not by the actions you take here and there, but by the habits you adopt and reinforce.

Everyone has physical goals – everyone. I've never met a person who told me they were 100 per cent satisfied with their body and physical habits. There's always room for improvement. So, get out your notebook and write your top five physical goals. Want some ideas? Here are the issues people tell me they want most in this realm:

1. To have more energy

2. To exercise more and be more fit, strong, and muscular

3. To lose weight

4. To get more sleep

5. To eat better

6. To drink more water

7. To age less, or at least more gracefully

8. To get more pampering

9. To have more sex

10. To heal from an illness or disorder

What is it you want most in this area? If you could wave a magic wand and have the body and health of your dreams, what would it look like? ⓘ Now write it down, including the feelings. What would it feel like to wear short shorts again and look down on your fit, lean legs? Call me when you get there, and I'll be the judge. (Again, just making sure you're awake.) What could you accomplish if you bounded out of bed in the morning with energy to spare? How much fun would it be to go clothes shopping and find that everything fits in your dream size? How easy would life be to crave salads over sweets or fried food every time? How rewarding would it be to be a fit, hip older adult, still sexual and attractive long after your peers have bought into being old and tired?

Do any of these statements excite you? Make it your physical intention or mission statement, and as you do so, lock onto a picture in your brain as you're writing it. Step into that picture and make it brighter, more colourful, more exciting. Give it more sound and feeling – all the things we've done already. Do them again and with greater conviction. You're probably really good at this by now. You've been visualising regularly, living in a state of expectation, taking your actions, and thinking and acting as the person you want to become.

Now that you've got the picture, what six action items would be a valuable investment of your time today? Maybe today's the day to call the dentist and schedule that long overdue appointment. Get a new hair-style – yes, even if you're a guy – that comb-over is really tired. Meet up with that neighbour who wants to walk with you in the mornings. Find the health food store in town that sells organic vegetables. You know the steps you need to take. Now write them down in sequential order, with number one being most important, and commit to taking those actions now. Just do it. Invest your time in the activities worthy of who you are and who you're becoming. It's your precious body, your temple. Treat it that way.

As you go through your day, get into the habit of checking in with yourself regularly and asking yourself these questions:

1. 'Does this activity fit in with my goals and intentions?'

2. 'Is this food or drink going to strengthen or weaken me?'

3. 'How am I spending or investing my time?'

4. 'How am I practising self-care today?'

5. 'Are my habits in line with the care and feeding of a champion?'

You're Worth It

People often tell me that it's expensive to do all the body work I do, eat organic, and take the best supplements, and they're right. I liken it to owning a Porsche. Mine runs like a bat out of hell, and anytime I take it into the garage it's going to be a couple of grand no matter what. It's high maintenance but also high performance. But it'll do anything I drive it to do – and more. The only limitations with a Porsche are the driver's limitations.

Anything that's truly high performance will also be high maintenance. A Hyundai probably costs little to keep up, but then again it's a Hyundai. There's nothing wrong with it; it just won't perform at the same level.

A high-performance body is no different. The more evolved and high performance you choose to become, the more effort you'll have to put into maintaining a high level of health, fitness, and vitality. You have to choose if you want to be a Porsche or a Hyundai. In my opinion, the money I spend on my health is an investment in myself, allowing me to run at top speed for the long haul. I hope you're convinced that you're never going to achieve what you're capable of achieving with a low-performance/low-maintenance physical body. Common sense (and the Law of Polarity) will tell you that the more you grow and evolve – the more high performance you become – the more little things can go wrong (notice that I didn't say big things). But you'll be ready because you'll be watching for signs, paying attention, and treating yourself like the treasure you are. Am I right?

I thought so. Good work!

PILLAR V

Spiritual

It was centuries ago that Blaise Pascal famously declared, 'The heart has its reasons whereof Reason knows nothing.' Call it heart, call it soul; the spirit within us connects us to our deepest, most unchanging truths, to the seat of the most ineffable love and amazement. Talk about a timeless truth. Here's another, this time from Pierre Teilhard de Chardin: 'We are not physical beings having a spiritual experience, but spiritual beings having a physical experience.' Keep these insights close. Know them in your heart.

We're all hard-wired to have a spiritual experience. I guarantee that you can have wealth in spades in all other pillars, and if you're lacking here, you'll end up feeling empty and unfulfilled. If you doubt me, my certainty overcomes your doubt. I've worked with hundreds of thousands of people over the years and I know what I know to be true. As a spiritual being, having a spiritual experience is part of your very nature. Without a connection to spirit, our greatest achievements fall flat. No matter the accomplishment or acclaim, it'll never be enough, never be fulfilling, not totally. You'll always be thirsty because you haven't fed the stream within.

This pillar will help you connect – or reconnect – to your source, to the grace, love, and light that give meaning to your life's journey, with all its joys and pains. I promise, I'm not here to tell you how to define your creative source – I'm not qualified to do that, nor, by the way, is anyone. Your relationship to your source is very personal and can only be defined by you. However, I also promise that when you've searched for your source and found it, you'll truly understand beyond doubt that you're guided and supported, that you are never alone. Never have been – never will be.

22

The Bridge to Spirit

If you think there's an important difference between being a Christian or a Jew
or a Hindu or a Muslim or a Buddhist, then you're making a division between
your heart, what you love with, and the way you act in the world.
– COLEMAN BARKS (TRANSLATING RUMI 1207–1273)

A Student First and Foremost

If you've been reading this book from the beginning, you know my history. You
know that I was raised in my father's Protestant church. You know that I've had
plenty of doubts and crises of faith along the way. You know that I've experienced
great longings of the spirit and the flesh, and that I've travelled the world looking
anywhere and everywhere for answers to help bring myself and others into greater
harmony. You may also know that my greatest wish is that some of the things I've
learned and experienced in my journey can assist you in some way along your
own.

Being a teacher and an author is a big responsibility. It's a precarious
dance I perform: provoking, encouraging, stimulating my students without disempowering them by becoming too large a presence in their
lives. I guess that's why I always try to keep in mind that, first and foremost, I am a student myself, doing my best to make sense of the many
mysteries we all face with the tools I've been given. That's why I'm
always wary of those spiritual leaders who encourage their students to

follow them in blind faith like ducklings, without questioning the path ahead or checking their own inner guidance system – spiritual leaders who are unaware that they may be leading their students right into oncoming traffic.

I don't want you to follow. I want you to explore. My aim is to teach you what I believe and what's worked for me, and most of all to encourage you to accelerate your own understanding and growth. Just so you know, I'm probably going to say a few things in this pillar that'll shock you or go against what you've been taught to believe. But in keeping with what I've repeatedly advised, take what feels right to you and leave the rest.

That's actually the Dalai Lama's advice. Practise whatever path speaks to you – not to dabble, but to embrace it fully and really commit so that you'll receive the benefits. Then leave the rest.

We Are All One

I'd like you to go back and read the quote at the start of this pillar. Why would Rumi – a thirteenth-century poet, the Shakespeare of Afghanistan – have such explosive beliefs when the Christian crusades were taking place in the Middle East? How did he have the presence of mind to embrace what was then such a heretical idea – that all religions were at heart the same?

I believe Rumi understood what science has proven in the 800 years since his birth: that whether we're comparing our DNA strands or discovering that everything in existence is 99.99999 per cent light, we're all ONE, all utterly alike and connected to each other and everything else.

Regardless of race, religion, or creed, no one can argue that we're more different than alike. It just doesn't wash. We all have the same needs: to take care of ourselves and our families, love one another, think and worship as we please. We all deserve to have our most basic needs met so we can find out who we are, what we love, and what our unique contribution is. Isn't that true for everyone?

I see religion as one way to cross the bridge to spirit, to connect to something within your that's larger than yourself. There are many ways to engage the spirit more fully within and without, but there's only one destination. All roads lead to Rome. I promise you, you'll never feel more vital, vibrant, and connected than when you're living an inspired life.

What Does It Mean to Be Spiritual, Anyway?

What is spirituality? Is it a belief system? A way of life? Something you tap into but then divorce yourself from when you hit the clubs? What does it mean to be spiritual?

I want you to think about what spirituality means to you. Does it mean being a member of a specific religion? Volunteering or giving your money to charity? Selfless service is an honourable path and it can lead you to a higher place. Perhaps you define your spirituality by your yogic practice, or maybe by studying with a guru or teacher, reading piles of books, walking in the woods, or strolling by the sea? Perhaps you're into going it alone, contemplating your personal experience through reflection or prayer?

Spirituality can be hard to define because it's really, really personal. I think of spirituality as that one-to-one relationship you have with your creative source, however you define him, her, or it. Your creative source is where you endlessly and tirelessly devote your heart, mind, and spirit. A well that never runs dry, a place of eternal abundance, your creative source is where your love is made manifest in the physical world. Connecting with your source allows you to feel like you're part of something bigger than the day-to-day routine, and you invest in it constantly – not for what you want to get, but what you want to give.

For simplicity's sake, I call my creative source God, but you may have one of a thousand other names for that spirit-that-runs-through-all-things. I'm not here to tell you how you should define your own source. That's up to you. I do want to tell you, however, that I absolutely believe you can advance spiritually without giving up the joys of the Earth. Whoever says you can't be wildly successful and highly spiritual at the same time probably has very little success in either area. Are there some paths that are faster and more efficient than others? Yes. Can some choices accelerate your unfolding and others not as much? Yes. But ultimately it's all there for your learning and reflection. Even the major disasters.

God One-to-One

As human beings, we operate on three levels of existence simultaneously: the spiritual level, the mental level, and the physical level. We cannot live on one level alone – say, concentrating on the spiritual at the expense of the mental and physical. That's why constantly switching between these three planes is one of our greatest challenges, and why harmonising this trinity presents the greatest opportunity for those of us who choose the integrated path. What we must do is to begin to tap into and harness the power of the spiritual plane of existence, while heeding the desires of the mental and physical. We can only do that through discipline, illumination, and understanding.

There's no way to know spirit until you experience spirit. You can read all the books and information in the world on Egypt but until you actually go and experience it for yourself, you still don't *know* Egypt – you know *about* Egypt. Big difference.

Worldwide, we gather together through our religious institutions to talk about God in the hope that by doing so we'll know God. But very few, if any, have direct personal experience of God. I read a study a few years ago in which hundreds of individuals who claimed to be religious, including clergy, were asked, and 95 per cent of them admitted to having had no personal experience of God. It's unfortunate; we're missing the point.

We've made quantum leaps in our technology in the West, but by and large we've taken baby steps spiritually. Church attendance is at an all-time low. Not only do most people define themselves as spiritual rather than religious, but they say that they follow their inner guidance before they follow the recommendations of a religious leader. What does that tell you? I believe the church (if you want to call it that) of the future will be a living laboratory where avid students in pursuit of their own evolution and potential come together to grow and expand experientially. This twenty-first-century spirituality is quite contrary to the old model of come, sit, listen, and learn, which has long outlived its value in today's world.

Live Above and Below

Some people credit Eastern spiritual traditions with being more advanced in achieving altered states of consciousness, while praising the West for its mastery of materialism and the GNP. Positron and electron, particle and wave. What we need here is harmony in both worlds, a rejection of the dualistic state that says either/or. We need to live above and below, in the world and beyond it, if we want to become fully integrated spiritual masters.

In quantum physics when the positron and electron merge, they annihilate each other and move to a new level of existence. When the spiritual and material areas of your life collide to become fully harmonised and integrated, you move to a new level of awakening and awareness.

Historically, there are two basic camps with regard to spirituality: the ascenders are the ones who believe they've got to disconnect from the physical (or at least sacrifice a lot of it) to move into spirit; the descenders are the ones who feel it's essential to live close to the Earth and embrace it fully and completely. Now, recall physics and how it tells us that all energy is either a particle or a wave. Simply put, light either manifests as a wave or a particle, the wave being energy in its pure potential state and the particle being the beginning of energy coming into form. I call the ascenders the wavy ones because the goal of ascension is to rise up to heaven or to attain enlightenment, both of which bring about freedom from the bonds of earthly life. The ascenders are the often ungrounded waves of no form. The descenders, on the other hand, are the ones who feel that it's essential to live close to the Earth, to celebrate, embrace, and harmonise with Mother Earth and all of her physical manifestations. These are the particle-minded people of form.

Of course I'm generalising here, but the basic belief of the ascender is that all things that provide physical enjoyment – like money, food, sex, power – are not spiritual, and therefore must be seen as the illusions they really are. Ascender traditions tend to suppress the physical part of nature, which can lead to a host of pathological behaviours, or at the very least, a lack of fulfilment. Keeping life all wavy and ethereal is fun for a time, but the physical aspects of life eventually come back to bite you. Believe me, I know.

After living with and learning from so many, I've experienced first-hand how the descenders believe, in direct opposition to the ascenders, that living out of sync with the Earth's rhythms is a kind of hell. I've spent time with the descendents of the great Incas in the highest peaks of the Peruvian Andes; camped in the dense jungles of the Amazon with indigenous people, sharing their rituals and teachings; abseiled miles into the Earth, into deep and treacherous caverns to visit powerful energy sites of old; and then journeyed to nearly forgotten spots in the South Pacific to study, understand, and apply some of the original spiritual teachings still in existence. The natives in all these places have everything invested in the Earth and their bonds with it. The descenders have a wisdom that is grounded and down to earth.

By the way, I've studied the ascending traditions as well. Raised in a Protestant household, I was immersed in fundamental Christian teachings. I began my study of Buddhism and the world's great religions in my early teens. I scaled Mount Sinai and spent the night in the cave where Moses received the Ten Commandments. I've trekked the path of the Mystery School Initiate up the Nile (through the seven sacred temples of ancient Egypt), while earning the honour of meditating alone between the paws of the Great Sphinx (followed by a solo journey into all three chambers of the Great Pyramid of Giza). This certainly doesn't mean I have all the truth in my possession or that I have it all completely together; what it does mean is that I've had a wide and diverse exposure to the world's traditions.

Interestingly enough, ascenders often describe the descending approach as pagan, which really means 'anything that doesn't agree with us'. Look around, and you'll notice that increasing numbers of people are drawn to the threatened traditions of shamanic, Native American, and indigenous teachings – those that embrace and celebrate the physical journey and joys of Earth. In contrast to the ethereal state of the waves, the descending focus is more upon the particle. But the answers aren't totally here either. The physical Earth can become a seduction and a place of escapism just as easily as soaring into the astral plane. Both of these approaches, particle and wave, are necessary, and yet, in and of themselves, incomplete.

So, here's the question: Which approach – ascending or descending – is correct?

Here's the answer? Both!

The Power of Heaven in the Body of Earth

Have you ever thought that the people who want to sit in front of the TV and just veg out all day are no different from the ceiling surfers? Think about it. There's spiritual escapism and there's mundane escapism. Sitting in front of the television is mundane escapism; not being grounded and just soaring into the ether is spiritual escapism. Guess what? They're both doing the same thing with a different approach, yet they tend to judge each other! One blasts materialism, money, and laziness, and the other blasts airy-fairy new agers. Mirror, mirror.

To fully realise your spirituality, you must be both an ascender *and* a descender. You need to keep your feet on the ground and work with the physical reality while simultaneously freeing your spirit to soar. Every tradition tells us that you, and everything around you, comes from one source. So, doesn't it stand to reason that everything should be held sacred, from a pine tree to a Porsche?

You're a spiritual being having a physical experience. If you weren't meant to experience the physical in full splendour, then why did you even bother coming here?

You must be master of Earth *and* heaven to become the spiritual being you were born to be.

The Base of the Mountain

The descent into matter must be complete before the ascent to spirit can commence.

— DION FORTUNE

Where does your spiritual evolution begin? Whether you choose to pursue it in a church, synagogue, or ashram, a yoga class or in the woods, you must first prepare the temple of your body and mind. Paramhansa Yogananda, the yogi and guru who was born in India in the late 1800s and became famous in America in the early part of the twentieth century, said that 90 per cent of the spiritual battle is psychological. My translation: you can't get to God if your mind is weighed down by darkness. Further translation: you can't get to God until you clean out your rubbish.

In many ways, the spiritual pillar and the mental pillar overlap to an even greater degree than the others. It's my experience that all pursuits of personal harmony carried through to completion bring the seeker/student to an eventual deep desire for spiritual experience. You've seen this play out over and over in interviews with those who've achieved the height of success and yet still feel empty. I call this the 'Is that all there is?' syndrome.

Notice how I said, 'carried through to completion'? I'm not talking about popping into a lecture or weekend seminar from time to time or reading a personal development book after some fleeting personal crisis. I'm talking about waking up and longing for a relationship that's both profound and timeless, one that, although physically intangible, is more potent than anything else and can never be equalled or replicated in the physical world and yet – interestingly enough – affects everything in your physical world.

If you want to evolve spiritually, you first have to deal with the stuff on the ground. In many cases that may mean seeking a qualified psychotherapist before you can move forward on your spiritual quest. Or you can do it simultaneously. I have yet to meet a traditional guru or shaman fully equipped to combine psychotherapy and spiritual growth as an approach to spiritual evolution. Yet, that's exactly what's desperately needed. Likewise, I've never met a psychological professional who's able to assist you in having a spiritual experience. In fact, many of them have traditionally shunned and seriously downplayed them. Again, if integration is your goal (which is the wave and particle of the future, my friend), you need both.

The typical guru or spiritual teacher has little ability to assist you in developing the ego/identity that's so necessary for healthy development. Imagine building a skyscraper without a foundation and yet expecting it to stand up. It's impossible.

When asked for assistance with problems of the physical world and identity, a typical response from a spiritual teacher may be things like: 'Be witness to it,' 'Be with it,' or 'Meditate.' But does this spiritual teacher know how to assist you with out-of-control family issues or a childhood spent hiding in a closet from an alcoholic parent? Quite frankly, you could witness those memories or meditate upon them your whole life and never overcome them. In fact, from what you now know about the Law of Attraction, with all that energy and attention focused their way, the memories will become even more powerful.

My friend Genpo, who is a Roshi in the Zen tradition (the highest-ranking Zen master outside Japan), recently told me, 'James, I cannot tell you how many times I've watched individuals in an ashram utilising their sitting practice [a Zen term for meditation] and yet after twenty to thirty years of daily practice, they're still just sitting on their stuff!'

Just because you can meditate really well doesn't mean you're highly functional. It doesn't mean that you're integrated or can master anything you want to pursue. The name of the game is integration. You've got to be able to take your practice and do something with it. But a lot of people in the spiritual pursuit get stuck out there in the worlds of the intangible.

In other words, just because you're committed to your spiritual path doesn't mean you're healthy *or* peaceful, or that you know how to let things go. I've met monks, preachers, and clergy who were as immature and undeveloped as people I knew back in high school. I'd go so far as to say that some were afflicted with mental health issues and a few were certifiably mad. Just because you can sit quietly for hours at a time and perform compassionate acts doesn't mean you don't need a good psychotherapist who can help you stop abusing yourself with self-defeating habits, habits that may actually be re-creating your personal pain, whatever the source.

This is where traditional psychotherapy can be invaluable in helping you achieve a healthy sense of self. Sometimes those introspective sessions are the quickest route to heaven on earth. I consider myself a spiritual teacher, yet at least 90 per cent of the work I do with people is psychological healing and awakening. The traditional therapist has very little ability, and as we discussed, sometimes even an aversion, to assisting an individual in moving beyond the ego or separate identity towards spiritual evolution. You need both approaches to achieve an integrated spirituality.

Contrary to accepted belief, psychotherapy and spiritual growth are not only *not* in conflict with one another, but much like science and spirituality, are completely interdependent. Like the wave and particle, they are two opposite poles of the same eternal dance.

One Light, One Passion

No matter what our religion or spiritual affiliation is, I think we can all agree that Jesus was, at the very least, a great teacher. Arguably, no one single person in history has made such a tremendous and lasting impact on the world – no one. In Luke 11:34, he said, 'The light of the body is the eye: therefore when thine eye is single, thy whole body also is full of light; but when thine eye is evil, thy body also is full of darkness.' Translation: if you focus like a laser on spiritual evolution and transformation, then your whole body will be full of truth and power. But if you split your attention, you won't achieve the heights of light attainment.

Please remember that *everything* in the universe is comprised of light. Therefore, the more light, the more everything – from the tangible to the intangible. That's exciting, isn't it? (An interesting side note is that the word *evil* is *live* spelt backwards. To be evil is to live in a backward way, to live in darkness – the opposite of light.)

I like this teaching. It tells us that you and I have to choose which master we're going to serve. Are we going to operate like the majority of the population in a physical world and hope for spirit to take pity on us and throw us a bone, or are we going to access who we truly are as spiritual beings and begin to co-create the results we choose in our life?

Which do you choose?

What are you singularly focused on? Frequently, I meet people who want to have their dreams, yet aren't willing to give up anything to achieve them. This is self-deception. Choosing to become great in any area means choosing to *not be great* in another area. Maybe you won't cook for your children when you get that job as a talk show host. Or master the guitar because your career keeps you travelling so much. Or build those bookshelves because you've got to get that manuscript done. There will always be a price to pay. There will always be a sacrifice. There is always a price for the prize, yet interestingly enough, when you're living the life you choose and following your calling, the sacrifice doesn't really feel like a sacrifice, it feels like a gift.

If your goal is integrated spiritual mastery, you need to engage in it with a single mind. Your work must be your passion and your love made manifest through action. To accomplish anything of consequence, anything magnificent and great, you must be willing to swap your life for it, to be so passionately focused and committed that nothing will divert you. Nothing and no one can stop you.

Now I know swapping your life sounds intense, and it is. But the hard reality is that you're already swapping your life – whether you love what you're doing or not. Inspiring or depressing, the hard fact is that you spend more time making your living than you do with the people you love most, more time than you do on your recreations or hobbies, holidaying, or relaxing. That's why it's so important to choose something worthy.

People often ask me, 'What do you do for fun and recreation?' There's an unspoken expectation that I come up with a whole list of activities I'm involved in: hiking, camping, going to movies, skiing. But I don't. The bottom line is that my work is my passion and my re-creation (notice the true meaning of the word). I can think of nothing more fulfilling and re-creating than to meditate, study, read, learn, write, create, help and coach others, talk to you and share insights. When someone asks me, 'How's work?' I can honestly answer, 'Work is play.' Work is my prayer and my love made manifest.

Every human being who's ever lived has a hard-wired need to be part of something meaningful, to be part of something that's bigger than this ordinary existence, to contribute some kind of value to the world, to feel like life has meaning and purpose. That's true for you, too, whether you know it or not.

Want to light up the path to spirit? Fall in love with someone or something and pursue this passion with a single mind. This is the true spiritual vibration. When you fall in love so completely that you give yourself totally to something, that's when your heart is open and the consciousness of Christ and Buddha is flowing through you. It doesn't matter what it is, but you must immerse yourself and give yourself completely to it. It could be Jesus, Buddha, Krishna, a mate, or your career, but it's that truly inspired state you're after. This is when you experience your true giving and Godly nature. It's a timeless state: time literally stands still.

The Master Embraces Joy and Pain

Walking a path lit by inspiration is the true path of the spiritual being, and finding your own unique purpose is a huge part of why you exist. However, I don't want to tell you that once you find your life's purpose, all will be rosy. You'll still have your challenges – that's part of life. The master understands this and embraces pain *and* pleasure in pursuit of his purpose. As the Buddha says, 'The light of truth's high noon is not for tender leaves.'You're always going to have challenges, self-doubt, uncertainty of sorts, disasters, pain as well as pleasure. But when you've defined your true life direction and surrender yourself completely to it, you'll have discovered the real secret. However, it's a secret only you can define.

No one said surrender would be easy. Sometimes wanting to understand everything cuts you off from the flow of spirit. So much of life occurs in the valleys and not the peaks, in the shadows and the chaos of our lives, particularly growth. We expand the most when we completely embrace the peaks as well as the valleys, the challenges as well as the joys.

Want to Be Spiritually Evolved? Get to Work!

As both a descender and ascender – that is, a fully integrated spiritual being – you need to live fully in the world even as you're continually working to transcend it. The integrated teacher may tell you that you need to change your diet, exercise, help you get a financial action plan, send you to relationship counselling, and assist you in releasing limiting beliefs and emotions that hinder you in all these areas and, by the way, still encourage you to keep up with your meditative practice. Do it all. Otherwise you'll get stuck being a ceiling surfer. Watch out for the chandelier.

Please understand, this doesn't mean you have to become the spiritual equivalent of a decathalon winner. For harmony and integration's sake, you must give attention to your whole being.

I often experience serious resistance from students who are so-called spiritual aspirants when I coach them to get to work in some area of their life that necessitates discipline and maybe even difficulty.

I recall one woman wanting to do more work in altered states of consciousness. I told her what she really needed first was a level of mastery in ordinary states of consciousness. This was evidenced clearly by the lack of tangible results in her life.

Her response? 'But I like the fun stuff!'

My point exactly.

The question for the true student of growth is: what has to happen for the stuff that strengthens you and moves you forward in life to be considered fun?

I remember reading of the spiritual teacher Adi Da Samraj, formerly Bubba Free John, approaching his teacher for the first time in his early years and asking the way to enlightenment. His teacher quickly responded, 'Lose twenty pounds and get a job. Then come talk to me.'

What does a job have to do with spirituality? Oh, just about everything. Unless you're born independently wealthy, you need a means of earning an income or you'll never attain the heights of your potential. That's part of getting your fingers into the earth. If you're with a spiritual leader who's all about rubbing crystals and navel gazing, smudging and moving your sofa and chairs around, and nothing about making a living and really being in the world, head for the hills.

I once asked one of my teachers, don José Luis Ruiz, to come to one of my workshops and teach some of my star students.

'No,' he told me, 'that's not my job, it's yours.' He continued, 'My challenge to you is to bring a cosmology of consciousness to the western world. The western world has lost their connection and it's not my job to do that. It's your job to do that.'

'How do I do that?'

'You have to be of the world you're teaching to put it into a language they'll understand. Because otherwise they won't recognise it.'

We're all teachers. We all have something unique to bring, and we all have to be of this world to transcend this world. You can't transcend something you've never mastered. Read that again.

Make no mistake about it: matter matters every bit as much as spirit. Do the work you need to do – get the job, lose the weight, get your house in order. This integrated approach guarantees you dominion of all realms.

23

The Universe Says Yes

Know from the bounteous heavens all riches flow;
And what man gives, the gods by man bestow.

– HOMER

It's All Good

A lot of my students struggle with the mistaken belief that there's a difference
between their material goals and their spiritual goals. This is an artificial distinc-
tion that won't help you. Every spiritual tradition tells us that all things come from
God. In the Judaeo-Christian-Muslim traditions (which all use the Old
Testament) the Creator stepped back on the seventh day to observe His handiwork
and decided 'it was ALL good'.

Therefore, where is God not? Where is spirit not? Where is energy not?

What I consistently hammer home to my students is that all goals are
spiritual goals. So, to say that you're going to abandon the material world
to become more spiritual is nothing more than escapism. In fact, it's total
nonsense. How do you measure being more spiritual? You can't. But
what you can measure are the results you're creating in the physical
world, all just a reflection of who you are. Jesus said, 'By their fruits you
shall know them.' (Matthew 7:15–16). When you're someone who
believes that we all have God within us and that everything happens for
a reason, then isn't *everything* spiritual?

Let's revisit science for a moment and the idea that all solid objects are really 99.99999 per cent light. This Zero Point Field, or field of nonform, is the place from which all form emerges. Wrap your brain cells around that one!

I call this energetic field Spirit.

Following this logic, everything is spiritual and comes from the same source. Therefore, all your goals and desires are ultimately spiritual goals and desires. This includes the goal to fit into those tight jeans, become a county councillor, and even find the right therapist for psychological help.

So, pursue all your goals with equal enthusiasm, knowing that they're all spiritual, and believe that God, your Higher Self, the universe always and only says 'Yes.'

We Are All One

No one can attach a schedule to your path to spirit, but I can say that the road will be smoother when you stop comparing yourself to others, creating an artificial distinction between me and you, and accept that we are all one.

One of the most profound spiritual moments of my life came totally unexpectedly in the Temple of Khnum in Egypt. Khnum was one of the earliest Egyptian gods and was considered the source of the Nile as well as the creator of the human body. His name literally translates as 'builder'. As I sat in the holy of holies in this temple, the place in each temple where the altar used to reside, I was thinking of how to use this primal energy I felt inside to build my own new beginning on the eve of my birthday. I could feel energies shooting up my spine. I was going deep.

Suddenly I heard the sound of feet walking towards me and figured that someone was going to ask me to leave this ancient site. I saw a Muslim gentleman, in full traditional attire, walking towards me, speaking. I couldn't understand a word he was saying, yet our eyes connected and he knelt in front of me and held out his hands, saying in a rough accent, 'Prayer.'

I held out my hands and we joined in yogic breath. Tears began to flow down my face and the strong energy I had felt minutes before continued. I was joining in prayer with a brother from a religious tradition so unlike my own, and yet beyond our religions, we were merely people – citizens of the human race. In that moment all I wanted to do was to unite with the whole planet. As above, so below.

After about twenty minutes, he stood and motioned for me to stand, holding out his arms to embrace. We did. It was a perfect metaphor for the union of East and West.

'What country?' he asked.

'America,' I said.

'You Christian?' he asked, then shook the thought away, 'No matter. Good man.' Backing away, he touched his palms together in front of him in prayer, bowed, and left. I could not consciously have created a more perfect experience.

We're all one. There's no such thing as separate parts in this world. When we truly appreciate this fact, there'll be no more terrorism. You and I both know that attention equals love, and we're terrorising ourselves with our obsession of evil empires, orange alerts, and the war on terror, following each and every media story as fast as they dish it out. We must change our focus. The more we become involved with and focus on peace, tranquility, unity, and harmony, the more we'll have peace, tranquility, unity, and harmony.

Wear Out Your Ego

When you're reaching and working for greater levels of awakening and awareness, one of the first reckonings is the battle to get beyond ego.

Remember, your ego is nothing more than the identity you've created for yourself. The human species has a need for consistency. The ego struggles against spiritual expansion and is tolerant – to a point. However, when the God force (or your Higher Self) has been patient enough, it'll often give an opportunity for expansion to the finite self. Ego, loving the familiar, usually despises the opportunity. Because it feels out of control, it'll try to knock the plan off track. Immortality is the ego's one objective, and it expresses that objective as the fear of death. To the degree that it can acquire many physical treasures – a bigger bank account, perhaps more accolades – the ego feels powerful. 'I'm in control,' it tells itself. 'I'm invincible!' But lying below the surface is the nagging promise of mortality. It was when my ego James was feeling invincible and the God force beckoned and called me that I had my humbling experience after Brazil.

In the West, the only way to truly transcend the ego is to build it, fully embody it, and then wear it out. In other words, if you don't fancy sitting in a monastery for twenty to thirty years, then play your silly ego games and take them to the limit until you get over it, then move on. Think of it this way. If you're really good at making money, writing music, being a philanthropist, parenting – whatever – then do it and do it with enthusiasm. Bring joy, well-being, and harmony to whatever you do and play that game to the end. Like a child with a new toy, eventually that path will come to a conclusion and you'll look for something else.

This is a defining moment, a moment of realising that it's time to transform, go deeper, play bigger. When your future-pull is calling, you'll either move forward in faith and power or backwards into fear. You've worn out the old, and only by setting it aside will you embrace the new. The apostle Paul said, 'When I was a child, I spoke as a child, I understood as a child, I thought as a child; but when I became a man, I put away childish things' (1 Corinthians 13:11). He'd worn out the old, familiar path and was ready to set out on an expanded one.

I once thought I was a special and chosen teacher and I wore that out, while wearing out many around me. I finally realised it was going to take a lifetime to play creator in my own universe, much less play creator in someone else's. I let it go and got over a lot of my own James Ray-ness. Now I know I'm just another guy doing my best to learn, love, and grow. That's my focus now, and to the degree I can do that and share value with others, I'm on the right path. In Zen they say that ordinary mind is the Zen mind. We're all special and have our unique spiritual gifts to bring.

Being reborn is dying to the smaller version/idea of yourself – death of the ego self. Please remember that the word *ego* is 'I' in Latin, so your ego is nothing more than the personal identity you've built for yourself.

You never fully let go of the ego — you can't and function in society. I've met many so-called enlightened beings and they all have an ego/personality. Your ego/personality is how you turn up and play. You're going to keep playing it until you wear it out. That's why I keep advising you to find what inspires you. It's every bit as spiritual for someone to play fully and give in their role as a parent as it is for someone who is teaching spiritual principles to do what they do. Finding something you totally love and immersing and merging with it is what's called bhakti yoga in the East, the path of love and devotion.

Peaks and Troughs

I once heard Ram Dass say, 'If you think you're really enlightened, go spend a weekend with your parents.' I think that's hilarious because no matter how much work I do on myself, my parents can still kick up my childhood stuff — and I love my mum and dad. The journey to enlightenment is long and continuous — it never ends. Some suggest that it happens in a blinding epiphany. Maybe it does. But for me, it's an experience of peaks and troughs, ups and downs. Typically, I experience a taste of unity and power followed by a fall where I lose any sense of unity and power.

You must go through a lot of pain and self-understanding when you begin the internal journey. Energy pouring in can tire you out. I recall once being in a profoundly altered state when I had a moment of inspiration — a divine download. In this profound moment, as I looked back across my entire life, I realised that while it often seemed as if the world was crashing down upon me, that I was certain to be crushed, in fact, I had *always* been caught by a net — often just in the nick of time.

The message that came into my consciousness was: 'James, you've always and only been guided, protected, and loved.' Tears rolled down my face in that moment, and I realised that this was the absolute truth and always would be no matter what.

This is true for each and every one of us. No matter how we stumble on the path to spirit, no matter how badly we seem to mess it up, we're never alone. *A Course in Miracles* states, 'If you knew who walks beside you at all times on this path that you have chosen, you would never experience fear again.' I have my own spin on this: 'If you knew who you really are, you'd never experience fear.' Know this in your heart and please repeat after me:

> I am the adventurer of life. I am eternal youth. I have come from the previous valleys of yesterday to the invigorating heights of today. I am the eternal traveller journeying into the miracle of self-discovery and infinite unfolding. I am always and only guided, protected, and loved.

Feeling Forsaken

I could give you all the reassurances in the world, but you'll most likely still have dark hours on the path to spirit when you feel lost and alone and believe me, I've been there too.

You're in good company. In a new book, *Mother Teresa: Come Be My Light,* author Brian Kolodiejchuk reveals for the first time that Mother Teresa lived through an immense personal struggle of faith. Incredibly, the most devoted nun in modern times admitted in letters to several confidants that she'd spent nearly fifty years without feeling the presence of God at all, and understandably hid that fact from a world enamoured with her supposed divine connection. This future saint wrote of feeling dryness, darkness, loneliness, and torture at believing she was being forsaken by her Lord and Saviour. An ice block was the way Mother Teresa described her soul. While some will use these shocking admissions to argue that religion fails to fulfill our sincere longing for a true relationship with the divine, others will feel validated that someone of her stature and commitment experienced feeling like a hypocrite and questioned the existence of God.

I guarantee to you that the esoteric traditions know that every single serious student experiences this very thing at some point in their lives. Many traditions speak of 'The Dark Night of the Soul' as a necessary stopping point on the journey to discover your ultimate infinite self. This is part of the journey, my friend; and from my experience the only way to get beyond it is to go through it. As the Buddha said, 'Enlightenment is nothing more than progressive disillusionment.'

As you progressively become more and more disillusioned with the things you once held as sacred and true – from the spiritual to the mundane – you wear them out and let them go. As more and more falls away you come to what Zen calls 'beginner's mind' – the curiosity, wonder, and amazement you possess regarding everything and everyone. With beginner's mind you embrace every single thing as glorious and amazing, finding buddhas (meaning 'the enlightened one') without number in every grain of sand, blade of grass, mound of money, and empty bank account. I believe this is what Jesus meant when he said, 'Except ye be converted, and become as little children ye shall not enter into the kingdom of heaven.' (Matthew 18:3)

When you stumble, have some compassion for yourself. That's how you learned to walk, one wobbly step at a time. Start again. Know that whatever is happening right now is part of a larger plan happening perfectly for your own personal growth, development, and betterment. The amateur hopes and wishes; the master knows. When asked, 'Do you believe in God?' Carl Jung answered, 'I don't believe – I know.' *Knowing is true power!*

Faith Is Action

In our world, results are created through our physical form. The only way God can allow us to experience all the fullness of this lifetime is through us taking massive action and understanding that we are co-creators of our own reality, of our own results. We are both cause and effect. We are the effect of the great Creative Source, yet we are the cause of our own results. The integrated master understands that he must study and master both divine poles to access truth and power. Cosmic illumination is achieved in the harmony and integration of the two pillars – that of Creator on one hand and that of Creation on the other.

If you read the ancient Kabbalah, you'll find the idea that man needs God, but God also needs man.

Again, I believe that our actions are meant to take us to all the glories God put on this earth. One thing in Kolodiejchuk's book on Mother Teresa stopped me cold. In 1951 Mother Teresa wrote, 'I want to . . . drink ONLY from His chalice of pain.' The caps in ONLY are her own.

I didn't know Mother Teresa and cannot pretend to comprehend the truth of what she was experiencing. I'm not debating her reasoning for wanting to experience a part of Jesus' darkness and pain on Earth, nor do I believe that she would have changed this path for any reason. I do believe, however, that saint or no saint, Mother Teresa's life operated under the same laws you and I adhere to, primarily: what you focus on expands and your wish is my command.

I ask you: as you put your faith into action, are you focusing on pain or joy? Are you even paying attention to what you're asking for? Every thought in your head and heart, every word out of your mouth, is a prayer. Every word casts a spell. Your thoughts are thunder and your word is law. You are that powerful. I don't know about you, but I only want to drink out of the chalice of joy. Knowing that life will have its ups and downs in the physical world, my experience of them is entirely up to me. Your wish is my command.

24

Turning Prayers to Thunder

Prayer is the spirit speaking truth to Truth.

– PHILIP JAMES BAILEY

Towards a Greater Awakening

Growing up in the church where my father preached, we often heard these words from Matthew 7:7: 'seek, and ye shall find; knock, and it shall be opened unto you. Ask, and it shall be given you.' They sounded good to me then and sound even better now. But how do you seek, knock, ask? I want to share some of the tools I use as I work towards greater awakening. These help me focus my attention and turn my prayers to thunder.

Meditation: True Prayer

Experiments have shown that experienced meditators have more activity in the left frontal lobe, the part of the brain associated with positive emotions such as happiness, joy, and contentment. These findings imply that happiness is something we can cultivate deliberately through mental training. Furthermore, research shows that regular meditators integrate the right and left hemispheres of the brain and are therefore able to use what's called whole brain thinking. So, not only will you be more happy and joyous, you'll be more intelligent and creative.

True prayer isn't getting on your knees and pleading – that's just noise on your knees. True prayer is the consistent control of the direction of your thoughts, feelings, and actions. Keep in mind that every thought is a prayer – and that goes for meditation as well. Prayer is not something you do – it's something you *are*.

Meditation is more than just sitting on a cushion. It's also the practice of directing and controlling your ongoing attention. It does little good to sit on a cushion (or your sofa, for that matter) and quieten your mind, only to get up and tremble in fear and uncertainty when your credit card bill arrives.

The apostle Paul of the Christian tradition exhorted us, 'Pray without ceasing' (1 Thessalonians 5:17). When I first heard this as a kid I thought, *How am I supposed to get anything else done?* I've since learned that you can do nothing else than what he advocates. Your prayers and meditations are your constant and consistent thoughts, feelings, and actions – and good or bad, they never cease.

Einstein said, 'Intuition does not come to an unprepared mind.' When he discovered the theory of relativity, it came to him in a flash of intuition, but only after he had studied and pondered the great mysteries of physics for years. This preparation allowed him to observe things that would have gone unnoticed to the unprepared mind. My advice to you is to get prepared. The best way I know how to do that is through study, practice, and traditional meditation. Hopefully some of the techniques I'm about to share with you are a little more practical than others you may have tried.

I start every day with meditation. In my meditations I'm doing a few things: I'm not only centring my energy vibration, I'm also setting my intentions for my day and how I'm going to create that day, so it's a brilliant way to start. In the best-case scenario, I meditate for an hour and then I like to go right into yoga because I've been sitting for an hour and I need to move my body before going to the gym.

Decades of meditation have really helped me focus my attention and bring much serenity and calm into my life. I was talking to my director of operations the other day and we were discussing how I can often get more done in a day than most people do in a month. The main reason for this is because I have incredible focus. When I sit down to do something, I'm like a laser, and it doesn't matter what's going on or what kind of distractions are happening around me. That's very powerful and practical. I know you want to be a powerful creator in the physical world, and having this power over your thoughts gives you a great advantage in life.

When you get to where you can control your thoughts that powerfully, things can't rattle you. I can be in the midst of a crisis at the office, and in the eye of the storm, I'm thinking, *Okay, what's good about this, how can I handle this, how can we do something differently?*

Meditation has multiple documented health benefits too. When you exercise any muscle intensely, what must you do afterwards? Let it rest. The mind is no different. Part of how it rests is going into a lower vibration via sleep. Meditation induces that same lower vibration. Twenty minutes of deep meditation has been shown to be the equivalent of two hours of sleep. Pretty impressive, and a good way to invest twenty minutes.

Meditation also reduces stress. Research on longevity proves that people with less stress in their lives have lower blood pressure and live longer and more fruitful lives. They also look better and age more slowly, so you benefit on many levels.

Focusing your attention gives you tremendous capabilities in real-world situations. This inner strength is available to everyone if they just know what to do.

Getting Started

Here's an important piece of advice: for God's sake, don't meditate in bed!

'I always fall asleep when I meditate,' people tell me time and time again. In many ways you're a stimulus–response being, and what we know from behavioural psychology is that when you do certain things repeatedly, it programs your unconscious mind into certain behaviours.

Getting into bed tells you that it's time to pass out or maybe that you're going to . . .

As long as you stay out of bed, you can use this fact of behavioural psychology to aid your technique. When you meditate, if you choose to sit in the same place, in the same way all the time, you're automatically giving yourself an advantage. On a mundane level, your body knows the drill, and on a metaphysical level, if you can keep the place where you meditate pristine (which can be difficult if you have kids or cats), then you'll build up a field of energy vibration (morphogenetic field) in that space. This'll make it much easier to get into your meditation because the space is unchanging. That's why my meditation room is locked and my housekeeper doesn't go in there – no one does. It's really easy for me to soar the minute I sit down in my chair because that's the only thing that's ever been done in that space.

Not everyone lives alone and can do this, but I encourage you to see if there's any small space in your home – it needn't be wider than a chair – that you can set aside for this purpose alone.

It's counterproductive to make your meditative practice one of drudgery or frustration. So whatever you do, make sure you have fun with this practice; life should be joyous and God is in everything – even chaos. For instance, some of my greatest meditative experiences have been at a casino down the street from my home in Las Vegas. Previously, I had thought it was amazing that I was experiencing soaring levels of oneness and non-duality in my meditation room, but like I always say, it's really easy to be the Buddha on the sofa.

I knew that if I could achieve those same meditative states in a casino, I'd really be soaring. So, on numerous occasions I went in and sat down at a slot machine to meditate. People didn't intentionally pester me but they were laughing, talking, cursing their luck, blowing cigarette smoke, and bumping into me. But I persisted with my practice, which was particularly amazing because in my normal everyday life I *really* don't enjoy people blowing smoke at me. You know what it taught me? If you can find peace in that environment, you can do it just about anywhere. No matter what your workplace, your mate, or your mortgage or landlord throw at you. Peace really is found within.

There are four categories of meditation I'd like to cover here:

1) The Focusing/Visualisation Meditation

2) Listening or Watching

3) Static Transcendence

4) Mobile Transcendence

Unless you have a lot of experience, I suggest that you try them in the order listed.

1) The Focusing/Visualisation Meditation

The Candle Meditation Focusing trains the thoughts to move in one controlled direction. Sit in a darkened room while staring at a candle flame. Your goal is to become the flame. When your thoughts wander in any direction, gently return them to the flame. Interestingly enough, once you get really good at this, you'll see that you can control the flame, make it grow brighter or weaker, flicker, and dance with your thoughts. If this sounds like hocus-pocus, remember that you and the flame are just energy, the same. All boundaries are illusion. Everything is energy.

Cloud Play Here's another meditation to do with your eyes open; it's really fun and a lot of people do this with their kids without realising it. Lie on your back in the garden and punch holes in clouds with your mind. It's pretty easy to do once you learn how to get focused because clouds are so ethereal. This teaches your children at an early age how powerful they really are and how their thoughts are impulses of energy. It's a good reminder for you too, so get outside and give it a test. Visualise a hole and keep it up intensely until it actually appears. It will!

Guided Meditations There are powerful CDs made especially for Westerners, who often have trouble focusing their train of thought. They work by entertaining your conscious mind – giving it something to listen to, visualise, and training it to focus in a certain direction. You can check out my website at www.harmonicwealthbook.com and choose between several ⓘ; probably my most popular is a six-CD set of different guided visualisations called *Collapse the World,* which helps listeners collapse the wave function we've discussed and choose to observe new particles from the unlimited waves of possibility in the Zero Point Field. You choose the world you're going to create and collapse anything you don't want.

The Grandfather Clock Meditation Sit with your eyes closed and visualise this clock in full detail: the smooth, dark finish, the pendulum swinging, the ticking sounds, all the bells and chimes. The idea is to get to the place where you can totally see this clock in your mind's eye. Then, when you get super-disciplined at this, you'll be able to open your eyes and really see and hear it – not as clearly as the desk in front of you, but it'll be there.

You can use this visualisation with any physical object. I happen to like a grandfather clock but you can use whatever you hope to create in your life as well – a new car, your dream home, whatever. Just be sure to see it vividly and add all the sensory factors: hear it, feel it, smell it, and so on.

The Counting Backwards Meditation With eyes closed, sit and count down, starting from 100 in your mind (not out loud). See and say (to yourself) 100, 99, 98, 97, and so on. This teaches you to focus the mind, but it also puts you into trance, which moves you into an altered state. If you find that starting at 100 is too difficult, count down from the number 10 or 20 instead. Be patient with yourself. This sounds easier than it is, but the effort is very rewarding.

Choose a Train of Thought The last visualisation technique I'll give is to train yourself to have one thought and to follow it without letting anything else come into your mind. For instance, if you want to write a book, with your eyes closed keep your attention on the physical writing of the book. Think about how you're going to handle every aspect of that: taking notes, gathering your research, composing an outline, writing a chapter, holding the finished manuscript, finding an agent, selling it, and so on. Follow that all the way to the best-seller lists, everything from A to Z. Just be sure to keep it in present time and bring it to a positive conclusion despite any negative thoughts that might come in during the meditation.

To be able to keep that train of thought for even a minute is a victory. The ultimate goal is to be able to do this exercise for thirty minutes.

2) Listening or Watching

This is traditional Eastern meditation, Zen sitting practice. In contrast to visualising, you don't attempt to control or direct your thoughts whatsoever, but rather just observe them. You pay attention to them and observe, listen, or watch what is going on inside your head. Do not judge or be attached to your thoughts, which is a challenge because all sorts of thoughts and feelings will arise. These should be interesting for you to observe but shouldn't hook you in. The minute you start to go down the path of 'Well, let me think this through,' you've stepped out of watching.

What is the goal of this form? To hear divine guidance and to recognise that you are so much more than your thoughts. You'll begin to realise that you are not the thinker.

When you're so immersed in something, you often can't observe it. A fish doesn't know it's in water; we don't stop and notice the oxygen we breathe, but the minute it's taken away, it becomes really important, doesn't it? Interestingly, you have thoughts, but you're not your thoughts. The minute you notice you're angry, you're no longer angry, you are noticing that you're angry – a good thing. The act of noticing something automatically pulls you out of *being* it. When you notice it you're not it.

As you think about this, if you can't control your thoughts, then who's really thinking? You have to ask yourself the question (which is really an interesting conundrum), *Are you doing the thinking or are you being thought?* The answer is that until you can focus your mind, you're not thinking but are rather being thought. You're a reactive being, an automaton operating upon the whim and whimsy of external circumstances. Your programming, either collective or individual, is running you, which is a big eye-opener for a lot of people. How about you?

This type of meditation is very difficult, and even though I started this way, for years I felt nothing but frustration and failure with this technique. I sat and sat and sat in my studio apartment, and got nowhere because I hadn't learned to control that puppy called my conscious mind. I wouldn't for years. I felt like such a failure because I wasn't having some transcendental experience, like the Buddha. That's why I recommend that students start with visualising meditations first. You'll most likely experience results more quickly.

Some will never want to even get this far and that's okay. It depends upon your karmic path in this lifetime. For many people, to learn to take control and responsibility for their physical life (in the focus meditations) is the grandest spiritual achievement of their entire life and I applaud that. To step outside the realm of victim and begin to control your own destiny, taking responsibility and accountability for that, is a huge accomplishment. That is why I say that for Ronaldo to score a hat-trick is every bit as spiritual as it is for me to meditate. Everybody comes with different capabilities for different experiences.

How do you know if you're ready for this step? Check out the biofeedback mechanism called your results. If you can focus your attention to the degree in your daily life that you can choose your emotions and create results in your world, you're living a highly functional and capable life. It doesn't mean you have to be a millionaire, but if you can't even go to work without getting annoyed because of triggers in your environment, or you can't achieve the goal of a new car, a certain salary, or a particular weight loss, then you still haven't descended fully into matter and need more integration, which the focusing meditations will help give you.

3) Static Transcendence

This is something very few people will get to because it involves years of practice to get beyond the mind chatter. Yogis are famous for this state; even for most of them, it takes at least twenty years of practice. This transcendental state, where you move beyond thought, isn't a realistic goal for most people. But don't get hung up on what kind of meditation you do.

The reality is that it's all meditation. It just depends what you're meditating on.

The Maharishi Mahesh Yogi popularised TM (Transcendental Meditation), or meditation with a mantra, which is an energy-based sound (like *Om* or *Aum,* which yogis believe to be the basic sound of the world). I've played with mantras, but only later on in my meditative practice. A mantra keeps your mind focused, so on a mundane level you're focusing the mind and on a metaphysical level you're getting the vibration of the mantra, which is changing your body's vibration. One of the best experiences I've had in more recent years was sitting for an hour in a crowd of close to two hundred people and chanting *Om* for an hour. It was awesome because of the vibration and the cohesion of the crowd.

4) Mobile Transcendence

This involves being able to move into a transcendental state at any time, but good luck trying to stay there or function in that capacity. Anyone who tells you this is possible is bonkers. Thank God there are other great thinkers who back me up on this, like Ken Wilber and my friend Genpo Roshi. You have to have some part of your personality in duality to function in this world.

People often come up to me in my seminars and say, 'I'm such a loser because I'm not doing my practice. I'm watching TV and eating crappy food.' Great, I say! My enthusiasm is because the only way you can observe that you're off your path is if *you're on* a path. That's not the case for everyone. The fact that you notice you've stumbled is an affirmation that you're on a path, so get excited, congratulate yourself, and make adjustments.

I want to make it really clear that I am not claiming to be fully enlightened. I do, however, have the ability at times to allow my body to move yet have my mind in a place of transcendence. I can sometimes turn my thoughts off. If you ever see me pause during one of my workshops where I'm working with someone, what's happening is that I'm moving into a state where I unify with them and come out with something from their childhood or life. They might think I just read their mind, but it's not me. I'm not in my mind at all. There's no James there. But after thirty years of practice, there are still times when I don't get there. It's not like I just sit down and go into the godhead every time I meditate. I really don't believe anyone does, not anyone who is highly functioning as an integrated human being in society. Maybe a guy sitting in a cave can do that, but if you're running a business and you've got a relationship, you just don't do that on a regular basis. We need to have realistic expectations of how we function in this body.

Yoga

Yoga is a meditative practice. It's a comprehensive body of study and living, as is Tantra, which is about so much more than sex. In the West we put yoga to rock music and turn the temperature up so we can sweat off calories, and that's cool (or hot, as the case may be), but it's not the objective of the original yoga.

There are all different kinds of yogas, but the one that fits this book, as I mentioned before, is bhakti yoga, the yoga of adoration. How do you find your spiritual path? Bhakti yoga is a great way. Again, it's about finding something you love and immersing yourself so completely in it that you become one with it. That is a transcendental state. The object of your adoration could be Buddha, Jesus, your partner, your work – it doesn't matter what the object of your affection is; it's about falling in love totally and completely. If it's football, you're no longer playing the game, you *are* the game. That's a spiritual and altered state. When you choose something you love completely, the lines of demarcation blur and you and it become one. You merge totally and completely into a unified whole. If you look long and hard enough at anything you'll find everything.

I do hatha yoga postures in the morning. It's part of my spiritual practice, but it's a bit more of a physical practice for me. Developed in the fifteenth century, it's a way to physically purify the body to make it

ready for long periods of meditation. You can often find classes in this
form of meditation.

Self-Reflection

We've discussed a lot of ideas regarding spirituality; let's pause for a moment and bring it back to you. I want you to take out your notepad and
write the answers to the following questions. This quick self-inventory
will bring insights into the harmony and integration you have in the
spiritual pillar of your life as well as where you may need some work.

- Do I regularly notice how other people, nature, or I reflect some-
thing magical and miraculous?
- Do I identify myself more frequently as a spiritual being connected
with all? Or am I in a category that excludes other people and things?
- Do I feel connected to the universe at large? Part of something
bigger than myself?
- Do I take time to be by myself and seek spirit?
- Do I find the good and God in all of life's circumstances, even the
most difficult?
- Do I share my unique spirituality with others? Is it a central point
in my life?
- Do I consistently set bigger and bolder intentions and goals to test
my level of spiritual development and creative ability?
- Am I able to walk my own path, to direct my life, without feeling
the victim of circumstance or the plaything of cultural conditioning?
- What spiritual disciplines make me happiest? When and how, specifically, will I do more of them?

How did you feel as you asked yourself these questions? Were they easily answered, or did they require some real contemplation? It's okay if
you're not sure where you stand in your spirituality or your disciplines.
The concepts in this chapter may be wrestling to find space in your
mind amidst other doctrines. Give yourself the time to let things settle

in. Keep an open mind and always trust that voice or feeling within that tells you what's right for you.

Merging Heaven and Earth: Unending Joy

At the end of our wanderings there is only the soul's yearning to return to God.

– RAM DASS

Again, every path is different; every path is perfect; all goals are spiritual goals. I am passionate about being involved and becoming integrated because you can sit on your sofa and be the Buddha all day long, and the minute you choose a tangible goal and start to go after it, you find out how Buddha you're not. That's really where you test your spiritual evolution – when you're engaged, whether you're succeeding or failing really makes no difference. It's all good. It gets really good when you can become fully engaged and yet remain detached. In other words, you do what you do for the sake of doing versus for the sake of the outcome.

The Tibetan tradition says we're so blessed *because we're so likely to get screwed up*. We've got to contend with both physical biology and spiritual potentiality. We regularly get seduced by the tangible world, yet we have the faculties for enlightenment. Think about how complex you are. You have a reptilian brain, which is literally the brain of a reptile at the top of your spine. You also have a paleomammalian horse brain (an inheritance from lower mammals), along with the neocortex, plus you have angels and demons – all carrying different operations and intentions – all vying to actualise their potential. We have all this stuff crammed into the small space of our bodies, which makes these bodies both wonderful learning grounds and simultaneously a potentially screwed-up mess. According to some esoteric traditions, there are souls upon souls queueing to get in here, because it's the greatest party in the cosmos – to learn, grow, and evolve in the great human experience. Our challenges are a gift because they help us grow!

My advice is to go within while also embracing the outer world – have a foot in both worlds. Recognise and utilise the immense power of the spiritual realm, and also address any problems on the level at which they appear to have been created. Embrace the Creator and Created; master the quantum world as well as the Newtonian world. Once you home in on the results you want (your spiritual prototype), then you must marshal all of your mental, emotional, and physical resources to support it, never letting yourself be distracted by what appear to be other causes in your life. Know that you are cause in this world – and only you. At the beginning and end of every day, you create your world, all that you see, taste, touch, and hear. Consider what you want, then work enthusiastically on all levels to create it.

Through it all, remember that you are guided, protected, and loved.

My friend Nicole Brandon was working with some acrobats. While preparing to be suspended twenty-five feet in the air on a trapeze and swung out into the void, her mind raced and she felt a knot building in her stomach. As she grabbed the first rung of the ladder to begin her climb, the catcher called out to her, 'Don't look for me, don't reach for me. I'm a catcher and I'll catch you. Your job is only to swing and let go.'

All you have to do is swing into the game of life – and let go.

A Call to Action

There's only one question you must answer: are you going to take what's rightfully yours?

It's Up to You

Most people leave this life with the greatest pain a human can experience – regret. Looking all the way back across their lives, they say, when it's too late, 'My God, I could have done something great. I had the chance, but I didn't have the courage.'

Let that not be you.

Over 2000 years ago, the Buddha said that sometimes you are so heavily conditioned in a lie that truth itself knocks at your door and you turn it away. Is that statement any less true today? No. Yet, we live at the most exciting time in our world history, a time in which science is proving exactly how we are co-creating our reality. We've broken down the science in this book, and now it's up to you to really understand all that you're capable of producing and living.

Let me ask you: what has to happen for you to unleash your potential and live up to your abilities?

It's always easier to do nothing, to maintain the status quo, at least in the short term. The naysayers are frightened by what they don't understand. While the status quo may feel familiar and comfortable *right now*, it brings long-term regret. The status quo brings death. As Carlos Santana got older, he continued growing and adapted his music to appeal to a new generation. If he had stayed with the status quo, he'd still be playing

'Black Magic Woman' in some bar. But because he kept up with the times and aligned himself with some of the greatest singers of the new era, younger generations now know his work. When asked why he'd continually made so many changes he reportedly replied, 'Predictability is death.'

We've taken quantum leaps in our technology but baby steps in our spiritual understanding. What appears to be new in the world is not really new at all. Electricity was there all the time; the ability to float and fly were present all the time. Quantum physics, the Internet, cellular and microwave technology – they too were there all the time. We just had to open our minds wide enough to tap into that knowledge. Look at history and you'll find that all profound transformation and growth begins with a shift in consciousness.

No one who was normal ever made history. In fact, history is full of examples of those who went against collective thinking and were ridiculed for it, some even killed. Galileo, Giordano Bruno, Jesus, bio-physicist Fritz-Albert Popp – all were outcasts who became heroes. Such is life. Such is the nature of growth and expansion.

The truth is that you have as much power to change the world as any of these luminaries. Your light is just as powerful. Your emotions, feelings, and attention have a direct effect on the world around you; they create your offer waves and affect the echo waves of your future-pull. You have the ability to participate in the universe of your own choosing. And so much more.

What Are You Creating?

Everything in your universe is 99.99999 per cent light. You are 99.99999 per cent light. Do you realise the power you have? You have a direct effect upon the very substance of the universe even beyond all time and space. Think about this long and hard. The implications are vast. As we've discussed numerous times, everything from a pine tree to a Porsche to a palace is comprised of energy or light. The energies that bring war are the same that bring peace. Pain or pleasure, poverty or prosperity – it's all made from the same energetic light substance in our universe. You affect it all – no exception.

Harold Saxon Burr, a physiologist from Yale, proved that every living entity is a transmitter and receiver of photons of light. Here's his most critical finding: *the level of consciousness* of the entity determines the level of transmission and reception. The greater one's level of consciousness, the greater the transmission and the reception. In simple terms: you grow, and your impact grows – individually and globally.

We're back to our original premise, aren't we? The more you grow, the more you gain. Expansion is everything – it's the only way to go.

My friends at the HeartMath Institute found that people who consistently experience what we would call negative emotions – anger, fear, worry, frustration, self-pity – are altering their DNA, actually making it tighten up. What do you think becomes of their potential when that happens? It dies. Conversely, when people experience what we would typically call the positive emotions of love, gratitude, appreciation, joy, fulfilment, and abundance, their DNA begins to loosen up and unwind. As that happens, what do you think becomes of their dormant potential? It awakens.

What I'm saying is that as you open up and experience more joy and power in your life (your natural state), you're alternately receiving and giving off more light, therefore becoming more of who you're supposed to be.

Every single thing you do in your body has a biochemical action that changes your vibratory rate, which in turn affects the substance of the entire universe. That's pretty profound, isn't it? As you think about it now, every single thought, feeling, and emotion you have creates a biochemical change in your body that's affecting not only your DNA, but the very fibre of reality. So, the question is: what are you creating in your life? What are you creating for the world?

Modern science now shows us in layer after layer that you've already been co-creating your entire life. I have one bold challenging question that I ask you to consider: are you going to continue to co-create on autopilot and refuse to embrace what all great spiritual traditions as well as now modern science are telling us, as so many unfortunately do? Or are you going to step up and become a Conscious Co-Creator? Because truth is knocking at your door.

You're More Than That

Let it never be said of you that change was happening all around you, that the signs of the times were readily apparent, and still you slept.

Consider this a call to action. I want you to join me in this new era, an era where forward thinkers like you and me begin to band together and redefine what it means to be truly wealthy and fulfilled. Redefine what it *really* means to be a spiritual being living in a physical world. To be in the world, but not *of* the world. As don José Luis says, *'To play the game, but not to buy in.'*

John Lennon once stated in an interview, 'From the first time that my buddies and I played together as the Beatles we *knew* we were the best band in the world . . . we were just waiting for the rest of the world to catch up.'

Your future and your destiny are patiently waiting for you to catch up. Do you hear the call? Your future-pull is beckoning: 'Come on. Let's *do* this! You're so much more than what you've settled for. So much more than what you're buying into.'

'But James,' you may be thinking, 'it's easy for some, but not for me. I don't have the right education to achieve my dreams.'

I understand. You're more than that.

'But I had an abusive childhood.'

I understand. You're more than that.

'I'm so far in debt that I can't even imagine light at the end of this tunnel.'

You're more than that.

'My husband cheated on me and left me.'

I appreciate your situation. You're more than that.

'I'm too old.'

More than that.

'I'm too young, not the right gender, race, or ethnicity.'

More.Than.That.You are eternal and beautiful and whole and vast and ancient and powerful and wise and made in the image and likeness of all that is.Want to try to get around that one? Just try me.

Okay. What if your answer is, 'James, my life is pretty wealthy right now in every single area.'

Congratulations. Seriously. You're more than that too. In fact, no matter how wealthy, successful, and fulfilled you may think you are or aren't right now, you haven't even scratched the surface of what you're capable.

Buried deep within you is a spark of greatness, a spark that's just waiting to be fanned into flames of unlimited passion and achievement.That flame is not outside you – it's born deep within you. It's all there for you, my friend, and it always has been. God, your Higher Self – the genie, if you will – is just patiently waiting, patiently thinking, *I wonder if he is going to wake up today? I wonder if she is going to grow and expand beyond her comfort zone today?*

Your future is just waiting for you to catch up. Know it. Live from the outcome; *be* it right now!

The Promise of a Bigger Life

You've got a lot to think about.You've just had your first exposure to so much of the magic that I'd like to share with you – a faithful rendition of some of the best that's taken me years and years of study, seeking, training, reading, and being mentored by some of the greats to understand. I offer it knowing that this information can save you time, heartache, and struggle. I offer it hoping that it acts as a mighty wind to ignite that flickering spark within you. I can't take you there. I can only show you the door; you have to be willing to walk through.

I don't know about you, but whenever I listen to a great new piece of music, particularly if it's in a style I'm not familiar with, I'm electrified, confused, excited, and unsure about it all at the same time. I'm feeling something, but I'm not sure what I'm feeling. I've got to listen to it a few times just to figure out why it moves me. I may not even hear this subtle harmony or that chord progression until the third or fifth listen.

Reading this book may be the same experience for you. Some of it excited you, some of it may have made you uncomfortable, some of it struck you as nonsense, some of it just confused you. That's all good. You're never totally comfortable when you're setting records – you're only comfortable when you're repeating. Stop and think. What parts did you resonate with the most? What struck you? Take a good, close look at those ah-ha moments, because there's gold in those flashes of insight. Now take a moment to think about what confused you, annoyed you, challenged you, made you say, 'Oh, no way!' because guess what? That's where the titanium resides. Remember, I'm not about easy. Achieving Harmonic Wealth isn't about easy. While the answers may be simple, implementing and living them is rarely easy. You have to live contrary to the conditioned norm. Many people you know, at least in the short term, may not understand you. The journey will be joyous and exciting, yes, but forging a new trail is never the most comfortable route. It's about growing to gain, fulfilling the promise of the power within you so you can move elegantly through a bigger life.

This isn't a book you just read once and you're done. This is a book I hope you'll return to again and again – for inspiration, education, motivation. This is a resource for creating your visions and putting them into action, a manual for your ultimate life. My goal is to get you to go 3 for 3 – align your thoughts, feelings, and actions – to achieve Harmonic Wealth in the five pillars: financial, relational, mental, physical, and spiritual. When you do that, my friend, sit back and watch the miracles unfold.

Living from the Outcome

Consider your thoughts the directional system for your life. If you spend just ten minutes a day reviewing an idea in this book, you'll see massive shifts in your life. That's how much the power of these pages will align with the power of your mind and the power of the vibrational universe in which we all live. What will you do next to feed that beautiful mind of yours, to raise your thoughts to the next quantum level? While you and I know that thoughts are not the entire equation, they are the beginning point. Thoughts, good and bad, set you in the direction of the outcome of your choosing. Control your thoughts and you point your life in the direction you choose.

Next let's talk about feelings. These are the vibrations in your body – the marriage of thoughts and emotions. Now that you know the universe is a big yes machine and good, bad, or indifferent the answer is always yes, does that excite you? Now that you realise you've successfully created exactly where you're at in this moment and you can create a bigger, bolder, braver existence beginning right now, do you feel powerful, motivated, confident? Now that you realise you have the ability to harness the Law of Attraction as well as other laws of this universe to bring every desire into your life, do you feel excited? Hold onto those feelings; love them, nurture them, and let them move you into bold, brave action.

Yes, action. You've got to work it, be it, go for it. I call this 'living from the outcome'. You must think, feel, and boldly act *from*, not towards, the outcome you choose to create in your life. This principle, or should I say the lack of it, is the reason most will never accomplish a fraction of their capability. The distinction is subtle and yet absolutely powerful. Think about it. If you're working *towards* an outcome, the energetic feeling you're putting forth is that you don't have it yet. Your wish is my command. If you're thinking, feeling, and acting *from* the outcome, the energy put into the universe is that you already have it. Your wish is my command. I believe this is the very reason that Jesus stated, 'Judge not according to the appearance.' (John 7:24) Appearances keep you focused upon what currently is versus what is triggered to spring forth perhaps only just moments away.

You don't take supplements once and see a complete change in your health, do you? No, you've got to take them over time, every day, in the right dose. You don't start a fitness programme and expect to win a beauty contest next week either. You build action upon action upon action and the results eventually unfold. I encourage you to return to every piece of wisdom you can find – this book, seminars, lectures, CDs, other educational resources, whatever works – to grow, expand, and attract the Harmonic Wealth that is your destiny. Immerse your thoughts and feelings continuously in the energies that keep you living from your outcome. Control your focus of attention and you change and control your life. What remains is for you to become the true student, the master who claims your destiny.

What an exciting time to be alive, a time in which future generations will look back upon us and state, 'They were the ones we were waiting for. They were the ones who figured it all out.'

I love mythologist Joseph Campbell's line: *'The big question is whether you are going to be able to say a hearty yes to your adventure.'*

You Can Change the World

While we've explored a tremendous amount of information regarding empowering your life, you also have the power within you to change the world, to make an impact on current and future generations. We spoke of Karl Pribram's Nobel Prize-winning research that proves your entire world is your own projection; this is true individually as well as collectively. Many forward scientific thinkers now strongly believe that our world is a hologram, a holographic projection of our own collective consciousness. Two things make this an extremely exciting concept. 1) In a hologram, the whole is contained in every single part – and this is true no matter how microscopically small you may go. Shining a light through the smallest sliver of a holographic film will reveal the entire image. 2) Making even a slight change in a hologram changes the entire holographic projection. All of it shifts accordingly, fully and completely.

Ervin Laszlo, the great thinker and systems theorist, states, 'All that happens in one place happens also in other places; all that happened at one time happens also at all times after that. Nothing is "local", limited to where and when it is happening.'

You've just explored some of our world's greatest minds. If even a fraction of what they believe and of what I believe to be true is in fact accurate, the implications are life changing. There are over six billion different manifestations of the human species currently on the planet today, yet there's only one of us here. In other words, every single thing you do to improve your life and your world improves mine as well. I want to thank you for that. Conversely, every time you choose to limit and disempower your life, it limits and disempowers the entire world.

The Christian prophet said: 'If I be lifted up from the Earth, I will draw all men unto me.' (John 12:32) What a responsibility you and I have – what an opportunity!

Only those willing to risk going too far can find out how far they can go.

– T. S. ELIOT

Farewell . . . Hello

Have a good journey! That's what *farewell* means in Old Saxon. Make no mistake about it, you and I are on a journey together, my friend, one in which we'll meet again and again on the page, in person, through the magic of technology, or through some as-yet-unknown venue that's just out there waiting for us to catch up. Every ending is also a new beginning: cause and effect, effect and cause. Each time, I'll wish you hello and farewell, and ask you to remember this truth:

You're greater than you can ever possibly imagine. You can do something great. This is your chance. Are you willing to go too far just to know how far you can go? You have the courage. Now is the time.

Go within and without and change the world. It begins with you. It begins with me. Let's do this together.

You are the one the world's been waiting for.